Good Housekeeping

Favourite Puddings, Desserts & Cakes

250 Tried, tested, trusted recipes ★ Delicious results

Good Housekeeping

Favourite
Puddings,
Desserts & Cakes

250 Tried, tested, trusted recipes ★ Delicious results

Compiled by Barbara Dixon

COLLINS & BROWN

First published in the United Kingdom in 2011 by
Collins & Brown
10 Southcombe Street
London
W14 0RA

An imprint of Anova Books Company Ltd

The Good Housekeeping website is
www.allaboutyou.com/goodhousekeeping

10 9 8 7 6 5 4 3

ISBN 978-1-84340-605-1

A catalogue record for this book is available from
the British Library.

Repro by Dot Gradations Ltd, UK
Printed and bound in Italy by G. Canale&C. S.p.A.

This book can be ordered direct from the publisher at
www.anovabooks.com

Recipes in this book are taken from the Good Housekeeping recipe
library and may have been reproduced in previous publications.

Picture Credits:
Neil Barclay (page 50); Martin Brigdale (pages 40, 41, 53, 71, 81,
153, 155, 157, 192, 195, 221, 222 and 267); Nicki Dowey (10, 11,
12, 13, 18, 21, 25, 26, 27, 29, 30, 31, 32, 34, 35, 36, 37, 38, 42,
43, 46, 47, 49, 51, 52, 54, 55, 56, 57, 58, 59, 61, 62, 64, 65, 66,
67, 68, 69, 70, 72, 73, 75, 76, 77, 79, 80, 82, 83, 84, 88, 89, 90,
91, 93, 94, 112, 134, 135, 137, 138, 139, 140, 141, 142, 143,
145, 146, 154, 156, 158, 164, 165, 166, 169, 172, 174, 175,
176, 177, 178, 179, 181, 182, 183, 184, 186, 187, 188, 189,
193, 194, 201, 203, 205, 206, 209, 211, 214, 223, 225, 226,
227, 232, 233, 237, 250, 252, 258, 262, 263 and 271); Will Heap
(page 33); Craig Robertson (pages 147, 161, 215, 236, 238, 240,
241, 244, 245, 246, 247, 248, 249, 251, 254, 255, 256, 259,
260, 261, 265, 268, 269, 270 and 272); Lucinda Symons (pages
14, 15, 16, 17, 19, 22, 24, 48, 60, 74, 78, 85, 92, 95, 96, 97, 98,
99, 100, 101, 102, 104, 105, 106, 107, 109, 110, 111, 113, 114,
115, 116, 117, 118, 119, 120, 121, 122, 123, 124, 125, 126,
127, 128, 129, 130, 131, 144, 148, 149, 159, 160, 162, 167,
168, 197, 198, 199, 200, 207, 212, 213, 216, 217, 229, 230,
242, 243, 253, 257, 264 and 273)
Home Economists: Joanna Farrow, Emma Jane Frost, Teresa
Goldfinch, Alice Hart, Lucy McKelvie, Kim Morphew, Bridget
Sargeson and Mari Mererid Williams
Stylists: Wei Tang, Helen Trent and Fanny Ward

★

NOTES

★ Both metric and imperial measures are given for the recipes. Follow either set of measures, not a mixture of both, as they are not interchangeable.

★ All spoon measures are level.
1 tsp = 5ml spoon; 1 tbsp = 15ml spoon.

★ Ovens and grills must be preheated to the specified temperature.

★ Medium eggs should be used except where otherwise specified.

DIETARY GUIDELINES

★ Note that certain recipes contain raw or lightly cooked eggs. The young, elderly, pregnant women and anyone with immune-deficiency disease should avoid these because of the slight risk of salmonella.

★ Note that some recipes contain alcohol. Check the ingredients list before serving to children.

Contents

Foreword

I've always thought that a back to front dinner party would suit me well – at least you wouldn't be full by the time pudding comes round! Most of the men in my life claim they aren't fussed by pudding, but somehow it always happens that when I triumphantly bring out a pillowy pavlova or a crisp crumble they are the first in line. Odd that.

I have my theory that there are many pitfalls when serving starters and mains – you have your vegetarians, pescatarians, confirmed carnivores and the picky eaters to mention but a few. But conspicuously, there don't seem to be half as many problems when it comes to puddings, it's usually one recipe fits all.

This cookbook is my ideal bedtime reading, leading you gently into dreams brimming with decadent chocolate cakes piled with satiny frosting and pies bursting with fresh fruit, nestled in flaky, buttery blankets. But aside from dreaming up which pudding I'm going to make next, the best bit of any Good Housekeeping cookery book is that every recipe has been triple tested in our dedicated kitchens so they are all guaranteed to work (and actually look like the pictures – we use no trickery in our photography).

Whether you want to have the ease of freeze-ahead desserts, or the comfort of throw-together family favourites, or indeed if you feel like attempting something a little more tricky, we have the recipe for you.

I hope you enjoy this book as much as I do.

Meike.

Meike Beck
Chief Home Economist

Baked and Steamed Puddings

Baked Apples with Butterscotch Sauce

Preparation Time 5 minutes, plus soaking • Cooking Time 15–20 minutes • Serves 6 • Per Serving 821 calories, 56g fat (of which 28g saturates), 70g carbohydrate, 0.4g salt • Gluten Free • Easy

125g (4oz) sultanas
2 tbsp brandy
6 large Bramley apples, cored
4 tbsp soft brown sugar
2 tbsp apple juice
125g (4oz) hazelnuts, chopped and toasted
ricotta cheese to serve

FOR THE BUTTERSCOTCH SAUCE
125g (4oz) butter
125g (4oz) soft brown sugar
2 tbsp golden syrup
2 tbsp black treacle
4 tbsp brandy
300ml (½ pint) double cream

1 Soak the sultanas in the brandy and put to one side for 10 minutes, then stuff each apple with equal amounts of soaked sultanas.

2 Preheat the oven to 220°C (200°C fan oven) mark 7. Put the apples into a roasting tin and sprinkle with the brown sugar and apple juice. Bake for 15–20 minutes until soft.

3 Meanwhile, make the sauce. Melt the butter, brown sugar, golden syrup and treacle in a heavy-based pan, stirring continuously. When the sugar has dissolved and the mixture is bubbling, stir in the brandy and cream. Bring back to the boil then remove from the heat and put to one side.

4 Remove the apples from the oven. Serve the apples with the butterscotch sauce, hazelnuts and a dollop of ricotta cheese.

 GET AHEAD
*To **prepare ahead** Complete step 1 up to 4 hours in advance. Make the sauce (step 3), then cool, cover and chill for up to one day.*
To use Complete the recipe and bring the sauce back to the boil to serve.

Baked Apricots with Almonds

Preparation Time 5 minutes • Cooking Time 20–25 minutes • Serves 6 • Per Serving 124 calories, 6g fat (of which 2g saturates), 16g carbohydrate, 0.1g salt • Gluten Free • Easy

12 apricots, halved and stoned
3 tbsp golden caster sugar
2 tbsp Amaretto liqueur
25g (1oz) unsalted butter
25g (1oz) flaked almonds
crème fraîche to serve

1 Preheat the oven to 200°C (180°C fan oven) mark 6. Put the apricot halves, cut side up, into an ovenproof dish. Sprinkle with the sugar, drizzle with the liqueur, then dot each apricot half with a little butter. Scatter the flaked almonds over them.

2 Bake for about 20–25 minutes or until the apricots are soft and the juices are syrupy. Serve warm, with crème fraîche.

★ TRY SOMETHING DIFFERENT
Use nectarines or peaches instead of apricots.

Oranges with Caramel Sauce

Preparation Time 15 minutes • **Cooking Time** 30–40 minutes • **Serves 6** • **Per Serving** 139 calories, 4g fat (of which 2g saturates), 24g carbohydrate, 0.1g salt • **Gluten Free** • **Easy**

6 oranges
25g (1oz) butter
2 tbsp golden caster sugar
2 tbsp Grand Marnier
2 tbsp marmalade
grated zest and juice of 1 large
    orange
crème fraîche to serve

1 Preheat the oven to 200°C (180°C fan oven) mark 6. Cut away the peel and pith from the oranges, then put them into a roasting tin just large enough to hold them.

2 Melt the butter in a pan and add the sugar, Grand Marnier, marmalade, orange zest and juice. Heat gently until the sugar dissolves. Pour the mixture over the oranges in the tin, then bake in the oven for 30–40 minutes or until the oranges are caramelised. Serve warm, with crème fraîche.

★ COOK'S TIP
Use thick-skinned oranges, such as navel oranges, as they are easier to peel.

Hot Spiced Fruit Salad

Preparation Time 10 minutes • Cooking Time 1½ hours • Serves 6 • Per Serving 185 calories, 1g fat (0g saturates), 44g carbohydrate, 0.1g salt • **Gluten Free** • **Dairy Free** • **Easy**

3 apples, cored and chopped

3 pears, cored and chopped

12 each ready-to-eat dried apricots
   and figs

juice of 2 large oranges

150ml (¼ pint) apple juice

a pinch of ground cinnamon

1 star anise

1 Preheat the oven to 180°C (160°C fan oven) mark 4. Put the apples and pears into a roasting tin with the apricots and figs, the orange juice, apple juice, ground cinnamon and star anise. Stir, cover with foil and bake in the oven for 1 hour.

2 Remove the foil and bake for a further 30 minutes. Discard the star anise before serving.

★ TRY SOMETHING DIFFERENT

Ready-to-eat prunes or 100g (3½ oz) dried cranberries may be substituted for the figs.

Apples with Oats and Blueberries

★

Preparation Time 15 minutes • Cooking Time 30–40 minutes • Serves 4 • Per Serving 164 calories, 5g fat (of which trace saturates), 29g carbohydrate, 0g salt • **Dairy Free** • **Easy**

4 Bramley apples
25g (1oz) pecan nuts, chopped
25g (1oz) rolled oats
50g (2oz) blueberries
2 tbsp light muscovado sugar
4 tbsp orange juice

1 Preheat the oven to 200°C (180°C fan oven) mark 6. Core the apples, then use a sharp knife to score around the middle of each (this will stop the apple from collapsing). Put the apples into a roasting tin.

2 Put the pecans into a bowl together with the oats, blueberries and sugar. Mix together, then spoon into the apples. Pour 1 tbsp orange juice over each apple and bake in the oven for 30–40 minutes or until the apples are soft.

Summer Fruit Compôte

Preparation Time 10 minutes • Cooking Time 20 minutes, plus cooling and chilling • Serves 4 • Per Serving 122 calories, trace fat (of which 0g saturates), 30g carbohydrate, 0g salt • **Gluten Free** • **Easy**

12 fresh, ripe apricots, halved and stoned
125g (4oz) fresh blueberries
50g (2oz) vanilla sugar
juice of 1 orange
200g (7oz) strawberries, hulled and halved
Greek yogurt to serve

1 Preheat the oven to 180°C (160°C fan oven) mark 4. Put the apricots, blueberries, sugar and orange juice into a large, shallow baking dish and bake, uncovered, in the oven for about 20 minutes until just tender.

2 Gently stir in the strawberries. Taste the cooking juices – you may want to add a little extra sugar – then leave to cool. Cover and chill. Serve with a spoonful of yogurt.

⭐ GET AHEAD
To prepare ahead *Make up to a day beforehand. Put into an airtight container and chill.*
To use *Take out of the fridge and allow to reach room temperature (about 30 minutes) before serving.*

Rice Pudding

★

Preparation Time 5 minutes • **Cooking Time** 1½ hours • **Serves** 6 • **Per Serving** 235 calories, 7g fat (of which 5g saturates), 35g carbohydrate, 0.2g salt • **Gluten Free** • **Easy**

butter to grease
125g (4oz) short-grain pudding rice
1.1 litres (2 pints) full-fat milk
4 tbsp golden caster sugar
grated zest of 1 small orange
2 tsp vanilla extract
whole nutmeg to grate

1 Preheat the oven to 180°C (160°C fan oven) mark 4. Lightly grease a 900ml (1½ pint) ovenproof dish. Add the pudding rice, milk, sugar, orange zest and vanilla extract and stir everything together. Grate a little nutmeg over the top.

2 Bake in the oven for 1½ hours or until the top is golden brown, then serve at once.

Rhubarb and Pear Crumble

Preparation Time 25 minutes • Cooking Time 40–45 minutes • Serves 6 • Per Serving 255 calories, 14g fat (of which 6g saturates), 32g carbohydrate, 0.2g salt • **Easy**

450g (1lb) rhubarb, cut into 2.5cm
   (1in) pieces
2 ripe pears, peeled, cored and
   roughly chopped
75g (3oz) demerara sugar
1 tsp ground cinnamon
50g (2oz) unsalted butter, chilled
75g (3oz) self-raising flour
2 shortbread fingers
50g (2oz) hazelnuts
Greek yogurt to serve

1 Preheat the oven to 180°C (160°C fan oven) mark 4. Put the fruit into a small shallow baking dish and sprinkle with 25g (1oz) sugar and the cinnamon. Mix together well.

2 Next, make the crumble mixture. Put the butter in a food processor, add the flour and the remaining sugar and whiz until it looks like rough breadcrumbs. (Alternatively, rub the fat into the flour by hand or using a pastry cutter, then stir in the sugar.)

3 Break the shortbread fingers into pieces and add to the processor with the hazelnuts, or crush the shortbread with a rolling pin and chop the hazelnuts. Whiz again for 4–5 seconds until the crumble is blended but still looks rough. Sprinkle the crumble over the fruit, spreading it up to the edges and pressing down with the back of a wooden spoon.

4 Bake for 40–45 minutes until the topping is golden brown and crisp. Serve with yogurt.

Pear and Blackberry Crumble

Preparation Time 20 minutes • Cooking Time 35–45 minutes • Serves 6 • Per Serving 525 calories, 21g fat (of which 9g saturates), 81g carbohydrate, 0.3g salt • Easy

450g (1lb) pears, peeled, cored and chopped, tossed with the juice of 1 lemon
225g (8oz) golden caster sugar
1 tsp mixed spice
450g (1lb) blackberries
cream, Vanilla Custard or Vanilla Ice Cream (see pages 269–70) to serve

FOR THE CRUMBLE TOPPING
100g (3½oz) butter, chopped, plus extra to grease
225g (8oz) plain flour
75g (3oz) ground almonds

1 Put the pears and lemon juice into a bowl, add 100g (3½oz) sugar and the mixed spice, then add the blackberries and toss thoroughly to coat.

2 Preheat the oven to 200°C (180°C fan oven) mark 6. Lightly grease a 1.8 litre (3¼ pint) shallow ovenproof dish, then carefully tip the fruit into the prepared dish in an even layer.

3 To make the topping, put the butter, flour, ground almonds and the remaining sugar into a food processor and pulse until the mixture begins to resemble breadcrumbs. Tip into a bowl. (Alternatively, rub the butter into the flour in a large bowl by hand or using a pastry cutter. Stir in the ground almonds and the remaining sugar.) Bring parts of the mixture together with your hands to make lumps.

4 Spoon the crumble topping evenly over the fruit, then bake for 35–45 minutes until the fruit is tender and the crumble is golden and bubbling. Serve with cream, Vanilla Custard or Vanilla Ice Cream.

★ COOK'S TIPS
● *This is a versatile recipe that can be popped in the oven while you whip up your main course.*
● *Make double the amount of crumble topping and freeze half for an easy pudding another day.*

★ TRY SOMETHING DIFFERENT
Crumble is a great way to use leftover, slightly overripe fruit. Replace the pears with apples, or omit the blackberries and use 700g (1½lb) plums or rhubarb instead. You could also use gooseberries (omit the spice), or try 450g (1lb) rhubarb with 450g (1lb) strawberries.

American-style Plum Cobbler

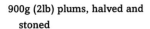

Preparation Time 25 minutes • Cooking Time 40 minutes • Serves 6 • Per Serving 451 calories, 15g fat
(of which 9g saturates), 76g carbohydrate, 0.3g salt • **Easy**

**900g (2lb) plums, halved and
  stoned**
**150g (5oz) golden caster sugar, plus
  3 tbsp**
1 tbsp cornflour
250g (9oz) self-raising flour
**100g (3½oz) chilled unsalted butter,
  diced**
**175ml (6fl oz) buttermilk or whole
  natural yogurt**

1 Preheat the oven to 200°C (180°C fan oven) mark 6. Cut the plums into chunky wedges. Tip into an ovenproof dish measuring 25.5 × 18 × 7.5cm (10 × 7 × 3in) and toss together with 3 tbsp sugar and the cornflour.

2 Whiz the flour, butter and 100g (3½oz) sugar in a food processor until the mixture forms fine crumbs. (Alternatively, rub the fat into the flour by hand or using a pastry cutter, then stir in the sugar.) Add the buttermilk or yogurt and blend for a few seconds until just combined.

3 Scatter clumps of the squidgy dough over the plums, leaving some of the fruit exposed. Sprinkle the cobbler with the remaining sugar and bake in the oven for 40 minutes or until the fruit is tender and the topping is pale golden.

★ FINISHING TOUCHES
A scoop of Vanilla Ice Cream (see page 270) makes an indulgent addition to a bowl of plum cobbler.

Cherry Clafoutis

Preparation Time 25 minutes, plus soaking • Cooking Time 1 hour, plus resting • Serves 6 • Per Serving 235 calories, 9g fat (of which 4g saturates), 32g carbohydrate, 0.2g salt • **Gluten Free** • **Easy**

350g (12oz) pitted cherries
3 tbsp Kirsch
100g (3½oz) caster sugar, plus
   1 tbsp and extra to dust
4 large eggs
25g (1oz) plain flour
150ml (¼ pint) milk
150ml (¼ pint) single cream
1 tsp vanilla extract
butter to grease
icing sugar to dust
double cream to serve

1 Put the cherries into a bowl with the Kirsch and 1 tbsp caster sugar. Mix together, then cover and put to one side for 1 hour.

2 Meanwhile, whisk the eggs with the remaining caster sugar and the flour. Bring the milk and cream to the boil, pour on to the egg mixture and whisk until combined. Add the vanilla extract and strain into a bowl, cover and put to one side for 30 minutes.

3 Preheat the oven to 180°C (160°C fan oven) mark 4. Lightly grease a 1.7 litre (3 pint) shallow ovenproof dish and dust with caster sugar. Spoon the cherries into the dish. Whisk the batter and pour it over them. Bake in the oven for about 50–60 minutes or until golden and just set. Dust with icing sugar and serve warm with cream.

★ TRY SOMETHING DIFFERENT
Use fresh apricots or greengages, halved and stoned, instead of the cherries.

Hot Pear and White Chocolate Puddings

★

Preparation Time 20 minutes • Cooking Time 20 minutes • Serves 4 • Per Serving 524 calories, 30g fat (of which 16g saturates), 61g carbohydrate, 0.5g salt • **Easy**

100g (3½oz) butter, softened, plus extra to grease
100g (3½oz) self-raising flour, sifted
100g (3½oz) light muscovado sugar
1 tsp cocoa powder
1 medium egg
2–3 drops of almond extract
50g (2oz) white chocolate, chopped
2 ripe pears
25g (1oz) flaked almonds

1 Preheat the oven to 180°C (160°C fan oven) mark 4. Lightly grease four 250ml (9fl oz) ramekins.

2 Put half the butter, half the flour and half the sugar into a bowl. Add the cocoa powder, egg and almond extract and beat together until smooth. Divide the mixture among the prepared ramekins. Scatter half the chocolate on top.

3 Peel, core and chop the pears and divide among the ramekins.

4 Rub the remaining butter, flour and sugar together in a bowl until the mixture resembles breadcrumbs. Stir in the flaked almonds and the remaining chocolate, then sprinkle over the pears and bake in the oven for 20 minutes or until golden.

Pear and Ginger Steamed Pudding

★

Preparation Time 20 minutes • Cooking Time 1 hour 35 minutes, plus cooling • Serves 8 • Per Serving 314 calories, 14g fat (of which 9g saturates), 45g carbohydrate, 0.6g salt • Easy

125g (4oz) unsalted butter, softened, plus extra to grease
1 large pear, peeled, cored and diced
2 tbsp golden caster sugar
2 balls preserved stem ginger, finely chopped, plus 2 tbsp ginger syrup
4 tbsp golden syrup
125g (4oz) light muscovado sugar
finely grated zest of 1 lemon
2 medium eggs, beaten
175g (6oz) self-raising flour
2 tsp ground ginger
3 tbsp perry or pear juice
cream to serve (optional)

1 Grease a 900ml (1½ pint) pudding basin. Put the pear into a pan with 2 tbsp water and the caster sugar and simmer for 5 minutes. Stir in the preserved stem ginger and the ginger and golden syrups and leave to cool. Tip the mixture into the basin.

2 Beat the butter, muscovado sugar and lemon zest in a bowl with a hand-held electric whisk until light and fluffy. Beat in the eggs a little at a time.

3 Fold in the flour and ground ginger, then fold in the perry or pear juice. Pour the mixture into the basin on top of the pear compote. Cut out a piece each of greaseproof paper and foil, each measuring 30.5 × 30.5cm (12 × 12in). Place the greaseproof on the foil and fold a pleat in the middle. Put on top of the pudding basin – it should overhang the sides. Tie the paper under the rim of the basin with string, using extra to make a knotted handle over the top. Trim off excess paper and foil.

4 Sit the basin on an upturned saucer in a large pan. Pour in enough boiling water to come halfway up the basin. Cover and steam for 1¼–1½ hours, topping up with boiling water as necessary. Turn out on to a plate and serve with cream if you like.

Cranberry Christmas Pudding

Preparation Time 20 minutes, plus soaking • Cooking Time 8½ hours • Serves 12 • Per Serving 448 calories, 17g fat (of which 7g saturates), 68g carbohydrate, 0.3g salt • Easy

200g (7oz) currants
200g (7oz) sultanas
200g (7oz) raisins
75g (3oz) dried cranberries or
   cherries
grated zest and juice of 1 orange
50ml (2fl oz) rum
50ml (2fl oz) brandy
1–2 tsp Angostura bitters
1 small apple, grated
1 carrot, grated
175g (6oz) fresh breadcrumbs
100g (3½oz) plain flour, sifted
1 tsp mixed spice
175g (6oz) light vegetarian suet
100g (3½oz) dark muscovado sugar
50g (2oz) blanched almonds,
   roughly chopped
2 medium eggs
butter to grease
fresh or frozen cranberries (thawed
   if frozen), fresh bay leaves and
   icing sugar to decorate
Brandy Butter (see Cook's Tip)
   to serve

1 Put the dried fruit, orange zest and juice into a large bowl. Pour the rum, brandy and Angostura bitters over. Cover and leave to soak in a cool place for at least 1 hour or overnight.

2 Add the apple, carrot, breadcrumbs, flour, mixed spice, suet, sugar, almonds and eggs to the bowl of soaked fruit. Use a wooden spoon to mix everything together well. Grease a 1.8 litre (3¼ pint) pudding basin and line with a 60cm (24in) square piece of muslin. Spoon the mixture into the basin and flatten the surface. Gather the muslin up and over the top, twist and secure with string. Put the basin on an upturned heatproof saucer or trivet in the base of a large pan, then pour in enough boiling water to come halfway up the side of the basin. Cover with a tight-fitting lid and simmer for 6 hours. Keep the water topped up with more boiling water.

3 Remove the basin from the pan and leave to cool. When the pudding is cold, remove from the basin, then wrap it in clingfilm and a double layer of foil. Store in a cool, dry place for up to six months.

4 To reheat, steam for 2½ hours; check the water level every 40 minutes and top up if necessary. Leave the pudding in the pan, covered, to keep warm until needed. Decorate with cranberries and bay leaves, dust with icing sugar and serve with Brandy Butter.

★ COOK'S TIP
Brandy Butter
Put 125g (4oz) unsalted butter into a bowl and beat until very soft. Gradually beat in 125g (4oz) light muscovado sugar until very light and fluffy, then beat in 6 tbsp brandy, a spoonful at a time. Cover and chill for at least 3 hours.

Bread and Butter Pudding

★

Preparation Time 10 minutes, plus soaking • **Cooking Time** 30–40 minutes • **Serves 4** • **Per Serving** 450 calories, 13g fat (of which 5g saturates), 70g carbohydrate, 1.1g salt • **Easy**

50g (2oz) unsalted butter, softened, plus extra to grease
275g (10oz) white farmhouse bread, cut into 1cm (½in) slices, crusts removed
50g (2oz) raisins or sultanas
3 medium eggs
450ml (¾ pint) milk
3 tbsp golden icing sugar, plus extra to dust

1 Lightly grease four 300ml (½ pint) gratin dishes or one 1.1 litre (2 pint) ovenproof dish. Butter the bread, then cut into quarters to make triangles. Arrange the bread in the dish(es) and sprinkle with the raisins or sultanas.

2 Beat the eggs, milk and sugar in a bowl. Pour the mixture over the bread and leave to soak for 10 minutes. Preheat the oven to 180°C (160°C fan oven) mark 4.

3 Bake the pudding(s) in the oven for 30–40 minutes. Dust with icing sugar to serve.

Panettone Pudding

Preparation Time 20 minutes, plus soaking • Cooking Time 35–45 minutes • Serves 6 • Per Serving 581 calories, 29g fat (of which 16g saturates), 73g carbohydrate, 0.9g salt • **Easy**

50g (2oz) butter, at room
    temperature, plus extra to grease
500g (1lb 2oz) panettone (see
    Cook's Tip), cut into slices about
    5mm (¼in) thick
3 large eggs, beaten
150g (5oz) golden caster sugar
300ml (½ pint) full-fat milk
150ml (¼ pint) double cream
grated zest of 1 orange

★ COOK'S TIP
Panettone is a yeasted fruit cake that is a traditional Christmas treat in Italy and is most widely available around Christmas time. If you can't find it, use brioche or cinnamon and raisin bread.

1 Grease a 2 litre (3½ pint) ovenproof dish. Lightly butter the panettone slices, then tear them into pieces and arrange in the dish.

2 Mix the eggs with the sugar in a large bowl, then whisk in the milk, cream and orange zest. Pour the mixture over the buttered panettone and leave to soak for 20 minutes. Preheat the oven to 170°C (150°C fan oven) mark 3.

3 Put the dish in a roasting tin and pour in enough hot water to come halfway up the sides. Bake in the oven for 35–45 minutes or until the pudding is just set in the middle and golden brown.

Steamed Syrup Sponge Puddings

Preparation Time 20 minutes • Cooking Time 35 minutes or 1½ hours • Serves 4 • Per Serving 580 calories, 29g fat (of which 17g saturates), 76g carbohydrate, 0.7g salt • **Easy**

125g (4oz) unsalted butter,
    softened, plus extra to grease
3 tbsp golden syrup
125g (4oz) golden caster sugar
few drops of vanilla extract
2 medium eggs, beaten
175g (6oz) self-raising flour, sifted
about 3 tbsp milk
custard or cream to serve

1 Half-fill a steamer or large pan with water and put it on to boil. Grease four 300ml (½ pint) basins or a 900ml (1½ pint) pudding basin and spoon the golden syrup into the bottom of the basin(s).

2 Cream the butter and sugar together in a bowl until pale and fluffy. Stir in the vanilla extract. Add the eggs, a little at a time, beating well after each addition.

3 Using a metal spoon, fold in half the flour, then fold in the remaining flour with enough milk to give a dropping consistency. Spoon the mixture into the prepared pudding basin(s).

4 Cover with greased and pleated greaseproof paper and foil (see page 26), and secure with string. Steam for 35 minutes for individual puddings or 1½ hours for one large pudding, checking the water level from time to time and topping up with boiling water as necessary. Turn out on to warmed plates and serve with custard or cream.

★ TRY SOMETHING DIFFERENT
Instead of syrup, try the following:
● ***Steamed Jam Sponge Puddings***
Put 4 tbsp raspberry or blackberry jam into the bottom of the basins instead of the syrup.
● ***Steamed Chocolate Sponge Puddings***
Omit the golden syrup. Blend 4 tbsp cocoa powder with 2 tbsp hot water, then gradually beat into the creamed mixture before adding the eggs.

Saucy Hot Lemon Puddings

Preparation Time 15–20 minutes • Cooking Time 35–40 minutes • Serves 4 • Per Serving 323 calories, 16g fat (of which 9g saturates), 40g carbohydrate, 0.4g salt • **Easy**

**50g (2oz) butter, plus extra to
  grease**
125g (4oz) golden caster sugar
**finely grated zest and juice of
  2 lemons**
2 medium eggs, separated
50g (2oz) self-raising flour, sifted
300ml (½ pint) semi-skimmed milk

1 Preheat the oven to 190°C (170°C fan oven) mark 5. Lightly grease four 200ml (7fl oz) ovenproof cups or glasses.

2 Cream the butter, sugar and lemon zest together in a bowl until pale and fluffy. Beat in the egg yolks, then the flour until combined. Stir in the milk and lemon juice – the mixture will curdle, but don't panic.

3 Put the egg whites into a clean, grease-free bowl and whisk until soft peaks form, then fold into the lemon mixture. (The mixture will still look curdled – don't worry.) Divide among the four cups and stand them in a roasting tin.

4 Add enough boiling water to the tin to come halfway up the sides of the cups and bake in the oven for 35–40 minutes until spongy and light golden. If you like softer tops, cover the entire tin with foil. When cooked, the puddings will have separated into a tangy lemon custard layer on the bottom, with a light sponge on top. Serve at once.

★ TRY SOMETHING DIFFERENT
Replace 1 lemon with a large lime for an added citrus twist.

Cherry and Tangerine Sticky Puddings

★

Preparation Time 20 minutes, plus soaking • **Cooking Time** 25 minutes • **Serves 8** • **Per Serving** 664 calories, 39g fat (of which 22g saturates), 79g carbohydrate, 0.7g salt • **Easy**

about 25g (1oz) white vegetable fat, melted
200g (7oz) dried cherries
2 tbsp orange-flavoured liqueur
¾ tsp bicarbonate of soda
75g (3oz) unsalted butter, softened
150g (5oz) golden caster sugar
2 medium eggs, beaten
175g (6oz) self-raising flour

FOR THE SAUCE
175g (6oz) light muscovado sugar
125g (4oz) unsalted butter
6 tbsp double cream
25g (1oz) pecan nuts, chopped
juice of 1 tangerine

1 Preheat the oven to 180°C (160°C fan oven) mark 4. Using the melted fat, lightly oil eight 175ml (6fl oz) metal pudding basins or ramekins, then put a circle of non-stick baking parchment into the base of each.

2 Put 175g (6oz) dried cherries into a bowl and pour 150ml (¼ pint) boiling water over them. Stir in the liqueur and bicarbonate of soda, then leave to soak for 1 hour.

3 Whisk the butter and sugar in a large bowl until pale and fluffy, then beat in the eggs a little at a time. Fold in the cherry mixture.

4 Add the flour and fold in with a large metal spoon. Divide the mixture equally among the basins, then place on a baking sheet and bake for about 25 minutes or until well risen and firm.

5 Meanwhile, make the sauce. Put the sugar, butter, cream, pecans and remaining cherries in a pan. Heat gently until the sugar has dissolved, then stir in the tangerine juice.

6 Leave the puddings to cool for 5 minutes, then turn out. Serve topped with the sauce.

★ FREEZING TIP
To freeze Cool the puddings completely. Wrap in clingfilm. Pour the sauce into a freezerproof container and leave to cool. Freeze both for up to one month.
To use Thaw the puddings and sauce overnight in the fridge. Warm the sauce. Meanwhile, put the puddings on a microwaveable plate. Spoon 1 tbsp sauce over each. Warm in the microwave on full power for 2 minutes. Serve with the remaining sauce.

Sticky Syrup Puddings

Preparation Time 20 minutes • Cooking Time 25–30 minutes, plus resting • Serves 4 • Per Serving 565 calories, 38g fat (of which 21g saturates), 53g carbohydrate, 0.9g salt • **Easy**

1 tbsp golden syrup
1 tbsp black treacle
150g (5oz) unsalted butter, softened
25g (1oz) pecan nuts or walnuts,
    finely ground
75g (3oz) self-raising flour
125g (4oz) caster sugar
2 large eggs, beaten
cream or custard to serve

1 Preheat the oven to 180°C (160°C fan oven) mark 4. Put the syrup, treacle and 25g (1oz) butter into a bowl and beat until smooth. Divide the mixture among four 150ml (¼ pint) timbales or ramekins and put to one side.

2 Put the nuts into a bowl, sift in the flour and mix together well.

3 Put the remaining butter and the sugar in a food processor and whiz briefly. (Alternatively, use a hand-held electric whisk.) Add the eggs and the flour mixture and whiz or

mix again for 30 seconds. Spoon the mixture on top of the syrup mixture in the timbales or ramekins. Bake in the oven for 25–30 minutes until risen and golden.

4 Remove the puddings from the oven and leave to rest for 5 minutes, then unmould on to warmed serving plates. Serve immediately with cream or custard.

Speedy Sticky Toffee Puddings

Preparation Time 15 minutes • **Cooking Time** 12 minutes • **Serves** 6 • **Per Serving** 720 calories, 38g fat (of which 22g saturates), 96g carbohydrate, 1g salt • **Easy**

75g (3oz) butter, softened, plus extra to grease

75g (3oz) mixed dried fruit

75g (3oz) pitted dates, roughly chopped

¾ tsp bicarbonate of soda

150g (5oz) light muscovado sugar

2 medium eggs, beaten

½ tsp vanilla extract

175g (6oz) self-raising flour

FOR THE TOFFEE SAUCE

125g (4oz) butter

175g (6oz) light muscovado sugar

4 tbsp double cream

25g (1oz) pecan nuts, roughly chopped

1 Grease and baseline six 250ml (9fl oz) cups. Put the dried fruit and bicarbonate of soda into a bowl and pour 175ml (6fl oz) boiling water over them. Put to one side.

2 Beat the sugar and butter in another bowl for 1–2 minutes until light and fluffy. Beat in the eggs and vanilla extract, then sift the flour over and fold it into the fruit mixture.

3 Spoon the mixture into the prepared cups. Cover very loosely with microwave film and cook three cups in the microwave oven on medium power or 600W for 6 minutes. Remove the microwave film from the puddings and leave to stand for 1 minute. Repeat with the remaining cups.

4 To make the sauce, put the butter, sugar and cream into a pan and heat gently, stirring well. Pour the sauce over the puddings and sprinkle with the chopped nuts.

⭐ COOK'S TIP

The puddings can also be baked in a conventional oven, although this takes a little longer. Preheat the oven to 200°C (180°C fan oven) mark 6. Spoon the mixture into greased heatproof cups and cover with foil, then put on to a baking sheet. Bake for 30 minutes or until soft and springy and a skewer inserted into the middle comes out clean.

Pies and Tarts

Rhubarb and Cinnamon Pie

Preparation Time 15 minutes, plus chilling • Cooking Time 50 minutes • Serves 6 • Per Serving 379 calories, 14g fat (of which 11g saturates), 55g carbohydrate, 0.3g salt • Easy

175g (6oz) plain flour, plus extra
    to dust
125g (4oz) butter, plus extra
    to grease
150g (5oz) golden caster sugar, plus
    extra to sprinkle
700g (1½lb) rhubarb, cut into bite-
    size chunks
2 tbsp cornflour
½ tsp ground cinnamon
a little milk to glaze

1 Put the flour, butter and 25g (1oz) sugar into a food processor and whiz until the pastry comes together. (Alternatively, rub the butter into the flour in a large bowl by hand or using a pastry cutter until it resembles fine crumbs. Stir in the sugar. Bring together and knead briefly to form a ball.) If the dough is slightly sticky, roll it in some flour. Chill for 20 minutes.

2 Grease a 23cm (9in) round ovenproof dish with sides at least 5cm (2in) deep. Roll out the pastry on a lightly floured worksurface to a large round, leaving the edges uneven. It should be large enough to line the dish and to allow the edges of the pastry to drape over the sides.

3 Preheat the oven to 200°C (180°C fan oven) mark 6. Toss the rhubarb in the remaining sugar, cornflour and cinnamon and spoon into the dish. Bring the pastry edges up and over the fruit, leaving a gap in the centre. Glaze with milk and sprinkle with sugar.

4 Put on a baking sheet and bake for 50 minutes or until the pastry is golden brown and the juice is bubbling up. Serve hot.

★ TRY SOMETHING DIFFERENT
Add the grated zest of 1 orange instead of the cinnamon.

Rustic Blackberry and Apple Pie

Preparation Time 25 minutes, plus chilling • Cooking Time 40 minutes • Serves 6 • Per Serving 372 calories, 19g fat (of which 11g saturates), 49g carbohydrate, 0.4g salt • Easy

200g (7oz) plain flour, plus extra
    to dust
125g (4oz) chilled unsalted butter,
    diced, plus extra to grease
1 medium egg, beaten
75g (3oz) golden caster sugar, plus
    3 tbsp
a pinch of salt
500g (1lb 2oz) eating apples,
    quartered, cored and cut into
    chunky wedges
300g (11oz) blackberries
¼ tsp ground cinnamon
juice of 1 small lemon

1 Pulse the flour and butter in a food processor until it resembles coarse crumbs. (Alternatively, rub the butter into the flour by hand or using a pastry cutter). Add the egg, 2 tbsp sugar and the salt, and pulse again to combine, or stir in. Wrap in clingfilm and chill for at least 15 minutes. Meanwhile, preheat the oven to 200°C (180°C fan oven) mark 6.

2 Put the apples, blackberries, 75g (3oz) sugar, the cinnamon and lemon juice in a bowl and toss together, making sure the sugar dissolves in the juice.

3 Grease a 25.5cm (10in) enamel or metal pie dish. Using a lightly floured rolling pin, roll out the pastry on a large sheet of baking parchment to a 30.5cm (12in) round. Lift up the paper, upturn the pastry on to the pie dish and peel away the paper.

4 Put the prepared fruit in the centre of the pie dish and fold the pastry edges up and over the fruit. Sprinkle with the remaining sugar and bake for 40 minutes or until the fruit is tender and the pastry golden.

Sugar-crusted Fruit Pie

Preparation Time 30 minutes, plus chilling • Cooking Time about 40 minutes, plus cooling • Serves 4 •
Per Serving 673 calories, 38g fat (of which 17g saturates), 79g carbohydrate, 0.5g salt • Easy

75g (3oz) hazelnuts
350g (12oz) cherries, pitted
75g (3oz) caster sugar, plus 2 tbsp
175g (6oz) plain flour, plus extra
   to dust
125g (4oz) butter
275g (10oz) cooking apples, peeled,
   cored and quartered

1 Preheat the grill. Spread the hazelnuts over a baking sheet. Toast under the hot grill until golden brown, turning them frequently. Put the hazelnuts in a clean teatowel and rub off the skins. Leave to cool.

2 Put the cherries into a bowl with 25g (1oz) sugar. Cover and put to one side. For the hazelnut pastry, put 50g (2oz) hazelnuts into a food processor with the flour and pulse to a powder. Remove and put to one side. Whiz the butter with 50g (2oz) sugar in the food processor. Add the flour mixture and pulse until it forms a dough. Turn out on to a lightly floured worksurface and knead lightly, then wrap in clingfilm and chill for 30 minutes. If the pastry cracks, just work it together.

3 Preheat the oven to 180°C (160°C fan oven) mark 4. Cut the apples into small chunks and put into a 900ml (1½ pint) oval pie dish. Spoon the cherries on top. Roll out the pastry on a lightly floured surface to about 5mm (¼in) thick. Cut into 1cm (½in) strips. Dampen the edge of the pie dish with a little water and press a few of the strips on to the rim to cover it. Dampen the pastry rim. Put the remaining strips over the cherries to create a lattice pattern. Brush the pastry with water and sprinkle with the extra sugar.

4 Bake for 30–35 minutes until the pastry is golden. Leave to cool for 15 minutes.

5 Chop the remaining toasted hazelnuts and sprinkle over the tart.

 GET AHEAD
To prepare ahead *Complete the recipe to the end of step 4, then cool, wrap and chill for up to three days.*
To use *Preheat the oven to 180°C (160°C fan oven) mark 4 and bake for about 20–25 minutes to heat through. Complete the recipe.*

 FREEZING TIP
To freeze *Complete the recipe to the end of step 3, then wrap and freeze.*
To use *Brush the pastry with egg and sprinkle the extra sugar on top. Bake from frozen at 180°C (160°C fan oven) mark 4 for 40–45 minutes until golden. Complete the recipe.*

Plum and Cardamom Pie

Preparation Time 15 minutes • Cooking Time 30 minutes, plus cooling • Serves 6 • Per Serving 275 calories, 12g fat (of which 4g saturates), 41g carbohydrate, 0.4g salt • **Easy**

250g (9oz) ready-rolled sweet
  shortcrust pastry
flour to dust
900g (2lb) mixed yellow and red
  plums, halved, stoned and
  quartered
2–3 green cardamom pods, split
  open, seeds removed and
  crushed or chopped
50–75g (2–3oz) caster sugar, plus
  extra to sprinkle
1 medium egg, beaten or milk
  to glaze

1 Preheat the oven to 220°C (200°C fan oven) mark 7 and put a flat baking sheet in to heat. Roll out the pastry on a lightly floured worksurface, into a 30.5cm (12in) round. Put it on a floured baking sheet, without a lip if possible.

2 Pile the fruit on to the pastry and sprinkle with the cardamom seeds and sugar (if the plums are tart you'll need all of it; less if they are ripe and sweet). Fold in the pastry edges and pleat together.

3 Brush the pastry with beaten egg or milk and sprinkle with sugar. Put on the preheated sheet and bake for 30 minutes until the pastry is golden brown and the plums just tender. The juices will begin to bubble from the pie as it cooks.

4 Leave to cool for 10 minutes, then carefully loosen the pastry around the edges. Cool for a further 20 minutes, then transfer very carefully to a serving plate. Sprinkle with a little sugar and serve warm.

⭐ TRY SOMETHING
DIFFERENT
Replace the plums with pears, toss them in a little lemon juice, and sprinkle with ½ tsp cinnamon instead of the cardamom seeds.

Classic Apple Pie

★

Preparation Time 20 minutes • Cooking Time 35–40 minutes • Serves 6 • Per Serving 268 calories, 11g fat (of which 4g saturates), 43g carbohydrate, 0.4g salt • Easy

900g (2lb) cooking apples, peeled, cored and sliced
50g (2oz) caster sugar, plus extra to sprinkle
Sweet Shortcrust Pastry (see page 268), made with 225g (8oz) plain flour, a pinch of salt, 100g (3½oz) chilled butter and 1 large egg
flour to dust
cream to serve

1 Preheat the oven to 190°C (170°C fan oven) mark 7.

2 Layer the apples and sugar in a 1.1 litre (2 pint) pie dish. Sprinkle with 1 tbsp water.

3 Roll out the pastry on a lightly floured worksurface to a round 2.5cm (1in) larger than the pie dish. Cut off a strip the width of the rim of the dish, dampen the rim of the dish and press on the strip. Dampen the pastry strip and cover with the pastry circle, pressing the edges together well. Decorate the edge of the pastry and make a slit in the centre to allow steam to escape.

4 Bake for 35–40 minutes until the pastry is lightly browned. Sprinkle with caster sugar before serving with cream.

★ COOK'S TIP
Apple pie is also great served cold, with Vanilla Ice Cream (see page 270).

Maple Pecan Tart

Preparation Time 40 minutes, plus chilling • **Cooking Time** 1¼ hours • **Serves 10** • **Per Serving** 748 calories, 57g fat (of which 24g saturates), 51g carbohydrate, 0.6g salt • **Easy**

250g (9oz) plain flour, sifted
a large pinch of salt
225g (8oz) unsalted butter, cubed
   and chilled
100g (3½oz) light muscovado sugar
125g (4oz) dates, stoned and
   roughly chopped
grated zest and juice of ½ lemon
100ml (3½fl oz) maple syrup, plus
   6 tbsp extra
1 tsp vanilla extract
4 medium eggs
300g (11oz) pecan nut halves
300ml (½ pint) double cream
2 tbsp bourbon whiskey

1 Put the flour and salt into a food processor. Add 125g (4oz) of the butter and whiz to fine crumbs. (Alternatively, rub the butter into the flour in a large bowl by hand or using a pastry cutter.) Add 2 tbsp water and whiz, or stir, until the mixture just comes together. Wrap in clingfilm and chill for 30 minutes. Use to line a 28 × 4cm (11 × 1½in) loose-based tart tin, then cover and chill for 30 minutes. Preheat the oven to 200°C (180°C fan oven) mark 6.

2 Prick the pastry all over, cover with greaseproof paper and fill with baking beans. Bake in the oven for 25 minutes, then remove the paper and beans and bake for a further 5 minutes or until the base is dry and light golden.

3 Meanwhile, whiz, or beat, the rest of the butter until soft. Add the sugar and dates and whiz, or beat, to cream together. Add the lemon zest and juice, 100ml (3½fl oz) maple syrup, the vanilla extract, eggs and 200g (7oz) nuts. Whiz until the nuts are finely chopped – the mixture will look curdled. Pour into the pastry case and top with the rest of the nuts.

4 Bake for 40–45 minutes until almost set in the middle. Cover with greaseproof paper for the last 10 minutes if the nuts turn very dark. Cool slightly before removing from the tin, then brush with 4 tbsp maple syrup. Lightly whip the cream with the whiskey and 2 tbsp maple syrup, then serve with the pie.

 TRY SOMETHING DIFFERENT
Replace the lemon with orange, the pecans with walnut halves and the whiskey with Cointreau.

Quick Apple Tart

Preparation Time 10 minutes • Cooking Time 20–25 minutes • Serves 8 • Per Serving 221 calories, 12g fat (of which 0g saturates), 29g carbohydrate, 0.4g salt • **Easy**

375g pack all-butter ready-rolled puff pastry

500g (1lb 2oz) Cox's Orange Pippin apples, cored, thinly sliced and tossed in the juice of 1 lemon

golden icing sugar to dust

1 Preheat the oven to 200°C (180°C fan oven) mark 6. Put the pastry on a 28 × 38cm (11 × 15in) baking sheet and roll lightly with a rolling pin to smooth down the pastry. Score lightly around the edge, to create a 3cm (1¼in) border.

2 Put the apple slices on top of the pastry, within the border. Turn the edge of the pastry halfway over, so that it reaches the edge of the apples, then press down and use your fingers to crimp the edge. Dust heavily with icing sugar.

3 Bake for 20–25 minutes until the pastry is cooked and the sugar has caramelised. Serve warm, dusted with more icing sugar.

Apple and Lemon Tartlets

Preparation Time 40 minutes, plus chilling • Cooking Time 1¼–1½ hours • Makes 8 • Per Tartlet 615 calories, 34g fat (of which 20g saturates), 77g carbohydrate, 0.6g salt • **Easy**

3 medium eggs

a pinch of salt

300g (11oz) plain flour, plus extra
   to dust

75g (3oz) icing sugar

175g (6oz) unsalted butter

FOR THE FILLING

700g (1½lb) Bramley or Granny
   Smith's apples

grated zest and juice of 2 lemons

150g (5oz) unsalted butter

225g (8oz) caster sugar, plus extra
   to dust

1 tsp arrowroot

1 Beat 1 egg with a pinch of salt, then set aside 1 tbsp. Put the flour, icing sugar and butter into a food processor and whiz until the mixture resembles fine crumbs. Add the remaining beaten egg with 3 tbsp water and pulse until the pastry comes together. (Alternatively, rub the butter into the dry ingredients in a large bowl by hand or using a pastry cutter. Stir in the egg and water.) Divide into eight balls and chill for 30 minutes. Roll out the pastry on a lightly floured worksurface and line eight 8cm (3¼in) loose-based fluted tartlet tins. Prick the bases all over with a fork and chill for 20 minutes.

2 Preheat the oven to 200°C (180°C fan oven) mark 6. Bake the tartlet cases blind (see step 2, page 44). Remove from the oven. Reduce the oven temperature to 180°C (160°C fan oven) mark 4.

3 Peel, core and thinly slice the apples, then toss in 2 tbsp lemon juice. Fry in 25g (1oz) butter for 1–2 minutes. Spoon the apple into the pastry cases.

4 Whiz, or beat, the remaining butter with the caster sugar for 3 minutes or until pale. Add the arrowroot, lemon zest and the remaining 2 eggs and blend for 2 minutes. With the food processor running, add the remaining lemon juice and blend for 1 minute. Pour the mixture over the apples, then dust with caster sugar.

5 Bake the tartlets for 45–50 minutes until the apples start to caramelise. Serve warm or cold.

Plum and Almond Tart

Preparation Time 30 minutes, plus chilling • **Cooking Time** 40 minutes, plus cooling and setting • **Cuts into 8 slices** •
Per Slice 535 calories, 35g fat (of which 16g saturates), 50g carbohydrate, 0.5g salt • **Easy**

150g (5oz) unsalted butter, chilled
    and diced
175g (6oz) plain flour, plus extra
    to dust
7 tbsp soured cream

FOR THE FILLING
50g (2oz) unsalted butter
50g (2oz) caster sugar, plus extra
    to dust
2 medium eggs, lightly beaten
100g (3½oz) ground almonds
1 tbsp Kirsch or 3–4 drops almond
    extract
900g (2lb) plums, stoned and
    quartered
50g (2oz) blanched almonds to
    decorate
175g (6oz) redcurrant jelly

1 To make the pastry, whiz the butter and flour in a food processor for 1–2 seconds. Add the soured cream and whiz for a further 1–2 seconds until the dough just begins to come together. (Alternatively, rub the butter into the flour in a large bowl by hand or using a pastry cutter, then mix in the soured cream.) Turn out on to a lightly floured worksurface and knead for about 30 seconds or until the pastry just comes together. Wrap in clingfilm and chill for 30 minutes.

2 To make the filling, put the butter into a bowl and beat until soft, then add the sugar and beat until light and fluffy. Beat in the eggs,

alternating with the ground almonds. Add the Kirsch or almond extract, cover and put to one side.

3 Roll out the pastry on a lightly floured worksurface to a 30.5cm (12in) round, then transfer to a baking sheet and prick all over with a fork. Spread the almond mixture over the pastry, leaving a 3cm (1¼in) border all round. Scatter the plums over the filling and fold the edges of the pastry up over the fruit. Dust with caster sugar, then chill for 20 minutes.

4 Preheat the oven to 220°C (200°C fan oven) mark 7 and put a baking tray in the oven to heat for 10 minutes. Put the tart, on its baking sheet, on top of the hot baking tray. Bake for 35–40 minutes until deep golden brown.

5 Leave the tart to cool for 10 minutes, then slide it on to a wire rack. Arrange the almonds among the fruit. Heat the redcurrant jelly gently in a pan, stirring until smooth, then brush generously over the tart. Leave to set.

Rhubarb and Orange Crumble Tart

Preparation Time 25 minutes, plus chilling • Cooking Time about 55 minutes, plus cooling • Cuts into 8 slices •
Per Slice 518 calories, 37g fat (of which 22g saturates), 45g carbohydrate, 0.3g salt • Easy

200g (7oz) plain flour, plus extra
   to dust
125g (4oz) unsalted butter, cut
   into small pieces
25g (1oz) golden caster sugar
cream to serve

FOR THE FILLING
550g (1¼lb) rhubarb, cut into
   2.5cm (1in) pieces
50g (2oz) golden caster sugar
grated zest of 1 orange
juice of ½ orange

FOR THE CRUMBLE TOPPING
50g (2oz) plain flour
25g (1oz) ground almonds
50g (2oz) light muscovado sugar
25g (1oz) unsalted butter, cut into
   small pieces

1 To make the pastry, whiz the flour, butter and caster sugar in a food processor until it resembles fine crumbs. (Alternatively, rub the butter into the flour in a large bowl by hand or using a pastry cutter until it resembles fine crumbs. Stir in the sugar.) Add 2 tbsp cold water and whiz briefly again, or stir with a fork, to form a soft pastry. Wrap the pastry in clingfilm and chill for at least 30 minutes.

2 Roll out the pastry on a lightly floured worksurface and use to line a 10 × 35.5cm (4 × 14in) loose-based tin, or a 23cm (9in) round loose-based tart tin. Chill for 30 minutes. Preheat the oven to 200°C (180°C fan oven) mark 6. Bake the tart case blind (see step 2, page 44).

3 Meanwhile, make the filling. Put the rhubarb, caster sugar, orange zest and juice into a pan and bring to the boil. Cook gently for 6–8 minutes until the rhubarb has just softened. Leave to cool.

4 To make the crumble topping, put the flour, almonds, muscovado sugar and butter into the food processor and whiz briefly until it resembles fine crumbs. (Alternatively, rub the butter into the flour in a bowl, by hand or using a pastry cutter, until it resembles fine crumbs. Stir in the almonds and sugar.)

5 Spoon the rhubarb filling into the pastry case and smooth the surface. Top with the crumble mixture and bake for 20 minutes or until pale golden. Leave to cool slightly before serving with cream.

★ COOK'S TIP
Elderflower Cream
Put 300ml (½ pint) double cream, 1 tbsp golden icing sugar and 1 tbsp elderflower cordial into a large bowl and whisk with a hand-held electric whisk until soft peaks form.

Caramelised Apple Tarts

Preparation Time 20 minutes, plus chilling • **Cooking Time** about 40 minutes • **Makes 6** • **Per Tart** 395 calories, 24g fat (of which 4g saturates), 45g carbohydrate, 0.6g salt • **Easy**

40g (1½oz) butter, plus extra to grease
1 pastry sheet from a 375g pack all-butter puff pastry
125g (4oz) white marzipan, chilled and coarsely grated
4 crisp dessert apples, quartered, cored and sliced
juice of 1 large lemon
25g (1oz) demerara sugar
½ tsp ground mixed spice

1 Preheat the oven to 200°C (180°C fan oven) mark 6. Grease six 7.5cm (3in) tartlet tins. Roll out the pastry a little more thinly. Cut out six 12.5cm (5in) rounds of pastry, using a saucer as a guide. Line the tins and prick the base twice with a fork. Chill for 10 minutes.

2 Bake the tartlet cases blind (see step 2, page 44). Sprinkle the marzipan over the pastry and bake in the oven for a further 5 minutes or until the marzipan melts and the pastry is cooked.

3 Meanwhile, heat the butter in a large non-stick frying pan. Add the apples, lemon juice, sugar and mixed spice and cook over a high heat for 5 minutes, turning the apples until just tender and most of the lemon juice has evaporated.

4 Pile the apples into the warm pastry cases, then put back in the oven for 2–3 minutes. Serve warm.

Tarte Tatin

★

Preparation Time 30 minutes, plus chilling • Cooking Time about 1 hour, plus cooling • Cuts into 6 slices •
Per Slice 727 calories, 39g fat (of which 24g saturates), 94g carbohydrate, 0.7g salt • Easy

Sweet Shortcrust Pastry (see page
   268), made with 225g (8oz) plain
   flour, ¼ tsp salt, 150g (5oz)
   unsalted butter, 50g (2oz) golden
   icing sugar, 1 medium egg and
   2–3 drops vanilla extract

FOR THE FILLING
200g (7oz) golden caster sugar
125g (4oz) chilled unsalted butter
1.4–1.6kg (3–3½lb) crisp dessert
   apples, peeled and cored
juice of ½ lemon

1 To make the filling, sprinkle
the caster sugar over the base of
a 20.5cm (8in) tarte tatin tin or
ovenproof frying pan. Cut the butter
into slivers and arrange on the
sugar. Halve the apples and pack
them tightly, cut side up, on top of
the butter.

2 Put the tin or pan on the hob
and cook over a medium heat for
30 minutes (making sure it doesn't
bubble over or catch on the bottom)
or until the butter and sugar turn a
dark golden brown (see Cook's Tip).
Sprinkle with the lemon juice,
then leave to cool for 15 minutes.
Meanwhile, preheat the oven to
220°C (200°C fan oven) mark 7.

3 Put the pastry on a large sheet of
baking parchment. Roll out the
pastry to make a round 2.5cm (1in)
larger than the tin or pan. Prick
several times with a fork. Lay the
pastry over the apples, tucking the
edges down the side of the tin.
Bake for 25–30 minutes until
golden brown. Leave in the tin for
10 minutes, then carefully upturn
on to a serving plate. Serve warm.

★ COOK'S TIP
When caramelising the apples in step 2,
be patient. Allow the sauce to turn a
dark golden brown – any paler and it
will be too sickly. Don't let it burn,
though, as this will make the caramel
taste bitter.

Easy Pear and Toffee Tarte Tatin

Preparation Time 15 minutes • Cooking Time 30–35 minutes, plus cooling • Cuts into 6 slices • Per Slice 294 calories, 12g fat (of which 2g saturates), 46g carbohydrate, 0.5g salt • **Easy**

4 small, rosy pears, quartered and cored – no need to peel them
8 tbsp dulce de leche toffee sauce
225g (8oz) ready-rolled puff pastry
flour to dust
cream or Vanilla Ice Cream (see page 270) to serve

1 Preheat the oven to 200°C (180°C fan oven) mark 6. Put the pears and toffee sauce into a large non-stick frying pan. Cook over a medium heat for 5 minutes or until the pears are well coated and the sauce has turned a slightly darker shade of golden brown.

2 Tip the pears and sauce into a 20.5cm (8in) non-stick sandwich or tart tin. Arrange the pears, skin side down, in a circle and leave to cool for 10 minutes.

3 If necessary, roll out the puff pastry on a lightly floured worksurface until it is wide enough to cover the tin. Lay it over the pears and press down on to the edge of the tin. Trim off any excess pastry. Prick the pastry all over, then bake for 20–25 minutes until well risen and golden.

4 Leave to cool for 5 minutes. To turn out, hold a large serving plate or baking sheet over the tart, turn over and give a quick shake to loosen. Lift off the tin. Serve the tart immediately, cut into wedges, with cream or Vanilla Ice Cream.

★ TRY SOMETHING DIFFERENT
Replace the pears with 3–4 bananas, thickly sliced on the diagonal. Cook the dulce de leche for 5 minutes in step 1, stir in the bananas to coat, then arrange in the tin in an overlapping circle. Complete the recipe.

Plum Tarte Tatin

★

Preparation Time 30 minutes, plus chilling • Cooking Time 30 minutes, plus cooling • Cuts into 6 slices • Per Slice 488 calories, 28g fat (of which 17g saturates), 59g carbohydrate, 0.5g salt • Easy

75g (3oz) unsalted butter
125g (4oz) caster sugar
700g (1½lb) plums, halved and stoned
350g pack all-butter dessert pastry
flour to dust
crème fraîche or cream to serve

1 Melt the butter and sugar in a heavy-based frying pan. Cook, stirring, for 2–3 minutes until the sugar begins to turn light brown. Immediately add the plums and cook for 5 minutes or until the juices begin to run and the plums start to soften. Increase the heat and bubble until the juices are very syrupy. Lift the plums out of the pan into a 23cm (9in) shallow ovenproof dish or cake tin, with some of them cut side up, and pour the juice over them. Leave to cool.

2 Roll out the pastry on a lightly floured worksurface into a round slightly larger than the dish and about 5mm (¼in) thick. Lay the pastry over the plums, tuck the edges down into the dish and make a few slits in the pastry with a knife to allow steam to escape. Chill for 20 minutes.

3 Preheat the oven to 220°C (200°C fan oven) mark 7. Bake for 20 minutes or until the pastry is golden. Cool for 5 minutes before carefully inverting on to a plate. Serve with crème fraîche or cream.

★ FREEZING TIP
To freeze Complete the recipe to the end of step 2, then cover, wrap and freeze.
To use Bake from frozen at 220°C (200°C fan oven) mark 7 for 40 minutes or until the pastry is golden. Complete the recipe.

Mango Tartes Tatin

Preparation Time 30 minutes • Cooking Time 30 minutes • Makes 4 • Per Tart 506 calories, 33g fat
(of which 5g saturates), 56g carbohydrate, 0.9g salt • Easy

2 small ripe mangoes, peeled, the
   flesh cut away in one piece from
   each side of the stone
40g (1½oz) golden granulated
   sugar
40g (1½oz) unsalted butter
375g pack ready-rolled puff pastry

1 Preheat the oven to 220°C (200°C fan oven) mark 7. Slice each piece of mango along most of the length, so that the slices remain joined at the top.

2 Put the sugar into a large heavy-based frying pan. Heat very gently until it starts to dissolve and turn brown. Add 25g (1oz) butter and stir with a wooden spoon to make a caramel. Add the mango and toss gently to coat in caramel. Cook for 2–3 minutes, then remove from the heat.

3 Grease four 8cm (3¼in) tart tins with the remaining butter. Unroll the pastry and put the tins upside down on it. Press a rolling pin over the tins to stamp out four pastry rounds.

4 Put one mango piece, curved side down, into each tin, pressing it gently to fan out, then divide any remaining caramel among them. Top each tin with a pastry round. Bake for 20–25 minutes until the pastry is golden brown. To serve, turn out the tartlets on to plates, with the mango uppermost.

Mincemeat and Ricotta Tart

★

Preparation Time 45 minutes, plus chilling • Cooking Time about 1¼ hours, plus cooling • Cuts into 8 slices •
Per Slice 594 calories, 29g fat (of which 13g saturates), 78g carbohydrate, 0.3g salt • Easy

175g (6oz) plain flour, plus extra
   to dust
125g (4oz) unsalted butter, cut into
   cubes
25g (1oz) ground almonds
25g (1oz) caster sugar
1 large egg yolk

FOR THE FILLING AND
   TOPPING
250g (9oz) ricotta cheese
25g (1oz) icing sugar, plus extra
   to dust
2 large egg yolks
3 tbsp double cream
700g (1½lb) mincemeat
grated zest of 1 lemon
1 tbsp brandy or lemon juice
25g (1oz) glacé cherries, sliced
2 tbsp flaked almonds

1 To make the pastry, whiz the flour
and butter in a food processor until
the mixture resembles fine crumbs.
Add the ground almonds, caster
sugar and egg yolk with 1 tbsp cold
water. Pulse until the mixture just
comes together. (Alternatively, rub
the butter into the dry ingredients in
a large bowl by hand or using a
pastry cutter. Mix in the egg yolk
and water.) Knead lightly, wrap and
chill for at least 30 minutes.

2 Roll out the pastry on a lightly
floured worksurface and use to line
a 10 × 33cm (4 × 13in) loose-based
tin. Prick the pastry base all over
with a fork and chill for 30 minutes.

3 Preheat the oven to 190°C
(170°C fan oven) mark 5. Bake the
tart case blind (see step 2, page 44).
Cool for 15 minutes. Reduce the
oven temperature to 180°C (160°C
fan oven) mark 4.

4 To make the filling, beat the
ricotta with the icing sugar, egg
yolks and cream. Spread over the
pastry and bake for 20–25 minutes
until lightly set.

5 Mix the mincemeat with the
lemon zest and brandy or lemon
juice and spoon over the tart.
Scatter the glacé cherries and
almonds on top and bake for
20 minutes. Cool slightly, then
dust with icing sugar.

Treacle Tart

Preparation Time 25 minutes, plus chilling • **Cooking Time** 45–50 minutes, plus cooling • **Cuts into 6 slices** •
Per Slice 486 calories, 15g fat (of which 8g saturates), 88g carbohydrate, 1.1g salt • **Easy**

Sweet Shortcrust Pastry (see page 268), made with 225g (8oz) plain flour, 150g (5oz) unsalted butter, 15g (½oz) golden caster sugar and 1 medium egg yolk
flour to dust

FOR THE FILLING
700g (1½lb) golden syrup
175g (6oz) fresh white breadcrumbs
grated zest of 3 lemons
2 medium eggs, lightly beaten

1 Preheat the oven to 180°C (160°C fan oven) mark 4. Roll out the pastry on a lightly floured worksurface and use to line a 25.5cm (10in), 4cm (1½in) deep, loose-based fluted tart tin. Prick the base all over with a fork and chill for 30 minutes.

2 To make the filling, heat the syrup in a pan over a low heat until thinner in consistency. Remove from the heat and mix in the breadcrumbs and lemon zest. Stir in the beaten eggs.

3 Pour the filling into the pastry case and bake for 45–50 minutes until the filling is lightly set and golden. Leave to cool slightly. Serve warm.

★ TRY SOMETHING DIFFERENT
For the pastry, replace half the plain flour with wholemeal flour. For the filling, use fresh wholemeal breadcrumbs instead of white.

Pinenut and Honey Tart

Preparation Time 50 minutes, plus chilling • Cooking Time 1 hour, plus cooling • Cuts into 6 slices • Per Slice 863 calories, 54g fat (of which 26g saturates), 88g carbohydrate, 0.6g salt • **Easy**

250g (9oz) plain flour, plus extra
    to dust
200g (7oz) unsalted butter, softened
40g (1½oz) icing sugar
4 large eggs
100g (3½oz) pinenuts
200g (7oz) muscovado sugar
100ml (3½fl oz) clear honey
150ml (¼ pint) double cream
Vanilla Ice Cream (see page 270)
    to serve

1 Put 225g (8oz) flour, 150g (5oz) butter and the icing sugar into a food processor and pulse until the mixture resembles fine crumbs. (Alternatively, rub the butter into the flour in a large bowl by hand or using a pastry cutter until it resembles fine crumbs. Stir in the icing sugar.) Add 1 egg. Pulse, or stir with a fork, until the mixture forms a ball. Wrap in clingfilm and chill for 30 minutes.

2 Preheat the oven to 200°C (180°C fan oven) mark 6. Roll out the pastry on a lightly floured worksurface and use to line a 23cm (9in) loose-based tart tin. Prick the base all over with a fork and bake blind (see step 2, page 44). Remove from the oven. Reduce the oven temperature to 190°C (170°C fan oven) mark 5.

3 Sprinkle 75g (3oz) pinenuts over the pastry base. Melt 25g (1oz) butter and whisk with 175g (6oz) muscovado sugar, the honey, remaining eggs and the cream. Pour into the pastry case and bake for 25–30 minutes.

4 Pulse the remaining pinenuts, flour, butter and sugar until the mixture forms a crumbly texture. (Alternatively, rub the butter into the flour in a large bowl and stir in the pinenuts and sugar.) When the tart is cooked, remove it from the oven, sprinkle with the crumble mixture and put it back into the oven for a further 8–10 minutes.

5 Remove from the oven and leave to cool slightly. Serve warm, with Vanilla Ice Cream.

Marzipan and Kumquat Tart

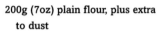

Preparation Time 1¼ hours, plus chilling • **Cooking Time** 1¼ hours, plus cooling • **Cuts into 12 slices** •
Per Slice 412 calories, 24g fat (of which 13g saturates), 46g carbohydrate, 0.5g salt • **Easy**

**200g (7oz) plain flour, plus extra
to dust**
125g (4oz) unsalted butter, chilled
**100g (3½oz) icing sugar, plus extra
to dust**
2 large egg yolks

FOR THE FILLING
250g (9oz) kumquats
150g (5oz) unsalted butter, softened
**300g (11oz) marzipan, chilled and
grated**
2 large eggs
50g (2oz) self-raising flour
25g (1oz) caster sugar

FOR THE BRANDY CREAM
300ml (½ pint) double cream
4 tbsp brandy
1 tbsp icing sugar

1 Whiz the plain flour and butter in
a food processor until the mixture
resembles breadcrumbs.
(Alternatively, rub the butter into
the flour in a large bowl by hand or
using a pastry cutter.) Add the icing
sugar, egg yolks and 1 tsp cold
water. Whiz, or stir, until the dough
just comes together. Tip on to a
clean worksurface and knead
lightly with your hands to bring it
together, then wrap and chill for at
least 1 hour.

2 To make the filling, put the
kumquats into a pan, cover with
water and bring to the boil. Reduce
the heat and simmer for 10 minutes.
Drain, reserving the liquid, and leave
to cool.

3 Roll out the pastry on a lightly
floured worksurface, then use to
line a 27cm (10½in) round, 2.5cm
(1in) deep loose-based flan tin. Chill
for 30 minutes. Preheat the oven to
200°C (180°C fan oven) mark 6.

4 Bake the tart case blind for
20 minutes (see step 2, page 44).
Remove the paper and beans and
put the tin back into the oven for
4–5 minutes until just dry to the
touch. Remove from the oven.
Reduce the oven temperature to
180°C (160°C fan oven) mark 4.

5 Beat the butter in a bowl until
creamy. Add the marzipan, eggs and
self-raising flour. Beat until smooth.
Keep 12 kumquats to one side and
chop the remainder, discarding the
pips. Add to the creamed mixture
and spread inside the case. Slice
each reserved kumquat into four.
Arrange the slices in a star shape on
top of the filling. Bake for 30 minutes
or until pale golden and the surface is
just firm.

6 Heat the caster sugar in a small pan
with 5 tbsp reserved cooking liquid
until the sugar dissolves, then cook
until syrupy. Brush the warm glaze
over the tart.

7 Whip the cream with the brandy
and icing sugar until thick. If you want
to dust the tart with icing sugar, cover
the kumquat 'star' with foil, then dust
the area outside with icing sugar.
Remove the foil and serve with the
brandy cream.

 GET AHEAD
To prepare ahead *Make the recipe to
the end of step 6. Cool, then cover with
foil and freeze for up to a month.*
To use *Complete the recipe.*

Macadamia and Maple Tart

Preparation Time 15 minutes, plus freezing • Cooking Time about 40 minutes, plus cooling • Cuts into 8 slices •
Per Slice 608 calories, 38g fat (of which 11g saturates), 60g carbohydrate, 0.9g salt • Easy

225g (8oz) macadamia nuts, halved
350g (12oz) ready-made shortcrust
   pastry, thawed if frozen
flour to dust
75g (3oz) unsalted butter, softened
75g (3oz) dark muscovado sugar
3 medium eggs, beaten
1 tsp cornflour
50ml (2fl oz) maple syrup, plus
   extra to drizzle
225ml (8fl oz) golden syrup
grated zest of 1 lemon and 2 tbsp
   lemon juice
1 tsp vanilla extract

1 Preheat the grill. Put the macadamia nuts on a baking sheet and toast under the hot grill until golden brown, turning them frequently. Leave to cool.

2 Roll out the pastry on a lightly floured worksurface and use to line a 23cm (9in), 4cm (1½in) deep, loose-based tart tin, leaving the pastry hanging over the edges to allow for shrinkage. Prick all over with a fork, then freeze for 30 minutes.

3 Preheat the oven to 200°C (180°C fan oven) mark 6. Bake the tart case blind (see step 2, page 44). Using a sharp knife, trim the overhanging pastry to a neat edge.

4 Beat the butter with the sugar until pale and creamy, then gradually add the beaten eggs and the cornflour. Stir in all the remaining ingredients. The mixture will look curdled, but don't panic. Stir in the toasted nuts and pour into the cooked pastry case.

5 Bake for 35–40 minutes until the filling is just set. Leave to cool for 10 minutes before serving.

 FREEZING TIP
To freeze Complete the recipe, wrap and freeze for up to one month.
To use Thaw overnight. Put on a baking sheet, cover loosely with foil and reheat at 200°C (180°C fan oven) mark 6 for 20 minutes.

Pear, Cranberry and Frangipane Tart

Preparation Time 30 minutes, plus chilling • Cooking Time 1 hour, plus cooling • Cuts into 8 slices • Per Slice 466 calories, 28g fat (of which 13g saturates), 48g carbohydrate, 0.6g salt • **Easy**

150g (5oz) caster sugar

2 small ripe pears

150g (5oz) unsalted butter, softened, plus extra to grease

175g (6oz) Hobnob biscuits, finely crushed (see page 225)

100g (3½oz) ground almonds

2 tbsp plain flour

1 tsp cornflour

1 tsp baking powder

2 medium eggs, beaten

1 tsp vanilla extract

25g (1oz) dried cranberries

25g (1oz) flaked almonds

icing sugar to dust

crème fraîche to serve

1 Put 50g (2oz) caster sugar in a pan with 500ml (18fl oz) water and dissolve over a low heat. Peel, halve and core the pears. Add to the sugar syrup. Cover the pan with a lid and simmer gently for 5–8 minutes, turning once. Transfer the pears and liquid to a bowl and leave to cool.

2 Lightly grease a 20.5cm (8in) loose-bottomed cake tin and line with greaseproof paper. Melt 25g (1oz) butter and mix in the crushed biscuits. Press into the base of the tin and chill for about 1 hour.

3 Preheat the oven to 180°C (160°C fan oven) mark 4. Cream the remaining butter and sugar together in a freestanding mixer (or use a hand-held electric whisk) until light and fluffy. Add the ground almonds,

flour, cornflour and baking powder and mix to combine. Add the eggs and vanilla extract. Mix until smooth. Stir in the cranberries and flaked almonds. Spoon the mixture on top of the biscuit base. Smooth the surface.

4 Remove the pears from the syrup and place on kitchen paper to soak up excess liquid. Slice one of the pear halves horizontally into 5mm (¼in) slices. Push down on the pear to fan out the slices slightly. Place on top of the filling. Repeat with the remaining pear halves, spacing them evenly apart on top of the filling.

5 Bake for 45–50 minutes until the frangipane is golden, puffed and firm to the touch. Dust with icing sugar and serve with crème fraîche.

★ FREEZING TIP

To freeze *Complete the recipe to the end of step 4, then leave the tart, still in its tin, to cool completely. Once cool, wrap the entire tin in clingfilm, then freeze for up to one month.*
To use *Thaw overnight in the fridge and serve as in step 5.*

Strawberry Tart

Preparation Time 40 minutes, plus chilling • **Cooking Time** 35–40 minutes, plus cooling • **Cuts into 6 slices** •
Per Slice 384 calories, 15g fat (of which 8g saturates), 57g carbohydrate, 0.2g salt • **Easy**

Sweet Shortcrust Pastry (see page
268), made with 125g (4oz) plain
flour, a pinch of salt, 50g (2oz)
golden caster sugar, 50g (2oz)
unsalted butter and 2 medium
egg yolks

FOR THE CRÈME PÂTISSIÈRE
300ml (½ pint) milk
1 vanilla pod, split, seeds separated
2 medium egg yolks
50g (2oz) golden caster sugar
2 tbsp plain flour
2 tbsp cornflour
50ml (2fl oz) crème fraîche

FOR THE TOPPING
450g (1lb) medium strawberries,
hulled and halved
6 tbsp redcurrant jelly

1 To make the crème pâtissière,
pour the milk into a pan with the
vanilla pod and seeds. Heat gently
to just below boiling, then remove
from the heat. Put the egg yolks and
sugar into a bowl, beat until pale,
then stir in the flours. Discard the
vanilla pod, then gradually mix the
hot milk into the yolk mixture. Put
back into the pan and slowly bring

to the boil, stirring, for 3–4 minutes
until thick and smooth. Scrape into
a bowl, cover with a round of damp
greaseproof paper and leave to cool.

2 Put the pastry between two
sheets of greaseproof paper and roll
out thinly. Use to line a 23cm (9in)
loose-based flan tin. Prick with a
fork, line with greaseproof paper
and chill for 30 minutes.

3 Preheat the oven to 190°C (170°C
fan oven) mark 5. Bake blind (see
step 2, page 44) for 10–15 minutes.
Remove the paper and beans,
put back in the oven and bake for
10 minutes or until golden. Cool for
5 minutes, then remove from the tin
and cool completely.

4 Add the crème fraîche to the
crème pâtissière and beat until
smooth. Spread evenly in the pastry
case. Arrange the strawberry halves
on top, working from the outside
edge into the centre.

5 Heat the redcurrant jelly in a pan
until syrupy, whisking lightly. Using a
pastry brush, cover the strawberries
with jelly. Serve within 2 hours.

★ COOK'S TIP
*Serve within 2 hours of putting the
tart together, otherwise the pastry will
go soggy.*

Classic Lemon Tart

Preparation Time 30 minutes, plus chilling • Cooking Time about 50 minutes, plus cooling • Cuts into 8 slices •
Per Slice 385 calories, 23g fat (of which 13g saturates), 42g carbohydrate, 0.2g salt • Easy

butter to grease
plain flour to dust
Sweet Shortcrust Pastry (see page
    268), made with 150g (5oz) plain
    flour, 75g (3oz) unsalted butter,
    50g (2oz) icing sugar and 2 large
    egg yolks
peach slices and fresh or frozen
    raspberries, thawed, to decorate
icing sugar to dust

FOR THE FILLING
1 large egg, plus 4 large egg yolks
150g (5oz) caster sugar
grated zest of 4 lemons
150ml (¼ pint) freshly squeezed
    lemon juice (about 4 medium
    lemons)
150ml (¼ pint) double cream

1 Grease and flour a 23cm (9in),
2.5cm (1in) deep, loose-based flan
tin. Roll out the pastry on a lightly
floured worksurface into a round –
if the pastry sticks to the surface,
gently ease a palette knife under it
to loosen. Line the tin with the
pastry and trim the excess. Prick the
base all over with a fork. Chill for
30 minutes.

2 Preheat the oven to 190°C (170°C
fan oven) mark 5. Put the tin on a
baking sheet and bake the pastry
case blind (see step 2, page 44).
Remove from the oven, leaving the
flan tin on the baking sheet. Reduce
the oven temperature to 170°C
(150°C fan oven) mark 3.

3 Meanwhile, to make the filling,
put the whole egg, egg yolks and
caster sugar into a bowl and beat
together with a wooden spoon or
balloon whisk until smooth.
Carefully stir in the lemon zest,
lemon juice and cream. Leave to
stand for 5 minutes.

4 Ladle three-quarters of the filling
into the pastry case, position the
baking sheet on the oven shelf and
ladle in the remainder. Bake for

25–30 minutes until the filling
bounces back when touched lightly
in the centre. Cool for 15 minutes
to serve warm, or cool completely
and chill. Decorate with peaches
and raspberries and dust with
icing sugar.

★ COOK'S TIP
*Remember that ovens vary, so check the
tart after 15 minutes of cooking. Turn
round if cooking unevenly, otherwise the
eggs might curdle.*

Almond and White Chocolate Tart with Pineapple

★

Preparation Time 1 hour, plus chilling • Cooking Time about 1 hour, plus cooling and setting • Cuts into 8 slices •
Per Slice 648 calories, 36g fat (of which 17g saturates), 77g carbohydrate, 0.5g salt • Easy

Sweet Shortcrust Pastry (see page
    268), made with 175g (6oz) plain
    flour, 50g (2oz) icing sugar,
    75g (3oz) butter, grated zest of
    1 large orange and 1 large
    egg yolk
flour to dust

FOR THE FILLING
100g (3½oz) white chocolate,
    broken into pieces
125g (4oz) unsalted butter
125g (4oz) icing sugar
2 large eggs, beaten
125g (4oz) ground almonds
1 tbsp plain flour
a few drops of vanilla extract

FOR THE TOPPING
1 medium pineapple, peeled and
    thinly sliced
icing sugar to sprinkle
125g (4oz) apricot jam

1 Roll out the pastry thinly on a lightly floured worksurface and use to line a 23cm (9in), 2.5cm (1in) deep, loose-based fluted tart tin. Chill for 20 minutes.

2 Preheat the oven to 200°C (180°C fan oven) mark 6. Prick the pastry base all over with a fork, then bake blind (see step 2, page 44). Remove from the oven. Reduce the oven temperature to 180°C (160°C fan oven) mark 4.

3 To make the filling, melt the chocolate in a heatproof bowl set over a pan of gently simmering water, making sure the base of the bowl doesn't touch the water. Remove the bowl from the pan and cool slightly.

4 Put the butter into a large bowl and, using a hand-held electric whisk, beat until creamy, then beat in the icing sugar until fluffy. Gradually beat the eggs into the butter mixture, a little at a time. Stir in the ground almonds, flour, melted chocolate and vanilla extract. Fill the pastry case with the mixture and smooth the top.

5 Bake for 25–30 minutes until just set in the middle. The mixture will puff in the oven and firm up on cooling. Cool for 15 minutes, then transfer to a wire rack to cool completely.

6 For the topping, preheat the grill. Sprinkle the pineapple heavily with icing sugar and put under the hot grill until the pineapple is glazed to a light caramel colour. Leave to cool. Put the jam into a small pan and warm over a low heat until melted. Simmer for 1–2 minutes, then sieve and put back in the pan (if the jam is a little thick, add a splash of water).

7 Arrange the pineapple over the tart and brush with a thin layer of warm jam. Leave the jam to set before serving.

Fruit and Walnut Tart

Preparation Time 25 minutes, plus chilling • Cooking Time 1 hour 5 minutes, plus cooling • Cuts into 8 slices •
Per Slice 646 calories, 40g fat (of which 18g saturates), 68g carbohydrate, 0.6g salt • Easy

Sweet Shortcrust Pastry (see page
  268), made with 225g (8oz) plain
  flour, 125g (4oz) butter, 2 tbsp
  golden icing sugar and 1 medium
  egg

FOR THE FILLING
200g (7oz) clear honey
125g (4oz) unsalted butter, softened
125g (4oz) light muscovado sugar
3 medium eggs, beaten
grated zest and juice of 1 lemon
125g (4oz) walnuts, roughly
  chopped
125g (4oz) ready-to-eat dried
  apples and pears, roughly
  chopped, plus 3 dried pear slices
  to decorate

1 To make the filling, warm 175g
(6oz) honey in a small pan over a
low heat. Put the butter into a large
bowl with the sugar and beat with a
hand-held electric whisk until light
and fluffy. Add the eggs, lemon zest
and juice, walnuts, chopped apples
and pears and the warm honey. Stir
well and put to one side.

2 Put the pastry between two
sheets of greaseproof paper and roll
out thinly. Peel off and discard the
top sheet of paper, then flip over
and use the pastry to line a 23cm
(9in) round or a 20.5cm (8in) square
loose-based tin. Prick all over with a
fork, cover with clingfilm and chill
for 30 minutes. Preheat the oven to
180°C (160°C fan oven) mark 4.

3 Bake the pastry case blind (see
step 2, page 44). Pour in the filling
and arrange the pear slices on top.
Brush with the remaining honey.
Put the tart on a baking sheet,
cover with foil and bake for
20 minutes. Remove the foil and
bake for a further 25 minutes or
until golden brown. Serve cool.

★ FREEZING TIP
*To freeze Complete the recipe.
Cool the tart completely in the tin.
Wrap in foil and freeze for up to
one month.
To use Remove from the freezer
12 hours before serving and thaw
in the fridge.*

Glazed Brandied Prune Tart

Preparation Time 25 minutes, plus soaking and chilling • Cooking Time about 1 hour • Cuts into 8 slices •
Per Slice 440 calories, 24g fat (of which 14g saturates), 47g carbohydrate, 0.2g salt • Easy

Sweet Shortcrust Pastry (see page
    268) made with 175g (6oz) plain
    flour, a pinch of salt, 75g (3oz)
    unsalted butter, 3 large egg yolks,
    75g (3oz) caster sugar, 1½ tsp
    water
flour to dust

FOR THE FILLING
250g (9oz) ready-to-eat dried
    prunes
5 tbsp brandy
1 vanilla pod, split
150ml (¼ pint) double cream
150ml (¼ pint) single cream
25g (1oz) caster sugar
2 large eggs
4 tbsp apricot jam and 2 tbsp
    brandy to glaze

1 To make the filling, put the prunes
into a small bowl, add the 5 tbsp
brandy, then cover and leave to soak
overnight or for several hours.

2 Roll out the pastry on a lightly
floured worksurface and use to line
a 23cm (9in), 2.5cm (1in) deep,
loose-based fluted flan tin. Chill for
30 minutes. Preheat the oven to
200°C (180°C fan oven) mark 6.
Prick the pastry base all over with a
fork, then bake blind (see step 2,
page 44). Remove from the oven.
Reduce the oven temperature to
180°C (160°C fan oven) mark 4.

3 Put the vanilla pod into a pan with
the double cream. Bring just to the
boil. Remove from the heat and
leave to infuse for 20 minutes.
Remove the vanilla pod, rinse, dry
and store for reuse. Pour the cream
into a bowl. Add the single cream,
sugar and eggs and beat well.

4 Scatter the prunes in the pastry
case, then pour the cream mixture
around them. Bake for 30 minutes
or until the custard is turning golden
and is just set in the centre.

5 Meanwhile, sieve the jam into
a pan, add the 2 tbsp brandy and
heat gently until smooth. Brush the
glaze over the tart and serve warm
or cold.

Sweet Ricotta Tart

Preparation Time 25 minutes, plus chilling • Cooking Time 1 hour, plus cooling • Cuts into 8 slices • Per Slice 404 calories, 15g fat (of which 9g saturates), 60g carbohydrate, 0.3g salt • **Easy**

Sweet Shortcrust Pastry (see page 268), made with 200g (7oz) plain flour, 75g (3oz) unsalted butter, 50g (2oz) golden caster sugar and 1 medium egg
flour to dust
icing sugar to dust

FOR THE FILLING
100g (3½oz) cracked wheat or bulgur wheat
200ml (7fl oz) milk
250g (9oz) ricotta cheese
150g (5oz) golden caster sugar
2 medium eggs
1 tbsp orange flower water
1 tsp vanilla extract
½ tsp ground cinnamon
1 piece – about 40g (1½oz) – candied peel, finely chopped

1 To make the filling, put the cracked wheat into a pan, add the milk, then cover and bring to the boil. Reduce the heat and simmer for 5–8 minutes until all the liquid has been absorbed and the wheat still has a slight bite. Leave to cool.

2 Preheat the oven to 190°C (170°C fan oven) mark 5. Roll out the pastry on a lightly floured worksurface and use to line a 20.5cm (8in) loose-bottomed sandwich tin. Prick the base all over with a fork. Cover and chill for 10 minutes. Knead together the trimmings, then wrap and chill. Bake the pastry case blind (see step 2, page 44). Remove from the oven.

3 Put the ricotta into a bowl and add the sugar, eggs, orange flower water, vanilla extract and cinnamon. Beat well. Add the peel and cracked wheat and mix.

4 Roll out the pastry trimmings. Cut out six strips, each measuring 1 × 20.5cm (½ × 8in). Pour the filling into the pastry case. Lay the strips on top. Bake for 45 minutes. Leave in the tin for 10 minutes. Leave to cool on a wire rack. Dust with icing sugar to serve.

Coconut and Mango Tart

⭐

Preparation Time 35 minutes, plus chilling • Cooking Time 50 minutes, plus cooling and chilling • Cuts into 10 slices •
Per Slice 253 calories, 18g fat (of which 11g saturates), 20g carbohydrate, 0.3g salt • Easy

125g (4oz) plain flour, plus extra
   to dust
75g (3oz) firm, unsalted butter
1 tbsp caster sugar
40g (1½oz) desiccated coconut
1 medium egg yolk
toasted coconut shreds to decorate
icing sugar to dust

FOR THE FILLING
2 small ripe mangoes, peeled,
   stoned and thinly sliced
75ml (2½fl oz) orange juice
2 tbsp caster sugar, plus 75g (3oz)
3 medium eggs
15g (½oz) cornflour
400ml can coconut milk
150ml (¼ pint) double cream

1 Whiz the flour and butter in a food processor until the mixture resembles fine crumbs. Stir in the caster sugar and coconut. Add the egg yolk and about 2 tbsp cold water and pulse to make a firm dough. (Alternatively, rub the butter into the dry ingredients in a large bowl by hand or using a pastry cutter. Mix in the egg yolk and water.) Knead lightly, wrap and chill for 30 minutes. Preheat the oven to 200°C (180°C fan oven) mark 6. Roll out the pastry on a floured worksurface and use to line a 23cm (9in), 4cm (1½in) deep, loose-based flan tin. Bake the pastry case blind (see step 2, page 44). Remove from the oven. Reduce the oven temperature to 150°C (130°C fan oven) mark 2.

2 Meanwhile, to make the filling, put the mango slices into a heavy-based pan with the orange juice and 2 tbsp caster sugar. Bring to a simmer and cook gently for 3–5 minutes until the mango slices are softened but still retain their shape. Cool slightly.

3 Beat the eggs and the remaining sugar together in a bowl. Blend the cornflour with a little of the coconut milk in a pan. Add the remaining coconut milk. Bring to the boil, stirring until thickened. Remove from the heat and stir in the cream.

Pour over the egg mixture, stirring until smooth.

4 Drain the mangoes, reserving the juice. Arrange in the pastry case. Stir the reserved juice into the coconut custard and ladle it over the mangoes. Bake for about 30 minutes or until the custard is just set; it will continue to firm up as it cools. Leave to cool, then chill for several hours or overnight.

5 Decorate with coconut shreds and dust with icing sugar to serve.

Caramelised Orange Tart

Preparation Time 15 minutes, plus chilling • Cooking Time about 1 hour, plus cooling • Cuts into 8 slices •
Per Slice 556 calories, 29g fat (of which 14g saturates), 70g carbohydrate, 0.5g salt • **Easy**

225g (8oz) plain flour, plus extra
   to dust
a pinch of salt
125g (4oz) unsalted butter, diced
2 tbsp golden icing sugar
1 medium egg yolk, beaten

FOR THE FILLING
juice of 1 lemon
juice of 1 orange
zest of 2 oranges
75g (3oz) unsalted butter
225g (8oz) golden granulated sugar
3 medium eggs, beaten
75g (3oz) ground almonds
2 tbsp orange liqueur

a few drops of orange food
   colouring (optional)

FOR THE DECORATION
100g (3½oz) golden caster sugar
pared zest of 1 orange, cut into
   slivers

1 Put the flour, salt, butter and icing sugar into a food processor and pulse until the mixture forms fine crumbs. (Alternatively, rub the butter into the flour by hand or using a pastry cutter, then stir in the icing sugar.) Beat the egg yolk with

2 tbsp cold water and add to the flour mixture. Whiz, or stir, until the crumbs make a dough. Knead lightly, wrap and chill.

2 To make the filling, put the juices, orange zest, butter, sugar and eggs into a heavy-based pan and heat gently, stirring, until thickened. Stir in the almonds, liqueur and food colouring, if using. Put to one side.

3 Preheat the oven to 200°C (180°C fan oven) mark 6. Roll out the dough on a lightly floured worksurface and use to line a 23cm (9in) tin. Prick the base all over with a fork. Cover and chill for 10 minutes. Bake the pastry case blind (see step 2, page 44). Remove from the oven. Reduce the oven temperature to 180°C (160°C fan oven) mark 4. Pour the filling into the pastry case and bake for 20 minutes or until just firm. Cool in the tin.

4 To decorate, preheat the grill. Dissolve 50g (2oz) caster sugar in a pan with 300ml (½ pint) water. Add the orange zest and simmer for 10–15 minutes until the liquid has reduced and the zest is tender. Drain. Sprinkle the rest of the caster sugar over the tart. Caramelise under the hot grill, then leave to cool. Spoon the orange zest around the edge to serve.

Glazed Cranberry and Orange Tart

Preparation Time 15 minutes • Cooking Time 6 minutes • Cuts into 8 slices • Per Slice 234 calories, 11g fat (of which 3g saturates), 29g carbohydrate, 0.2g salt • Easy

350g (12oz) fresh or frozen cranberries, thawed
grated zest and juice of 1 orange
125g (4oz) golden caster sugar
½ tbsp arrowroot
250g tub mascarpone cheese
200ml (7fl oz) ready-made fresh custard with real vanilla
20.5cm (8in) cooked shortcrust pastry case

1 Tip the cranberries into a pan with the orange zest, juice and sugar and bring to the boil. Reduce the heat and simmer for 5 minutes or until the cranberries are just softened and the syrup has reduced slightly. Using a slotted spoon, strain off the cranberries and put to one side in a bowl, leaving the syrup in the pan.

2 Mix the arrowroot with 1 tbsp cold water, add to the pan and cook for 1 minute, stirring, until the syrup has thickened. Pour over the cranberries and leave to cool.

3 Tip the mascarpone and custard into a bowl and, using a hand-held electric whisk, mix until smooth. Spoon into the pastry case, top with the cranberry mixture and serve.

★ COOK'S TIP
A shop-bought pastry case helps to cut corners but, if you prefer, you can make a pie crust using the Sweet Shortcrust Pastry recipe on page 268.

Almond Bakewell Tarts

Preparation Time 25 minutes, plus chilling • **Cooking Time** 50 minutes, plus cooling • **Makes 6** •
Per Tart 931 calories, 52g fat (of which 24g saturates), 104g carbohydrate, 0.8g salt • **Easy**

Sweet Shortcrust Pastry (see page
    268), made with 200g (7oz) plain
    flour, 100g (3½oz) unsalted
    butter, 75g (3oz) caster sugar,
    3 large egg yolks and ½ tsp
    vanilla extract
flour to dust
Plum Sauce (see Cook's Tip) to serve

FOR THE FILLING
125g (4oz) unsalted butter, softened
125g (4oz) caster sugar
3 large eggs
125g (4oz) ground almonds
2–3 drops almond extract
6 tbsp redcurrant jelly

FOR THE CRUMBLE TOPPING
25g (1oz) unsalted butter
75g (3oz) plain flour
25g (1oz) caster sugar

1 Roll out the pastry thinly on a
lightly floured worksurface and line
six 10cm (4in), 3cm (1¼in) deep
tartlet tins. Chill for 30 minutes.
Preheat the oven to 190°C (170°C
fan oven) mark 5.

2 Prick the bases all over with a fork,
then bake blind (see step 2, page
44). Leave to cool.

3 To make the filling, beat the
butter and sugar together until light
and fluffy. Gradually beat in 2 eggs,
then beat in the remaining egg with
one-third of the ground almonds.
Fold in the remaining almonds and
the almond extract.

4 Melt the redcurrant jelly in a small
pan and brush over the inside of
each pastry case. Spoon in the
almond filling. Put the tarts on a
baking sheet and bake for 20–25
minutes until golden and just firm.
Leave in the tins for 10 minutes,
then unmould on to a wire rack and
leave to cool completely.

5 To make the crumble topping,
preheat the grill. Rub the butter into
the flour and add the sugar. Spread
evenly on a baking sheet and grill
until golden. Cool, then sprinkle
over the tarts. Decorate with
plums (see Cook's Tip) and serve
with Plum Sauce.

⭐ COOK'S TIP
Plum Sauce
Put 450g (1lb) halved and stoned ripe
plums, 50–75g (2–3oz) soft brown sugar
and 150ml (¼ pint) sweet white wine
into a pan with 150ml (¼ pint) water.
Bring to the boil, then reduce the heat
and simmer until tender. Remove 3 plums
to decorate; slice and put to one side.
Cook the remaining plums until very soft
(about 15 minutes). Put into a food
processor and whiz until smooth. Sieve,
if you like, adding more sugar to taste.
Leave to cool.

Cinnamon Custard Tart

Preparation Time 50 minutes, plus chilling and infusing • Cooking Time 1½ hours, plus standing and cooling •
Cuts into 8 slices • Per Slice 664 calories, 34g fat (of which 20g saturates), 87g carbohydrate, 0.4g salt • Easy

250g (9oz) plain flour, plus extra
   to dust
100g (3½oz) unsalted butter
100g (3½oz) icing sugar
4 large eggs
450ml (¾ pint) milk
285ml (9½fl oz) double cream
1 vanilla pod, split
1 cinnamon stick, crumbled
275g (10oz) caster sugar
1 mango, 1 small pineapple,
   2 clementines and 125g (4oz)
   kumquats to serve

1 Put the flour, butter and icing sugar into a food processor and pulse until the mixture forms fine crumbs. (Alternatively, rub the butter into the flour by hand or using a pastry cutter, then stir in the icing sugar.) Beat 1 egg and add to the flour mixture with 1 tbsp water. Whiz, or stir, until the crumbs make a dough. Wrap in clingfilm and chill for 30 minutes.

2 Use the pastry to line a 23cm (9in) loose-based tart tin. Prick the base all over with a fork. Chill for 30 minutes.

3 Preheat the oven to 200°C (180°C fan oven) mark 6. Bake the pastry case blind (see step 2, page 44). Lightly whisk the remaining eggs. Use 1 tbsp egg to brush over the pastry. Put back into the oven for 2 minutes. Remove from the oven. Reduce the oven temperature to 150°C (130°C fan oven) mark 2.

4 Put the milk, cream, vanilla pod and cinnamon into a pan and slowly bring to the boil. Leave to infuse for 20 minutes. Mix the whisked eggs with 150g (5oz) caster sugar. Stir the milk into the egg mixture, strain into a jug and pour into the tart. Bake for 40–50 minutes or until the filling has just set. Turn the oven off and leave the tart in the oven for 15 minutes. Remove and cool in the tin for 20–30 minutes. Transfer to a wire rack to cool completely.

5 Make the caramelised fruit (see Finishing Touches below). Cut the tart into portions and spoon the fruit over the top to serve.

⭐ FINISHING TOUCHES
To decorate, cut the fruits into thick slices and arrange on two non-stick baking sheets. Put the remaining caster sugar into a small, heavy-based pan and cook over a low heat until the sugar begins to dissolve, then turn up the heat and cook to a pale caramel. Cool a little and drizzle over the fruit. Leave to set. (The caramel will stay brittle for 1–2 hours.)

Sticky Banoffee Pies

Preparation Time 15 minutes, plus chilling • Serves 6 • Per Serving 827 calories, 55g fat (of which 32g saturates), 84g carbohydrate, 1.2g salt • Easy

150g (5oz) digestive biscuits

75g (3oz) unsalted butter, melted, plus extra to grease

1 tsp ground ginger (optional)

450g (1lb) dulce de leche toffee sauce

4 bananas, peeled, sliced and tossed in the juice of 1 lemon

300ml (½ pint) double cream, lightly whipped

plain chocolate shavings

1 Put the biscuits into a food processor and whiz until they resemble fine crumbs. (Alternatively, put them in a plastic bag and crush with a rolling pin.) Transfer to a bowl. Add the melted butter and ginger, if using, then whiz, or stir well, for 1 minute to combine.

2 Grease six 10cm (4in) rings or tartlet tins and line with greaseproof paper. Press the biscuit mixture evenly into the bottom of each ring. Divide the toffee sauce equally among the rings and top with the bananas. Pipe or spoon on the cream, sprinkle with chocolate shavings and chill. Remove from the rings or tins to serve.

★ COOK'S TIP

Slightly overripe bananas are ideal for this recipe.

Vanilla Egg Custard Tart

Preparation Time 40 minutes, plus chilling • Cooking Time 1 hour, plus cooling • Cuts into 6 slices •
Per Slice 497 calories, 36g fat (of which 21g saturates), 36g carbohydrate, 0.4g salt • **Easy**

Sweet Shortcrust Pastry (see page
268), made with 175g (6oz) plain
flour, 125g (4oz) unsalted butter,
25g (1oz) vanilla sugar, 1 tsp
grated orange zest and 1 medium
egg yolk
flour to dust
175g (6oz) raspberries (optional)
to serve
vanilla sugar to dust

FOR THE VANILLA CUSTARD
2 large eggs, plus 2 large egg yolks
40g (1½oz) golden caster sugar
450ml (¾ pint) single cream
½ vanilla pod, split lengthways

1 Roll out the pastry on a lightly
floured worksurface and use to line
a 20.5cm (8in), 4cm (1½in) deep,
loose-based fluted tart tin. Prick the
base all over with a fork. Chill for
30 minutes.

2 Preheat the oven to 200°C
(180°C fan oven) mark 6. Bake the
pastry case blind (see step 2, page
44). Remove from the oven and
leave to cool for 15 minutes. Reduce
the oven temperature to 150°C
(130°C fan oven) mark 2.

3 Meanwhile, make the vanilla
custard. Put the whole eggs, egg
yolks and sugar into a bowl and
beat well. Put the cream and vanilla
pod into a small pan over a very low
heat until the cream is almost
boiling. Pour on to the egg mixture,
whisking constantly, then strain into
the pastry case.

4 Put the tart back into the oven.
Bake for 45 minutes or until the
centre is softly set. Leave until cold,
then carefully remove from the tin.
Top with raspberries if you like, and
dust with vanilla sugar.

★ TRY SOMETHING
DIFFERENT
Chocolate Custard Tart
*Replace 25g (1oz) of the flour with sifted
cocoa powder. For the custard, omit the
vanilla pod and heat 375ml (13fl oz)
single cream with 100g (3½oz) chopped
plain chocolate (70% cocoa solids), until
melted and just simmering.*

Bramley Apple and Custard Tart

Preparation Time 30 minutes, plus chilling • **Cooking Time** about 2 hours, plus cooling • **Cuts into 12 slices** •
Per Slice 472 calories, 32g fat (of which 15g saturates), 46g carbohydrate, 0.5g salt • **Easy**

750g (1lb 11oz) Bramley apples,
   peeled, cored and roughly
   chopped
175g (6oz) golden caster sugar
500g pack shortcrust pastry, chilled
flour to dust
400ml (14fl oz) double cream
1 cinnamon stick
3 large egg yolks, plus 1 large egg,
   beaten together
2 dessert apples to decorate
Apple Sauce (see Cook's Tip) to
   serve

1 Cook the apples with 2 tbsp water over a low heat until soft. Add 50g (2oz) sugar and beat to make a purée. Leave to cool.

2 Roll out the pastry on a lightly floured worksurface and use to line a 20.5cm (8in), 4cm (1½in) deep, loose-based fluted flan tin. Cover and chill for 1 hour. Preheat the oven to 180°C (160°C fan oven) mark 4. Bake the pastry case blind (see step 2, page 44). Remove from the oven.

3 Put the cream into a pan with 50g (2oz) sugar and the cinnamon stick. Bring slowly to the boil, then take off the heat and remove the cinnamon. Cool for 2–3 minutes then beat in the egg yolks and egg.

4 Reduce the oven temperature to 170°C (150°C fan oven) mark 3. Put the tart on a baking sheet, then spoon the apple purée over the

pastry. Pour the cream mixture on top and bake for 1–1½ hours or until the custard is just set. Remove the tart from the oven and leave to cool in the tin, then chill.

5 To decorate, preheat the grill. Cut the dessert apples into 5mm (¼in) thick slices and lay them on a lipped baking sheet. Sprinkle with 50g (2oz) sugar and grill for 4–5 minutes until caramelised, turn over and repeat on the other side, then cool. Remove the tart from the tin and decorate with the apple slices. Serve with Apple Sauce.

★ COOK'S TIP
Apple Sauce
Pour 300ml (½ pint) apple juice into a measuring jug. Mix 2 tbsp of the apple juice with 1 tbsp arrowroot to make a smooth paste. Pour the remaining apple juice into a small pan and bring to a gentle simmer. Add the arrowroot paste and continue to heat, stirring constantly, for 2–3 minutes until the sauce has thickened slightly.

Hot Fruit Puddings and Desserts

Cinnamon Pancakes

Preparation Time 5 minutes, plus standing • Cooking Time 20 minutes • Serves 6 • Per Serving 141 calories, 5g fat
(of which 1g saturates), 20g carbohydrate, 0.1g salt • Easy

150g (5oz) plain flour
½ tsp ground cinnamon
1 medium egg
300ml (½ pint) skimmed milk
olive oil to fry
fruit compote or sugar and Greek
   yogurt to serve

1 Whisk together the flour, cinnamon, egg and milk in a large bowl to make a smooth batter. Leave to stand for 20 minutes.

2 Heat a heavy-based frying pan over a medium heat. When the pan is really hot, add 1 tsp oil, pour in a ladleful of batter and tilt the pan to coat the base with an even layer. Cook for 1 minute or until golden. Flip over and cook for 1 minute. Repeat with the remaining batter, adding more oil if necessary, to make six pancakes. Serve with a fruit compote or a sprinkling of sugar, and a dollop of yogurt.

★ TRY SOMETHING DIFFERENT
Serve with sliced bananas and Vanilla Ice Cream (see page 270) instead of the fruit compote and yogurt.

Pears with Hot Fudge Sauce

★

Preparation Time 5 minutes • Cooking Time 15 minutes • Serves 4 • Per Serving 301 calories, 16g fat
(of which 10g saturates), 40g carbohydrate, 0.4g salt • Gluten Free • Easy

75g (3oz) butter
1 tbsp golden syrup
75g (3oz) light muscovado sugar
4 tbsp evaporated milk or single or
   double cream
4 ripe pears, cored, sliced and
   chilled

1 Melt the butter, syrup, sugar and
evaporated milk or cream together
over a very low heat. Stir thoroughly
until all the sugar has dissolved,
then bring the fudge mixture to the
boil without any further stirring.

2 Put each pear in a serving dish and
pour the hot fudge sauce over it.
Serve immediately.

Lemon and Blueberry Pancakes

Preparation Time 15 minutes • Cooking Time 10–15 minutes • Serves 4 • Per Serving 290 calories, 13g fat (of which 6g saturates), 39g carbohydrate, 0.6g salt • Easy

125g (4oz) wholemeal plain flour
1 tsp baking powder
¼ tsp bicarbonate of soda
2 tbsp golden caster sugar
finely grated zest of 1 lemon
125g (4oz) natural yogurt
2 tbsp milk
2 medium eggs
40g (1½oz) butter
100g (3½oz) blueberries
1 tsp sunflower oil
natural yogurt and fruit compote
**   to serve**

1 Sift the flour, baking powder and bicarbonate of soda into a bowl, tipping in the contents left in the sieve. Add the sugar and lemon zest. Pour in the yogurt and milk. Break the eggs into the mixture and whisk together.

2 Melt 25g (1oz) butter in a pan, add to the bowl with the blueberries and stir everything together.

3 Heat a dot of butter with the oil in a frying pan over a medium heat until hot. Add four large spoonfuls of the mixture to the pan to make four pancakes. After about 2 minutes, flip them over and cook for 1–2 minutes. Repeat with the remaining mixture, adding a dot more butter each time.

4 Serve with natural yogurt and some fruit compote.

⭐ TRY SOMETHING DIFFERENT
Instead of blueberries and lemon, use 100g (3½oz) chopped ready-to-eat dried apricots and 2 tsp grated fresh root ginger.

Barbecued Figs with Marsala

★

Preparation Time 10 minutes • Cooking Time 12–20 minutes • Serves 4 • Per Serving 106 calories, trace fat, 22g carbohydrate, 0g salt • **Gluten Free** • **Easy**

12 large ripe figs
melted butter to brush
1 cinnamon stick, roughly broken
6 tbsp clear Greek honey
6 tbsp Marsala
crème fraîche to serve

1 Preheat the barbecue. Make a small slit in each fig, three-quarters of the way through. Take two sheets of foil large enough to hold the figs in one layer. With the shiny side uppermost, lay one piece on top of the other and brush the top piece all over with the melted butter.

2 Stand the figs in the middle of the foil and scatter the broken cinnamon stick over them. Bring the sides of the foil together loosely and pour in the honey and Marsala. Scrunch the edges of the foil together so that the figs are loosely enclosed.

3 Put the foil parcel on the barbecue and cook for 10–15 minutes.

4 Just before serving, open up the foil slightly at the top and barbecue for a further 2–3 minutes to allow the juices to reduce and become syrupy. Serve the figs with a large dollop of crème fraîche and the syrupy juices spooned over them.

Figs in Cinnamon Syrup

★

Preparation Time 15 minutes • Cooking Time 35 minutes, plus cooling and chilling • Serves 4 • Per Serving 336 calories, 2g fat (of which 0g saturates), 68g carbohydrate, 0.2g salt • Gluten Free • Dairy Free • Easy

1 orange
1 lemon
300ml (½ pint) red wine
50g (2oz) golden caster sugar
1 cinnamon stick
450g (1lb) ready-to-eat dried figs
mascarpone cheese or Vanilla Ice
    Cream (see page 270) to serve

1 Pare the zest from the orange and lemon and put into a medium pan. Squeeze the orange and lemon and add their juice, the wine, sugar and cinnamon stick to the pan. Bring very slowly to the boil, stirring occasionally.

2 Add the figs. Reduce the heat and simmer very gently for 20 minutes until plump and soft. Remove the figs, zest and cinnamon with a slotted spoon and transfer to a serving bowl.

3 Bring the liquid to the boil once again and bubble for 5 minutes until syrupy. Pour over the figs, then cool, cover and chill.

4 If you like, warm the figs in the syrup for 3–4 minutes, then serve with mascarpone cheese or Vanilla Ice Cream.

Ginger-glazed Pineapple

Preparation Time 10 minutes • Cooking Time 10 minutes • Serves 6 • Per Serving 88 calories, trace fat, 22g carbohydrate, 0g salt • Gluten Free • Dairy Free • Easy

2 pineapples
2 tbsp light muscovado sugar
2 tsp ground ginger
natural yogurt (optional) and honey
   to serve

1 Preheat the grill. Cut the pineapples into quarters lengthways, leaving the stalk intact. Remove the core, extract the flesh and put the skin to one side. Cut the flesh into pieces and return to the pineapple shell. Wrap the green leaves of the stalk in foil.

2 Mix the sugar with the ginger. Sprinkle each pineapple quarter with the sugar mixture. Put on foil-lined baking sheets and grill for 10 minutes until golden and caramelised. Serve with yogurt, if you like, and a drizzle of honey.

★ COOK'S TIP
This is the perfect dessert after a heavy or rich meal. Fresh pineapple contains an enzyme, bromelin, which digests protein very effectively and helps balance any excess acidity or alkalinity. Ginger is a well-known digestive and has many therapeutic properties.

Caramelised Pineapple

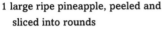

Preparation Time 10 minutes • Cooking Time about 20 minutes • Serves 6 • Per Serving 187 calories, 4g fat
(of which trace saturates), 31g carbohydrate, 0g salt • Gluten Free • Dairy Free • Easy

**1 large ripe pineapple, peeled and
  sliced into rounds**
6 tbsp brown sugar
6 tbsp rum
2 tbsp olive oil

1 Cut each pineapple round in half
and remove the core. Put the sugar
and rum into a bowl with the
pineapple and toss to coat.

2 Heat the oil in a non-stick frying
pan until hot. Using a slotted spoon,
lift the pineapple out of the bowl,
keeping the liquid to one side, and
fry over a medium heat for 4–5
minutes on each side until golden
and caramelised.

3 Divide the pineapple among six
plates. Add the rum and sugar to
the pan and bubble for 1 minute.
Drizzle over the pineapple to serve.

★ COOK'S TIP
*To check whether a pineapple is ripe,
pull on one of the leaves in the centre of
the crown. If it pulls out easily, the fruit
is ripe.*

Fruit Kebabs with Spiced Pear Dip

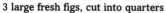

Preparation Time 20 minutes, plus soaking • Cooking Time 8 minutes • Serves 6 • Per Serving 122 calories, 3g fat (of which trace saturates), 23g carbohydrate, 0g salt • Gluten Free • Easy

3 large fresh figs, cut into quarters

1 large ripe mango, peeled, stoned and cut into cubes

1 baby pineapple or 2 thick slices, peeled and cut into cubes

1 tbsp clear honey

FOR THE SPICED PEAR DIP

150g (5oz) ready-to-eat dried pears, soaked in hot water for about 30 minutes

juice of 1 orange

1 tsp finely chopped fresh root ginger

½ tsp vanilla extract

50g (2oz) very low-fat natural yogurt

½ tsp ground cinnamon, plus extra to dust

1 tsp clear honey

25g (1oz) hazelnuts, toasted and roughly chopped

1 Soak six 20.5cm (8in) wooden skewers in water for 30 minutes. To make the dip, drain the pears and put into a food processor or blender with the orange juice, ginger, vanilla extract, yogurt, cinnamon and 50ml (2fl oz) water, then whiz until smooth. Spoon the dip into a bowl. Drizzle with the honey, sprinkle with the toasted hazelnuts and dust with a little ground cinnamon. Cover and put to one side in a cool place until ready to serve.

2 To make the kebabs, preheat the grill until very hot. Thread pieces of fruit on to the soaked skewers, using at least two pieces of each type of fruit per skewer. Put the skewers on a foil-covered tray. Drizzle with honey and grill for about 4 minutes on each side, close to the heat, until lightly charred. Serve warm or at room temperature with the spiced pear dip.

★ GET AHEAD

To prepare ahead *Make the dip as in step 1 and spoon the dip into a bowl, but don't drizzle with the honey. Cover and chill for up to two days. Thread the fruit on to the soaked skewers as in step 2. Cover and chill for up to one day.*

To use *Drizzle the dip with honey, sprinkle with toasted nuts and dust with cinnamon. Allow the chilled kebabs to come to room temperature. Finally, complete step 2.*

Sticky Maple Syrup Pineapple

★

Preparation Time 15 minutes • Cooking Time 5 minutes • Serves 4 • Per Serving 231 calories, trace fat, 60g carbohydrate, 0.3g salt • Gluten Free • Dairy Free • Easy

1 large pineapple
200ml (7fl oz) maple syrup

1 Peel the pineapple and cut into quarters lengthways. Cut away the central woody core from each pineapple quarter. Slice each one lengthways into four to make 16 wedges.

2 Pour the maple syrup into a large non-stick frying pan and heat for 2 minutes. Add the pineapple and fry for 3 minutes, turning once, until warmed through.

3 Divide the pineapple among four plates, drizzle the maple syrup over and around the pineapple and serve immediately.

Griddled Peaches

Preparation Time 15 minutes • Cooking Time 6–8 minutes • Serves 4 • Per Serving 94 calories, 5g fat
(of which 1g saturates), 11g carbohydrate, 0g salt • Gluten Free • Dairy Free • Easy

**4 ripe but firm peaches, halved
and stoned
1 tbsp maple syrup
1 tsp light olive oil
25g (1oz) pecan nuts, toasted**

1 Cut the peaches into thick slices,
then put into a bowl with the maple
syrup and toss to coat.

2 Heat the oil in a griddle or large
frying pan, add the peaches and
cook for 3–4 minutes on each side
until starting to char and caramelise.
Sprinkle with the toasted pecans
and serve at once.

★ TRY SOMETHING
DIFFERENT
*Use nectarines instead of peaches,
or 8 plump plums.*

Peach Brûlée

Preparation Time 10 minutes • **Cooking Time** about 10 minutes • **Serves 4** • **Per Serving** 137 calories, 6g fat (of which 4g saturates), 21g carbohydrate, 0.1g salt • **Gluten Free** • **Easy**

4 ripe peaches, halved and stoned
8 tsp soft cream cheese
8 tsp golden caster sugar

1 Preheat the grill until very hot. Fill each stone cavity in the fruit with 2 tsp cream cheese, then sprinkle each one with 2 tsp caster sugar.

2 Put the fruit halves on a grill pan, and cook under the very hot grill until the sugar has browned and caramelised to create a brûlée crust. Serve warm.

★ TRY SOMETHING DIFFERENT
Use nectarines instead of peaches.

Summer Gratin

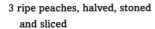

Preparation Time 15 minutes • Cooking Time 10–12 minutes • Serves 4 • Per Serving 168 calories, 4g fat (of which 1g saturates), 27g carbohydrate, 0g salt • **Gluten Free** • **Dairy Free** • **Easy**

3 ripe peaches, halved, stoned and sliced
225g (8oz) wild strawberries or raspberries
3 tbsp Kirsch or eau de vie de Mirabelle
4 large egg yolks
50g (2oz) caster sugar

1 Put the peach slices into a bowl with the strawberries or raspberries and 2 tbsp Kirsch or eau de vie.

2 Put the egg yolks, sugar, the remaining Kirsch or eau de vie and 2 tbsp water into a heatproof bowl set over a pan of barely simmering water. Whisk for 5–10 minutes until the mixture leaves a trail when the whisk is lifted, and is warm in the centre. Remove from the heat. Preheat the grill.

3 Arrange the fruit in four shallow heatproof dishes and spoon the sauce over them. Cook under the hot grill for 1–2 minutes or until light golden. Serve immediately.

⭐ TRY SOMETHING DIFFERENT
Use mango slices and blueberries and replace the Kirsch with Cointreau.

Drunken Pears

★

Preparation Time 15 minutes • Cooking Time 50 minutes • Serves 4 • Per Serving 305 calories, trace fat, 52g carbohydrate, 0g salt • Gluten Free • Dairy Free • Easy

4 Williams or Comice pears
150g (5oz) granulated sugar
300ml (½ pint) red wine
150ml (¼ pint) sloe gin
1 cinnamon stick
zest of 1 orange
6 star anise
Greek yogurt or whipped cream to
    serve (optional)

1 Peel the pears, cut out the calyx at the base of each and leave the stalks intact. Put the sugar, wine, sloe gin and 300ml (½ pint) water into a small pan and heat gently until the sugar dissolves.

2 Bring to the boil and add the cinnamon stick, orange zest and star anise. Add the pears, then cover, reduce the heat to low and poach for 30 minutes or until tender.

3 Remove the pears with a slotted spoon, then continue to heat the liquid until it has reduced to about 200ml (7fl oz) or until syrupy. Pour the syrup over the pears. Serve warm or chilled with Greek yogurt or whipped cream, if you like.

★ GET AHEAD
To prepare ahead Complete the recipe, cool, cover and chill for up to three days.

Sweet Kebabs

★

Preparation Time 5 minutes • Cooking Time 3 minutes • Serves 4 • Per Serving 521 calories, 23g fat (of which 12g saturates), 77g carbohydrate, 0.3g salt • **Easy**

chocolate brownie, about 10 × 5cm (4 × 2in), cut into eight chunks
8 large strawberries
whipped cream to serve

1 Preheat the barbecue or grill. Spear alternate chunks of chocolate brownie and strawberries on to metal skewers.

2 Barbecue or grill for 3 minutes, turning occasionally. Serve with whipped cream.

Barbecue Banoffee

Preparation Time 5 minutes • Cooking Time 4–5 minutes • Serves 4 • Per Serving 210 calories, 3g fat (of which 2g saturates), 38g carbohydrate, 0.1g salt • Gluten Free • Easy

4 bananas, peeled
75g (3oz) vanilla fudge, roughly chopped
butter to grease
4 tbsp rum or brandy
thick cream or Vanilla Ice Cream (see page 270) to serve

1 Preheat the barbecue or grill. Make a long slit in each banana. Divide the fudge among the bananas, then place the bananas on four large squares of buttered foil. Spoon 1 tbsp rum or brandy over each banana and scrunch the edges of the foil together to make loose parcels.

2 Put the foil parcels on the barbecue or under the hot grill and cook for 4–5 minutes. Serve with thick cream or Vanilla Ice Cream.

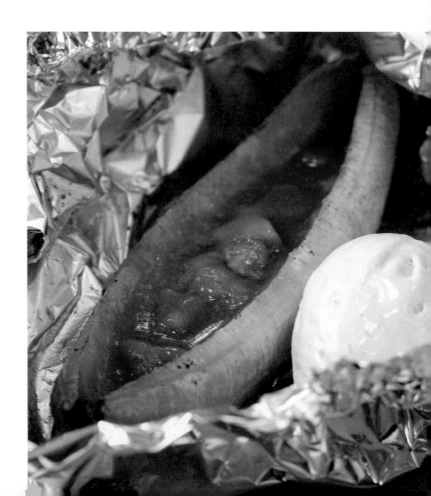

Papaya with Lime Syrup

Preparation Time 10 minutes • Cooking Time 10 minutes • Serves 4 • Per Serving 200 calories, trace fat
(of which 0g saturates), 50g carbohydrate, 0g salt • Gluten Free • Dairy Free • Easy

75g (3oz) golden caster sugar
zest and juice of 2 limes, plus extra
 zest to decorate
2 papayas, peeled, halved and
 seeded

1 Put the sugar into a small pan
with 100ml (3½ fl oz) water and
the lime zest and juice. Heat
gently to dissolve the sugar, then
bring to the boil and bubble rapidly
for 5 minutes or until the mixture is
reduced and syrupy.

2 Cut the papayas into slices
and arrange on a large serving
plate. Drizzle the lime syrup over
them and serve decorated with
extra lime zest.

⭐ TRY SOMETHING
DIFFERENT
This is just as good with mangoes and
orange syrup: use 1 orange instead of
2 limes.

Tropical Fruit Pots

Preparation Time 15 minutes • Cooking Time 5 minutes • Serves 8 • Per Serving 192 calories, 1g fat (of which trace saturates), 45g carbohydrate, 0.1g salt • Gluten Free • Easy

400g can apricots in fruit juice
2 balls of preserved stem ginger in
    syrup, finely chopped, plus
    2 tbsp syrup from the jar
½ tsp ground cinnamon
juice of 1 orange
3 oranges, cut into segments
1 mango, peeled, stoned and
    chopped
1 pineapple, peeled, cored,
    and chopped
450g (1lb) coconut yogurt
3 tbsp lemon curd
3–4 tbsp light muscovado sugar

1 Drain the juice from the apricots into a pan and stir in the syrup from the ginger. Add the chopped preserved stem ginger, the cinnamon and orange juice. Put over a low heat and stir gently. Bring to the boil, then reduce the heat and simmer for 2–3 minutes to make a thick syrup.

2 Roughly chop the apricots and put into a bowl with the segmented oranges, the mango and pineapple. Pour the syrup over the fruit. Divide among eight 300ml (½ pint) glasses or dessert bowls.

3 Beat the yogurt and lemon curd together in a bowl until smooth. Spoon a generous dollop over the fruit and sprinkle with muscovado sugar. Chill if not serving immediately.

★ GET AHEAD
To prepare ahead *Complete the recipe to the end of step 2 up to 2 hours before you plan to eat – no need to chill.*
To use *Complete the recipe.*

Mango Gratin with Sabayon

★

Preparation Time 5 minutes, plus optional resting • Cooking Time 10 minutes • Serves 6 • Per Serving 249 calories, 5g fat (of which 1g saturates), 45g carbohydrate, 0g salt • Gluten Free • Dairy Free • A Little Effort

3 large ripe mangoes, peeled, stoned and sliced
5 medium egg yolks
6 tbsp golden caster sugar
300ml (½ pint) champagne or sparkling wine
6 tbsp dark muscovado sugar to sprinkle
crisp sweet biscuits to serve

1 Arrange the mangoes in six glasses. Whisk the egg yolks and caster sugar in a large heatproof bowl over a pan of gently simmering water until the mixture is thick and falls in soft ribbon shapes. Add the champagne or sparkling wine and continue to whisk until the mixture is thick and foamy again. Remove from the heat.

2 Spoon the sabayon over the mangoes, sprinkle with the muscovado sugar, then blow-torch the top to caramelise or leave for 10 minutes to go fudgey. Serve with biscuits.

Golden Honey Fruits

....★

Preparation Time 5 minutes • Cooking Time 5–8 minutes • Serves 4 • Per Serving 160 calories, trace fat, 40g carbohydrate, 0g salt • Gluten Free • Easy

900g (2lb) selection of tropical fruit, such as pineapple, mango, papaya and banana
3 tbsp runny honey
Greek yogurt to serve
mixed spice to sprinkle

1 Preheat the grill to high. Peel the fruit as necessary and cut into wedges.

2 Put the fruit on to a foil-lined grill pan, drizzle with the honey and cook under the hot grill for 5–8 minutes until caramelised.

3 Serve with the yogurt, sprinkled with a little mixed spice.

Polenta and Plum Gratin

⭐

Preparation Time 10 minutes • **Cooking Time** about 20 minutes, plus cooling • **Serves 6** • **Per Serving** 390 calories, 15g fat (of which 9g saturates), 58g carbohydrate, 0.1g salt • **Gluten Free** • **Easy**

150g (5oz) demerara sugar
a pinch of salt
175g (6oz) polenta
25g (1oz) butter
700g (1½ lb) plums, stoned and
   quartered
1 tsp ground cinnamon
150ml (¼ pint) red wine
150g (5oz) crème fraîche

1 Line a baking sheet with greaseproof paper. Bring 900ml (1½ pints) water to the boil and add 25g (1oz) sugar and the salt. Gradually add the polenta, stirring constantly for 2–4 minutes.

2 Stir in the butter, then spread the polenta in a layer about 1cm (½in) thick on the baking sheet. Cover with greaseproof paper and cool.

3 Melt 50g (2oz) sugar in a pan over a medium heat until golden, then add the plums, cinnamon, wine and 50ml (2fl oz) water. Simmer for 2–3 minutes until the caramel has dissolved and the plums are tender.

4 Preheat the grill. Cut the polenta into large triangles and put into a deep 1.7 litre (3 pint) heatproof dish. Pour the warm plums over. Dot with the crème fraîche and sprinkle the remaining sugar over the top. Grill for 7 minutes or until golden, then serve.

⭐ TRY SOMETHING DIFFERENT
Use apricots instead of plums, and white wine instead of red.

Warm Plum Brioche Toasts

★

Preparation Time 10 minutes • Cooking Time 10 minutes • Serves 8 • Per Serving 46 calories, trace fat, 10g carbohydrate, 0g salt • **Easy**

8 plums, halved and stoned
butter to grease
2 tbsp fruit liqueur, such as Kirsch
2 tbsp golden caster sugar
1 vanilla pod, split lengthways
grilled brioche and mascarpone
   cheese to serve

1 Preheat the barbecue. Put the halved plums on a large piece of buttered foil. Sprinkle with the fruit liqueur and sugar and add the split vanilla pod. Scrunch the edges of the foil together to make a loose parcel.

2 Put the foil parcel on the barbecue and cook for 10 minutes. Serve hot, with lightly grilled brioche slices and mascarpone cheese.

Poached Plums with Port

★

Preparation Time 5 minutes • Cooking Time 20 minutes • Serves 4 • Per Serving 97 calories, 0g fat, 23g carbohydrate, 0g salt • Gluten Free • Dairy Free • Easy

75g (3oz) golden caster sugar
2 tbsp port
6 large plums, halved and stoned
1 cinnamon stick
Vanilla Ice Cream (see page 270) to serve (optional)

1 Put the sugar into a pan with 500ml (18fl oz) water. Heat gently until the sugar dissolves. Bring to the boil and simmer rapidly for 2 minutes without stirring.

2 Stir in the port. Add the plums to the pan with the cinnamon stick, and simmer gently for 5–10 minutes until the fruit is tender but still keeping its shape.

3 Remove the plums and put to one side, discarding the cinnamon. Simmer the syrup until it has reduced by two-thirds. Serve the plums warm or cold, drizzled with syrup and with a scoop of Vanilla ice Cream alongside, if you like.

Fruit Desserts, Creams, Mousses and Jellies

Apple Compôte

Preparation Time 10 minutes, plus chilling • Cooking Time 5 minutes • Serves 2 • Per Serving 188 calories, 7g fat (of which 1g saturates), 29g carbohydrate, 0g salt • Gluten Free • Easy

250g (9oz) cooking apples, peeled
 and chopped
juice of ½ lemon
1 tbsp golden caster sugar
ground cinnamon

TO SERVE
25g (1oz) raisins
25g (1oz) chopped almonds
1 tbsp natural yogurt

1 Put the cooking apples into a pan with the lemon juice, sugar and 2 tbsp cold water. Cook gently for 5 minutes or until soft. Transfer to a bowl.

2 Sprinkle a little ground cinnamon over the top, cool and chill. It will keep for up to three days.

3 Serve with the raisins, chopped almonds and yogurt.

★ COOK'S TIP
To microwave, put the apples, lemon juice, sugar and water into a microwave-proof bowl, cover loosely with clingfilm and cook on full power in an 850W microwave oven for 4 minutes or until the apples are just soft.

Poached Peaches and Strawberries

Preparation Time 15 minutes, plus chilling • Cooking Time 10 minutes, plus cooling • Serves 4 • Per Serving 78 calories, trace fat, 18g carbohydrate, 0g salt • Gluten Free • Dairy Free • Easy

4 ripe peaches, halved, stoned and
   quartered
250ml (9fl oz) orange juice
½ tbsp golden caster sugar
a small pinch of ground cinnamon
225g (8oz) strawberries, hulled
   and halved

1 Put the peaches into a pan with the orange juice, sugar and cinnamon. Simmer gently for 5 minutes. Remove the peaches with a slotted spoon and put into a large bowl.

2 Let the juice bubble until it is reduced by half. Pour over the peaches, then cool, cover and chill. Remove from the fridge about 2 hours before serving and stir in the halved strawberries.

★ TRY SOMETHING DIFFERENT
Use nectarines instead of peaches and whole raspberries instead of the strawberries.

Spiced Nectarines

Preparation Time 10 minutes, plus cooling • Serves 4 • Per Serving 95 calories, trace fat, 23g carbohydrate, 0g salt • Gluten Free • Easy

4 tbsp clear honey
2 star anise
1 tbsp lemon juice
4 ripe nectarines or peaches, halved and stoned
cream or Vanilla Ice Cream (see page 270) to serve

1 Put the honey, star anise and lemon juice into a heatproof bowl. Stir in 150ml (¼ pint) boiling water and leave until just warm.

2 Add the nectarines or peaches to the warm honey syrup and leave to cool. Serve with cream or Vanilla Ice Cream.

 TRY SOMETHING DIFFERENT
Use a cinnamon stick instead of the star anise.

Eton Mess

Preparation Time 10 minutes • Serves 6 • Per Serving 198 calories, 5g fat (of which 3g saturates), 33g carbohydrate, 0.1g salt • Gluten Free • Easy

200g (7oz) fromage frais, chilled
200g (7oz) low-fat Greek yogurt, chilled
1 tbsp golden caster sugar
2 tbsp strawberry liqueur
6 meringues, roughly crushed
350g (12oz) strawberries, hulled and halved

1 Put the fromage frais and yogurt into a large bowl and stir to combine.

2 Add the sugar, strawberry liqueur, meringues and strawberries. Mix together gently and divide among six dishes.

★ TRY SOMETHING DIFFERENT
Caribbean Crush
Replace the sugar and liqueur with dulce de leche toffee sauce and the strawberries with sliced bananas.

Marinated Strawberries

Preparation Time 5 minutes, plus marinating • Serves 4 • Per Serving without ice cream 47 calories, trace fat, 12g carbohydrate, 0g salt • Gluten Free • Easy

350g (12oz) strawberries
juice of ½ lemon
2 tbsp golden caster sugar
Vanilla Ice Cream (see page 270)
   to serve

1 Hull the strawberries and cut in half, if large. Put into a bowl with the lemon juice and sugar. Stir to mix, then put to one side for 30 minutes.

2 Serve with Vanilla Ice Cream.

Strawberry Compôte

Preparation Time 15 minutes, plus chilling • Cooking Time 10 minutes • Serves 4 • Per Serving 156 calories,
0g fat, 40g carbohydrate, 0g salt • Gluten Free • Dairy Free • Easy

175g (6oz) raspberry conserve
juice of 1 orange
juice of 1 lemon
1 tsp rosewater
350g (12oz) strawberries, hulled
   and thickly sliced
150g (5oz) blueberries

1 Put the raspberry conserve into a
pan with the orange and lemon
juices. Add 75ml (2½fl oz) boiling
water. Stir over a low heat to melt
the conserve, then leave to cool.

2 Stir in the rosewater and taste –
you may want to add a squeeze
more lemon juice if it's too sweet.
Put the strawberries and blueberries
into a large serving bowl, then strain
the raspberry conserve mixture over
them. Cover and chill overnight.
Remove the bowl from the fridge
about 30 minutes before serving.

Vanilla Chilled Risotto

Preparation Time 5 minutes, plus chilling • **Cooking Time** 40 minutes, plus cooling • **Serves** 10 • **Per Serving** 280 calories, 14g fat (of which 9g saturates), 34g carbohydrate, 0.1g salt • **Gluten Free** • **Easy**

900ml (1½ pints) full-fat milk
1 vanilla pod, split lengthways
75g (3oz) risotto rice
40g (1½oz) caster sugar
200ml (7fl oz) double cream
ground cinnamon to sprinkle
Orange Poached Peaches (see
   Cook's Tip) to serve

1 Put the milk and vanilla pod in a large pan and bring slowly to the boil. Stir in the rice, reduce the heat and simmer gently for 40 minutes, stirring from time to time, until the rice is soft and most of the liquid has been absorbed. You might need to add a little more milk during the cooking time.

2 Stir in the sugar, remove the vanilla pod and leave to cool. Once the mixture has cooled, stir in the cream, pour into a large bowl, cover and chill.

3 Just before serving, sprinkle with a little ground cinnamon. Serve with Orange Poached Peaches.

★ COOK'S TIP
Orange Poached Peaches
Put 100g (3½oz) caster sugar into a pan with 600ml (1 pint) water and the grated zest and juice of 2 oranges. Bring to the boil and bubble for 5 minutes. Add 10 ripe peaches, bring back to the boil, then cover the pan, reduce the heat and simmer for 10–15 minutes until they're almost soft, turning from time to time. Carefully lift out the peaches with a slotted spoon, reserving the liquid. Leave to cool slightly, then remove the skins and put the peaches into a serving dish. Bring the reserved liquid to the boil and bubble for 10 minutes until syrupy. Strain the syrup over the peaches and leave to cool. Cover and chill.

Fruity Rice Pudding

Preparation Time 10 minutes, plus chilling • Cooking Time 1 hour, plus cooling • Serves 6 • Per Serving 323 calories, 17g fat (of which 10g saturates), 36g carbohydrate, 0.2g salt • **Gluten Free** • **Easy**

125g (4oz) pudding rice
1.1 litres (2 pints) full-fat milk
1 tsp vanilla extract
3–4 tbsp caster sugar
200ml (7fl oz) whipping cream
6 tbsp wild lingonberry sauce

1 Put the rice into a pan with 600ml (1 pint) cold water and bring to the boil, then reduce the heat and simmer until the liquid has evaporated. Add the milk and bring to the boil, then reduce the heat and simmer for 45 minutes or until the rice is very soft and creamy. Leave to cool.

2 Add the vanilla extract and sugar to the rice. Lightly whip the cream and fold through the pudding. Chill for 1 hour.

3 Divide the rice mixture among six glass dishes and top with 1 tbsp lingonberry sauce.

★ TRY SOMETHING DIFFERENT

● *Although wild lingonberry sauce is used here, a spoonful of any fruit sauce or compote such as strawberry or blueberry will taste delicious.*
● *For an alternative presentation, serve in tumblers, layering the rice pudding with the fruit sauce; you will need to use double the amount of fruit sauce.*

Cherry Yogurt Crush

★

Preparation Time 10 minutes, plus chilling • Serves 4 • Per Serving 390 calories, 18g fat (of which 9g saturates), 45g carbohydrate, 0.5g salt • **Easy**

400g can pitted cherries, drained, or 450g (1lb) fresh cherries, pitted
500g (1lb 2oz) Greek yogurt
150g (5oz) ratafia biscuits
4 tbsp cherry brandy (optional)

1 Spoon some cherries into the base of each of four 400ml (14fl oz) glasses. Top with a dollop of yogurt, some ratafia biscuits and a drizzle of cherry brandy, if you like. Continue layering up each glass until all the ingredients have been used.

2 Chill for 15 minutes–2 hours before serving.

Cherry and Chocolate Layer

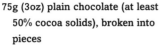

Preparation Time 5 minutes • **Cooking Time** 15 minutes • **Serves 6** • **Per Serving** 440 calories, 29g fat (of which 12g saturates), 42g carbohydrate, 0.4g salt • **Easy**

75g (3oz) plain chocolate (at least 50% cocoa solids), broken into pieces
142ml carton double cream
400g can pitted black cherries, strained and juice reserved
1 tbsp Kirsch
1 tbsp vanilla bean paste
4 × 40g (1½oz) brownies, roughly chopped
Vanilla Ice Cream (see page 270)
25g (1oz) chopped toasted hazelnuts

1 Put the chocolate and cream into a heatproof bowl set over a pan of gently simmering water, making sure the base of the bowl doesn't touch the water, and leave to melt. Stir to combine.

2 Put the cherries into a separate pan with the Kirsch and vanilla bean paste and heat gently for 5 minutes.

3 Divide half the brownies among six sundae glasses and spoon the reserved cherry juice on top. Add half the poached cherries, then half the chocolate sauce. Repeat with another layer of each and top with a scoop of Vanilla Ice Cream. Sprinkle each with the hazelnuts and serve.

Boozy Oranges with Orange Cream

Preparation Time 15 minutes • Serves 20 • Per Serving 160 calories, 14g fat (of which 9g saturates), 7g carbohydrate, 0.2g salt • Gluten Free • Easy

8 large juicy oranges
6 tbsp Cointreau (optional)
600ml (1 pint) double cream
1 tbsp golden icing sugar, sifted

1 Grate the zest from two oranges into a bowl and put to one side.

2 Put the oranges on a board and use a sharp knife to cut the top and bottom off each. Next, cut off all the peel and white pith. Cut the flesh into rounds, pouring any juice into a large serving bowl. Put the slices in the bowl, add 3 tbsp Cointreau, if you like, and put to one side.

3 Whip the cream in a bowl until just thick, then stir in the remaining Cointreau, almost all the orange zest and the icing sugar. Scatter the remaining zest on top and serve with the oranges.

 COOK'S TIP
Take care not to overwhip the cream when you're whisking it first; it will thicken a lot once you add the remaining ingredients.

★ GET AHEAD
To prepare ahead *Complete the recipe to the end of step 2 up to one day ahead, then cover and chill. Make the cream up to 4 hours ahead, cover and chill until ready to serve.*
To use *Complete the recipe.*

Summer Fruit with Raspberry Cream

★

Preparation Time 5 minutes • Serves 6 • Per Serving 270 calories, 23g fat (of which 14g saturates), 15g carbohydrate, 0.1g salt • Gluten Free • Easy

600g (1lb 5oz) mixed summer fruit
   (such as strawberries,
   raspberries and blueberries)
juice of ½ orange
150g (5oz) raspberries
2 tbsp icing sugar
284ml carton double cream

1 Put the summer fruit into a large bowl. Add the orange juice and toss gently, then divide among four serving bowls.

2 Put the raspberries and icing sugar into a food processor and whiz to form a purée. Lightly whip the cream, add the purée and fold together gently to produce a marbled effect.

3 Spoon a dollop of cream over the fruit and serve.

Exotic Fruit Salad

★

Preparation Time 30 minutes, plus infusing and chilling • Cooking Time 7 minutes • Serves 6 • Per Serving 232 calories, 1g fat (of which 0g saturates), 58g carbohydrate, 0.1g salt • Gluten Free • Dairy Free • Easy

1 pineapple, about 900g (2lb), peeled, cored and cut into chunks
2 papayas, peeled, seeded and sliced
1 Galia melon, seeded, and flesh cut into chunks
fresh mint leaves to decorate

FOR THE SYRUP
125g (4oz) caster sugar
6 fresh mint sprigs
¼ tsp Chinese five-spice powder
2 small fresh bay leaves
4 lemongrass stalks, split in half and bruised
½ tsp grated fresh root ginger

1 To make the syrup, put the sugar into a pan with 600ml (1 pint) water and the remaining syrup ingredients. Heat gently until the sugar has dissolved. Bring to the boil, then reduce the heat and simmer for 5 minutes. Remove from the heat and leave to infuse for at least 1 hour.

2 Put all the fruit into a bowl, strain the cooled syrup over the top, then cover and chill for at least 2 hours. Decorate with mint leaves.

Watermelon with Feta and Honey

Preparation Time 10 minutes • **Cooking Time** 3 minutes • **Serves 4** • **Per Serving** 182 calories, 8g fat (of which 2g saturates), 24g carbohydrate, 0.5g salt • **Gluten Free** • **Easy**

2 tbsp pinenuts
½ watermelon
50g (2oz) feta cheese
2 tbsp clear honey
a handful of freshly chopped mint

1 Put the pinenuts into a small pan and toast over a medium-high heat, tossing occasionally for about 2–3 minutes, until golden brown all over. Leave to cool.

2 Cut the rind off the watermelon, then cut the melon into chunks and arrange on a serving plate. Crumble the feta cheese over the melon and drizzle with the honey.

3 Scatter with the toasted pinenuts and chopped mint.

⭐ TRY SOMETHING DIFFERENT
If watermelon is not in season use another variety of melon, such as Charentais, Canteloupe or Galia. If you are using one of the sweeter varieties, reduce the honey to about 1 tbsp.

Summer Pudding

★

Preparation Time 10 minutes, plus chilling • Cooking Time 10 minutes • Serves 8 • Per Serving 173 calories,
1g fat (of which trace saturates), 38g carbohydrate, 0.4g salt • **Dairy Free** • **Easy**

**800g (1lb 12oz) mixed summer
    berries, such as 250g (9oz) each
    redcurrants and blackcurrants
    and 300g (11oz) raspberries**
125g (4oz) golden caster sugar
3 tbsp crème de cassis
**9 thick slices slightly stale white
    bread, crusts removed**
**crème fraîche or clotted cream
    to serve**

1 Put the redcurrants and
blackcurrants into a medium pan.
Add the sugar and cassis. Bring to
a simmer and cook for 3–5 minutes
until the sugar has dissolved. Add
the raspberries and cook for
2 minutes. Once the fruit is cooked,
taste it – there should be a good
balance between tart and sweet.

2 Meanwhile, line a 1 litre (1¾ pint)
bowl with clingfilm. Put the base of
the bowl on one piece of bread and
cut around it. Put the circle of bread
in the base of the bowl.

3 Line the inside of the bowl with
more slices of bread, slightly
overlapping them to prevent any
gaps. Spoon in the fruit, making
sure the juice soaks into the bread.
Keep back a few spoonfuls of juice
in case the bread is unevenly soaked
when you turn out the pudding.

4 Cut the remaining bread to fit the
top of the pudding neatly, using a
sharp knife to trim any excess bread
from around the edges. Wrap in
clingfilm, weigh down with a saucer
and a can and chill overnight.

5 To serve, unwrap the outer
clingfilm, upturn the pudding on
to a plate and remove the inner
clingfilm. Drizzle with the reserved
juice and serve with crème fraîche or
clotted cream.

Winter Fruit Compôte

Preparation Time 10 minutes • Cooking Time 50 minutes, plus cooling • Serves 6 • Per Serving 150 calories, trace fat, 28g carbohydrate, 0.1g salt • **Gluten Free** • **Dairy Free** • **Easy**

75g (3oz) ready-to-eat dried pears
75g (3oz) ready-to-eat dried figs
75g (3oz) ready-to-eat dried apricots
75g (3oz) ready-to-eat prunes
about 300ml (½ pint) apple juice
300ml (½ pint) dry white wine
1 star anise
½ cinnamon stick
light muscovado sugar, to taste
crème fraîche or thick Greek-style yogurt to serve

1 Put the dried fruits into a pan with the apple juice, wine, star anise and cinnamon stick. Slowly bring to the boil.

2 Reduce the heat, cover and simmer for 45 minutes until the fruits are plump and tender. Check the liquid during cooking to ensure there is sufficient; add a little more apple juice if necessary.

3 Turn the compote into a bowl. Taste the cooking liquid for sweetness, adding a little sugar if necessary. Leave to cool to room temperature.

4 Serve the compote with crème fraîche or thick Greek-style yogurt.

★ TRY SOMETHING DIFFERENT
Replace the figs with dried apple rings and the pears with raisins.

Spiced Winter Fruit

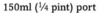

Preparation Time 20 minutes • Cooking Time about 20 minutes • Serves 6 • Per Serving 222 calories, 0g fat, 48g carbohydrate, 0g salt • **Gluten Free** • **Dairy Free** • **Easy**

150ml (¼ pint) port
150ml (¼ pint) freshly squeezed orange juice
75g (3oz) light muscovado sugar
1 cinnamon stick
6 whole cardamom pods, lightly crushed
5cm (2in) piece fresh root ginger, peeled and thinly sliced
50g (2oz) large muscatel raisins or dried blueberries
1 small pineapple, peeled, cored and thinly sliced
1 mango, peeled, stoned and thickly sliced
3 tangerines, peeled and halved horizontally
3 fresh figs, halved

1 First, make the syrup. Pour the port and orange juice into a small pan, then add the sugar and 300ml (½ pint) water. Bring to the boil, stirring all the time. Add the cinnamon stick, cardamom pods and ginger, then bubble gently for 15 minutes.

2 Put all the fruit into a serving bowl. Remove the cinnamon stick and cardamom pods from the syrup, then pour the syrup over the fruit. Serve warm or cold.

★ FREEZING TIP

To freeze *Tip the fruit and syrup into a freezerproof container, leave to cool, then cover with a tight-fitting lid. Freeze for up to three months.*
To use *Thaw overnight in the fridge and serve cold.*

★ COOK'S TIPS

● *It might sound odd freezing a fruit salad, but it saves all the last-minute chopping and slicing.*
● *Not suitable for children due to the alcohol content.*

Apple and Raspberry Mousse

★

Preparation Time 10 minutes, plus chilling • Cooking Time 15 minutes • Serves 6 • Per Serving 127 calories, trace fat,
32g carbohydrate, 0g salt • **Gluten Free** • **Dairy Free** • **Easy**

900g (2lb) cooking apples, peeled,
    cored and sliced
4 tbsp orange juice
grated zest of 1 lemon
225g (8oz) raspberries
6 tbsp golden caster sugar
1 large egg white
mint sprigs to decorate

1 Put the apples and orange juice
into a pan and cook over a low heat,
uncovered, for 10 minutes until soft.
Add the lemon zest, then use a fork
to mash to a purée. Cover and chill
for at least 1 hour.

2 Gently heat the raspberries and
2 tbsp sugar in a pan until the juices
start to run.

3 Put the egg white in a clean,
grease-free bowl and whisk until
stiff, adding the remaining sugar
gradually until stiff peaks form. Fold
the mixture into the apple purée.

4 Divide the raspberries and any
juice among six glasses, spoon the
apple mixture on top and decorate
with mint sprigs.

Mango and Lime Mousse

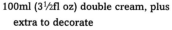

Preparation Time 25–35 minutes, plus soaking, freezing and chilling • Cooking Time 1–2 minutes • Serves 6 •
Per Serving 209 calories, 14g fat (of which 7g saturates), 16g carbohydrate, 0.1g salt • Gluten Free • A Little Effort

100ml (3½fl oz) double cream, plus
    extra to decorate
2 very ripe mangoes, peeled,
    stoned and sliced
finely grated zest and juice of
    2 limes, plus zest of 1 lime to
    decorate
1 sachet powdered gelatine (see
    Cook's Tips, page 142)
3 large eggs, plus 2 large egg yolks
50g (2oz) golden caster sugar

1 Whip the cream until just thick, then chill. Purée the mango flesh in a blender to give 300ml (½ pint).

2 Put 3 tbsp lime juice into a small heatproof bowl, sprinkle the gelatine on top and leave to soak for 10 minutes.

3 Whisk the eggs, extra yolks and sugar together in a large bowl for 4–5 minutes until very thick and mousse-like. Very gently fold in the mango purée, whipped cream and lime zest.

4 Put the gelatine and lime mixture over a pan of boiling water for 1–2 minutes, stir until the gelatine dissolves, then lightly fold into the mango mixture until evenly combined. Divide among six glasses and freeze for 20 minutes, then transfer to the fridge to chill for at least 1 hour.

5 To serve, decorate with whipped cream and lime zest.

★ TRY SOMETHING DIFFERENT
Replace the mango with 300ml (½ pint) mixed berry purée and decorate with extra berries.

Quick Lemon Mousse

Preparation Time 1–2 minutes • Serves 4 • Per Serving 334 calories, 30g fat (of which 18g saturates), 16g carbohydrate, 0.1g salt • Gluten Free • Easy

6 tbsp lemon curd
300ml (½ pint) double cream, whipped
fresh blueberries to decorate

1 Gently stir the lemon curd through the cream until combined, then decorate with blueberries.

Zabaglione

★

Preparation Time 5 minutes • Cooking Time 20 minutes • Serves 4 • Per Serving 193 calories, 6g fat (of which 2g saturates), 28g carbohydrate, 0g salt • Gluten Free • Dairy Free • Easy

4 medium egg yolks
100g (3½oz) caster sugar
100ml (3½fl oz) sweet Marsala wine

1 Heat a pan of water to boiling point. Put the egg yolks and sugar into a heatproof bowl large enough to rest over the pan without its base touching the water. With the bowl in place, reduce the heat so that the water is just simmering.

2 Using a hand-held electric whisk, whisk the yolks and sugar for 15 minutes until pale, thick and foaming. With the bowl still over the heat, gradually pour in the Marsala, whisking all the time.

3 Pour the zabaglione into four glasses or small coffee cups and serve immediately.

Baked Orange Custard

Preparation Time 10 minutes, plus infusing and chilling • Cooking Time 50 minutes or 1 hour 10 minutes, plus cooling • Serves 6 •
Per Serving 268 calories, 20g fat (of which 10g saturates), 18g carbohydrate, 0.2g salt • Gluten Free • Easy

zest of 1 orange
450ml (¾ pint) milk
150ml (¼ pint) double cream
75g (3oz) clear honey (see
   Cook's Tips)
2 large eggs, plus 4 large egg yolks
25g (1oz) caster sugar
slivers of orange zest to decorate

1 Put the orange zest, milk and cream into a pan, then bring to the boil. Remove from the heat and leave to infuse for 30 minutes.

2 Preheat the oven to 150°C (130°C fan oven) mark 2. Warm a 1.7 litre (3 pint) soufflé dish or six 150ml (¼ pint) coffee cups in the oven. Bring the honey to the boil in a small heavy-based pan. Bubble for 2–3 minutes until it begins to caramelise (see Cook's Tips). Pour the caramel into the warmed dish or cups and rotate to coat the base. Leave to cool and harden.

3 Put the eggs, yolks and sugar into a bowl and beat together until smooth. Add the infused milk mixture, stir until well combined, then strain into the dish(es). Put the dish or cups into a roasting tin, adding enough hot water to come halfway up the side(s). Bake for 1 hour 10 minutes for the soufflé dish or 45–50 minutes for the coffee cups until just set in the middle (see Cook's Tips). Cool and chill for at least 6 hours or overnight. Decorate with orange zest.

⭐ COOK'S TIPS
● *Look for a mild flower honey such as lavender or orange blossom; a strong honey will be overpowering.*
● *The honey needs to be cooked to a golden brown caramel – any darker and it will become bitter.*
● *The custard may still be wobbly after cooking, but don't worry, it firms up on cooling and chilling.*

Baked Raspberry Creams

Preparation Time 15–20 minutes, plus chilling • Cooking Time 30–35 minutes, plus cooling • Serves 6
Per Serving 347 calories. 30g fat (of which 17g saturates), 15g carbohydrate, 0.1g salt • Gluten Free • Easy

250g (9oz) raspberries
2 large eggs, plus 2 large egg yolks
50g (2oz) caster sugar
300ml (½ pint) double cream
oil to oil
450g (1lb) mixed raspberries,
   strawberries and redcurrants
   to decorate
icing sugar to serve

1 Preheat the oven to 170°C (150°C fan oven) mark 3. Purée the raspberries in a food processor, then press through a sieve with the back of a spoon to remove the pips.

2 Whisk the eggs, yolks and caster sugar together in a bowl. Strain into the puréed raspberries, pour in the cream and stir well.

3 Divide the mixture among six 150ml (¼ pint) ramekins, put into a roasting tin and pour enough water around the dishes to come halfway up the sides. Cover with oiled greaseproof paper and bake for 30–35 minutes until just set. Lift the dishes out of the roasting tin, then cool, cover and chill overnight.

4 To serve, spoon the mixed fruit on top of the creams and dust with icing sugar.

 COOK'S TIP
Save 150 calories by replacing the double cream with whipping cream.

★ GET AHEAD
***To prepare ahead** Make the creams, but don't top with the berries and icing sugar. Chill for up to two days.*
***To use** Complete the recipe, then decorate with berries and icing sugar.*

Coffee Semifreddi

Preparation Time 20 minutes, plus freezing • Serves 6 • Per Serving 367 calories, 32g fat (of which 17g saturates), 14g carbohydrate, 0g salt • **Gluten Free** • **Easy**

2 tbsp instant espresso coffee

2 tbsp Sambuca or Amaretto, plus extra to serve

3 large egg yolks

75g (3oz) caster sugar

300ml (½ pint) double cream, whipped to soft peaks

40g (1½oz) ground almonds, lightly toasted and cooled

1 Line the bases of six 150ml (¼ pint) pudding moulds with greaseproof paper. Dissolve the coffee in 100ml (3½fl oz) water then stir the Sambuca or Amaretto into the coffee.

2 Whisk the egg yolks and sugar together in a large bowl until pale and fluffy. Gradually whisk the coffee into the egg mixture.

3 Gently fold in the cream and almonds until combined. Divide the mixture among the lined moulds and freeze for at least 6 hours.

4 To serve, upturn the moulds on to six plates and drizzle a little extra Sambuca or Amaretto around each one. Eat immediately.

★ COOK'S TIP
Sambuca is an anise-flavoured Italian liqueur, while Amaretto is an almond-flavoured liqueur.

Classic Tiramisu

★

Preparation Time 20 minutes, plus chilling • Serves 8 • Per Serving 420 calories, 33g fat (of which 18g saturates),
24g carbohydrate, 0.3g salt • Easy

4 medium egg yolks
75g (3oz) golden caster sugar
200g tub mascarpone cheese
1 tbsp vanilla extract
300ml (½ pint) double cream,
    whipped to soft peaks
100ml (3½fl oz) grappa
200g pack sponge fingers or
    Savoiardi biscuits
450ml (¾ pint) warm strong
    black coffee
1 tbsp cocoa powder

1 Using an electric hand-held whisk, whisk the egg yolks and sugar in a large bowl for about 5 minutes until pale and thick. Add the mascarpone and vanilla extract and beat until smooth. Fold in the whipped cream and grappa.

2 Spread half the mascarpone mixture over the base of eight small serving dishes. Dip the sponge fingers, in turn, into the warm coffee and arrange on the mascarpone layer. Top with the remaining mascarpone mixture.

3 Cover and chill in the fridge for at least 2 hours. Dust with cocoa, just before serving.

Boozy Pannacotta

Preparation Time 10 minutes, plus soaking and chilling • Cooking Time 10 minutes • Serves 2 • Per Serving 622 calories, 45g fat (of which 25g saturates), 50g carbohydrate, 0.2g salt • Gluten Free • Easy

oil to oil
140ml (4½fl oz) double cream
150ml (¼ pint) semi-skimmed milk
3 tbsp light muscovado sugar
1 tbsp instant espresso coffee
  powder
50ml (2fl oz) Tia Maria or other
  coffee liqueur
40g (1½oz) plain chocolate (at least
  70% cocoa solids), chopped
1½ tsp powdered gelatine (see
  Cook's Tips, page 142)
1 tsp vanilla extract
2 chocolate-coated coffee beans
  (optional)

1 Oil two 150ml (¼ pint) individual pudding basins and line them with clingfilm. Pour 100ml (3½fl oz) cream into a small pan with the milk, sugar, coffee, 1 tbsp liqueur and the chocolate. Heat gently until the chocolate has melted, then bring to the boil.

2 Remove the pan from the heat, sprinkle the gelatine over the surface and leave for 5 minutes. Stir well to ensure the gelatine is fully dissolved, then add the vanilla extract and mix well. Strain the mixture through a sieve into a jug, then pour into the lined basins and chill for 2 hours.

3 To serve, unmould the pannacottas on to plates and remove the clingfilm. Stir the rest of the liqueur into the remaining cream and drizzle around the pannacottas. Top with chocolate-coated coffee beans, if you like.

Plum and Cardamom Fool

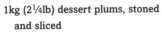

Preparation Time 15–20 minutes, plus standing and chilling • Cooking Time 30 minutes • Serves 4 •
Per Serving 365 calories, 11g fat (of which 5g saturates), 63g carbohydrate, 0.2g salt • Gluten Free • Easy

1kg (2¼lb) dessert plums, stoned
   and sliced
125g (4oz) caster sugar
4 cardamom pods, split, seeds
   removed and crushed
2 tbsp lemon juice
150g (5oz) fresh Vanilla Custard
   (see page 269)
400g (14oz) Greek yogurt
amaretti biscuits to serve (optional)

1 Put the plums, sugar, cardamom seeds and lemon juice into a pan. Cover and bring to the boil, then reduce the heat and simmer for 20–25 minutes until the plums are soft but still holding their shape. Pour into a cold bowl and leave for 30 minutes. Remove four slices for the decoration and put to one side.

2 Strain the plums, reserving the juices. Purée the plums in a food processor and pour into a bowl. Boil the juices for 3–4 minutes until reduced to 3 tbsp, then stir into the plum purée with the custard and half the yogurt until smooth. Spoon into four glasses and chill for up to 2 hours.

3 Decorate with the remaining yogurt and the reserved plum slices and serve with amaretti biscuits, if you like.

Fruity Fool

★

Preparation Time 1–2 minutes • Serves 6 • Per Serving 159 calories, 2g fat (of which trace saturates), 31g carbohydrate, 0.1g salt • Gluten Free • Easy

500g carton summer fruit compote
500g carton fresh custard

1 Divide half the compote among six glasses, then add a thin layer of custard. Repeat the process until all the compote and custard have been used.

2 Stir each fool once to swirl the custard and compote together, then serve.

Rhubarb Fool

Preparation Time 5 minutes, plus chilling • Cooking Time about 15 minutes, plus cooling • Serves 6 •
Per Serving 107 calories, 3g fat (of which 1g saturates), 20g carbohydrate, 0.1g salt • Gluten Free • Easy

450g (1lb) rhubarb, thickly chopped
50ml (2fl oz) orange juice
1 cinnamon stick
25g (1oz) golden caster sugar
1 tbsp redcurrant jelly
150g (5oz) fat-free Greek-style
  yogurt
2 tbsp soft brown sugar

1 Put the rhubarb, orange juice, cinnamon stick and caster sugar into a pan. Cover and cook gently for 10 minutes or until tender.

2 Remove the lid and cook for 5 minutes or until the liquid has evaporated. Discard the cinnamon stick. Stir in the redcurrant jelly, then leave to cool.

3 Roughly fold in the yogurt, then spoon the mixture into six glasses and sprinkle with the soft brown sugar. Chill for 2 hours.

★ TRY SOMETHING DIFFERENT
Blackberry Fool
Use blackberries instead of rhubarb – you will need 400g (14oz) – and a squeeze of lemon juice instead of the orange juice. Blend in a food processor after stirring in the redcurrant jelly.

Lemon and Passion Fruit Fool

Preparation Time 20 minutes • Serves 6 • Per Serving 210 calories, 17g fat (of which 10g saturates), 14g carbohydrate, 0.1g salt • Gluten Free • Easy

6 tbsp lemon curd
4 ripe passion fruits
150ml (¼ pint) double cream
1 tbsp icing sugar
200g (7oz) Greek yogurt
toasted flaked almonds to decorate

1 Put the lemon curd into a small bowl. Halve the passion fruits and spoon the pulp into a sieve resting over a bowl. Stir to separate the seeds from the juice. Add 1 tbsp of the passion fruit juice to the lemon curd and mix well.

2 Whip the cream and icing sugar together in a large bowl until soft peaks form. Stir in the yogurt.

3 Put a dollop of yogurt cream into each of six small glasses. Layer with a spoonful of lemon curd mixture and 1 tsp passion fruit juice. Repeat to use up all the ingredients. Scatter some toasted flaked almonds on top and serve immediately.

★ COOK'S TIP
Using a good-quality lemon curd will make all the difference to the final flavour of this fool.

Strawberry Brûlée

Preparation Time 15 minutes, plus chilling (optional) • **Cooking Time** 5 minutes, plus cooling • **Serves 4** •
Per Serving 240 calories, 10g fat (of which 5g saturates), 35g carbohydrate, 0.2g salt • **Gluten Free** • **Easy**

250g (9oz) strawberries, hulled
   and sliced
2 tsp golden icing sugar
1 vanilla pod, split in half
   lengthways
400g (14oz) Greek yogurt
100g (3½oz) golden caster sugar

1 Divide the strawberries among four ramekins and sprinkle with icing sugar.

2 Scrape the seeds from the vanilla pod and stir into the yogurt, then spread the mixture evenly over the fruit.

3 Preheat the grill to high. Sprinkle the caster sugar evenly over the yogurt until it is well covered.

4 Put the ramekins on a baking sheet or into the grill pan and grill until the sugar turns dark brown and caramelises. Leave for 15 minutes or until the caramel is cool enough to eat, or chill for up to 2 hours before serving.

★ TRY SOMETHING DIFFERENT
Use raspberries or blueberries instead of the strawberries.

Champagne Jellies

Preparation Time 15 minutes, plus soaking and chilling • Cooking Time 15 minutes • Serves 8 • Per Serving 165 calories, trace fat, 21g carbohydrate, 0g salt • **Gluten Free** • **Dairy Free** • **Easy**

125g (4oz) golden caster sugar
pared zest of 1 orange
5 sheets leaf gelatine (see Cook's
    Tips, page 142)
75cl bottle champagne or
    sparkling wine
2–3 tbsp orange-flavoured liqueur,
    such as Grand Marnier
edible gold leaf to decorate

1 Put the sugar into a pan. Add the orange zest and 250ml (9fl oz) cold water. Heat gently until the sugar dissolves. Bring the mixture to the boil, then reduce the heat and simmer gently for 2–3 minutes until slightly reduced and syrupy. Remove the pan from the heat and discard the orange zest.

2 Meanwhile, put the gelatine into a shallow bowl and cover with cold water. Leave to soak for 5 minutes.

3 Lift the gelatine out of the bowl, squeeze out excess water, then add it to the pan. Stir gently for about 2–3 minutes until the gelatine dissolves completely.

4 Pour the champagne or wine and liqueur into the pan, then transfer the mixture to a jug. Fill eight wine glasses with the jelly mixture, then chill for 4 hours or until set. Decorate with gold leaf to serve.

 GET AHEAD
To prepare ahead *Complete the recipe, cover and chill for up to two days.*

Elderflower and Fruit Jelly

Preparation Time 15 minutes, plus chilling • Cooking Time 10 minutes, plus cooling • Serves 6 • Per Serving 189 calories, 0g fat, 42g carbohydrate, 0g salt • Gluten Free • Dairy Free • Easy

2–3 tbsp elderflower cordial
200g (7oz) caster sugar
4 gelatine leaves (see Cook's Tips)
150g (5oz) raspberries
150g (5oz) seedless grapes, halved

1 Put the elderflower cordial into a large pan and add 750ml (1¼ pints) water and the sugar. Heat gently, stirring to dissolve the sugar.

2 Put the gelatine leaves in a bowl. Cover with cold water and leave to soak for 5 minutes. Lift out the gelatine, squeeze out the excess water, then add to the liquid in the pan. Stir to dissolve, then strain into a jug.

3 Divide the raspberries and grapes among six 200ml (7fl oz) glass dishes. Pour the liquid over the fruit, then cool and chill for at least 4 hours or overnight.

★ COOK'S TIPS
● *Gelatine is available in leaf and powdered forms. Both must be soaked in liquid to soften before being dissolved in a warm liquid. Always add dissolved gelatine to a mixture that is warm or at room temperature – if added to a cold liquid, it will set in fine threads and spoil the final texture of the dish.*
● *Gelatine is derived from meat bones, but there are also several vegetarian alternatives, such as agar agar and gelazone.*

Strawberry Fizz Jellies

Preparation Time 10 minutes, plus chilling • Cooking Time 1–2 minutes • Serves 10 •
Per Serving without cream 140 calories, 0g fat, 23g carbohydrate, 0.1g salt • Gluten Free • Easy

10 sheets leaf gelatine (see Cook's
   Tips, opposite)
700g (1½lb) strawberries, hulled
150g (5oz) caster sugar
600ml (1 pint) sparkling white wine
strawberry slices or double cream
   to decorate

1 Put the gelatine in a bowl. Cover
with cold water and leave to soak
for 5 minutes.

2 Put the strawberries and sugar
into a food processor and whiz until
smooth. Push through a fine sieve
set over a pan, discarding the pips.

3 Lift out the softened gelatine and
squeeze out excess water, then add
to the strawberry mixture. Put the
pan over a low heat and cook for
1–2 minutes, whisking constantly,
until the gelatine dissolves.

4 Empty the mixture into a large jug
and stir in the wine. Divide among
ten champagne flutes and chill for
at least 4 hours or overnight.

5 Top each with strawberry slices or
a little cream just before serving.

Clementine and Cranberry Jellies

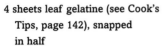

Preparation Time 30 minutes, plus soaking and chilling • Cooking Time 5 minutes, plus cooling • Serves 6 •
Per Serving 152 calories, 5g fat (of which 3g saturates), 21g carbohydrate, 0g salt • Gluten Free • A Little Effort

4 sheets leaf gelatine (see Cook's
    Tips, page 142), snapped
    in half
600ml (1 pint) cranberry juice
2 tbsp golden caster sugar
    (optional)
8 clementines or mandarins, about
    700g (1½lb)
150ml (¼ pint) single cream
    (optional)

1 Put the gelatine into a bowl and
cover with cold water. Leave to soak
for a few minutes until the gelatine
softens. Meanwhile, pour 150ml
(¼ pint) cranberry juice into a pan
and add the sugar, if using. Gently
bring to the boil, then remove from
the heat.

2 Lift the softened gelatine out of
the water and add to the heated
cranberry juice. Stir until dissolved.
Tip into a large jug and add the
remaining cranberry juice. Leave to
cool, stirring from time to time so it
doesn't set.

3 Pour some of the jelly into six
150ml (¼ pint) tall glasses, to come
2.5cm (1in) up the sides of each
glass. Chill for 1 hour until set. Leave
the remaining jelly out of the fridge.

4 Meanwhile, peel the clementines
or mandarins, break the fruit into
segments and remove as much of
the white pith as possible.

5 Divide a third of the fruit among
the glasses, packing the segments in
tightly. Carefully pour over another
layer of jelly so it just covers the fruit
in each glass. Chill for 30 minutes
until set. Repeat the layering and
chilling process, finishing with a thin
jelly layer.

6 Remove the set jellies from the
fridge 15 minutes before serving
and flood the surfaces with a thin
layer of single cream, if you like.

★ GET AHEAD
To prepare ahead *Complete the recipe*
to the end of step 5 up to two days
ahead. Cover and chill.
To use *Complete the recipe.*

Chocolate ★

Chocolate Mousse

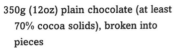

Preparation Time 20 minutes, plus chilling • **Serves 8** • **Per Serving** 309 calories, 17g fat (of which 9g saturates), 28g carbohydrate, 0.1g salt • **Gluten Free** • **Easy**

350g (12oz) plain chocolate (at least 70% cocoa solids), broken into pieces
6 tbsp rum, brandy or cold black coffee
6 large eggs, separated
a pinch of salt
chocolate curls, to decorate (see page 273)

1 Put the chocolate with the rum, brandy or black coffee into a heatproof bowl set over a pan of gently simmering water, making sure the base of the bowl doesn't touch the water. Leave to melt, stirring occasionally. Take the bowl off the pan and leave to cool slightly for 3–4 minutes, stirring frequently.

2 Beat the egg yolks with 2 tbsp water, then beat into the chocolate mixture until evenly blended.

3 Put the egg whites and salt into a clean, grease-free bowl and whisk until firm peaks form, then fold into the chocolate mixture.

4 Pour the mixture into a 1.4–1.7 litre (2½–3 pint) soufflé dish or divide among eight 150ml (¼ pint) cups or ramekins. Chill for at least 4 hours, or overnight, until set. Decorate with chocolate curls.

White Chocolate Mousse

Preparation Time 15 minutes, plus chilling • Cooking Time 15 minutes, plus cooling • Serves 6 • Per Serving 515 calories, 41g fat (of which 25g saturates), 31g carbohydrate, 0.2g salt • Gluten Free • Easy

100ml (3½fl oz) full-fat milk
1 cinnamon stick
250g (9oz) white chocolate, broken into pieces
300ml (½ pint) double cream
3 large egg whites
50g (2oz) plain chocolate
a little cocoa powder and ground cinnamon to decorate

1 Put the milk and cinnamon stick into a small pan and warm over a medium heat until the milk is almost boiling. Remove the pan from the heat and put to one side.

2 Melt the white chocolate in a heatproof bowl over a pan of gently simmering water, making sure the base of the bowl doesn't touch the water. Take the bowl off the pan and leave to cool a little.

3 Strain the warm milk on to the melted chocolate and stir together until completely smooth. Leave to cool for 10 minutes.

4 Whip the cream until it just begins to hold its shape. Whisk the egg whites in a clean, grease-free bowl until soft peaks form. Fold the whipped cream into the chocolate mixture with a large metal spoon, then carefully fold in the egg whites. Spoon the mixture into six 150ml (¼ pint) bowls or glasses and chill for 4 hours or overnight.

5 Make curls using plain chocolate (see page 273). Sprinkle over the mousse. Dust with cocoa and a pinch of cinnamon and serve.

★ GET AHEAD
To prepare ahead Complete the recipe to the end of step 4 up to one day ahead. Cover and chill until needed.
To use Complete the recipe.

Rich Chocolate Pots

Preparation Time 10 minutes, plus chilling • Cooking Time 10 minutes • Serves 6 • Per Serving 895 calories, 66g fat (of which 41g saturates), 66g carbohydrate, 0g salt • Gluten Free • Easy

300g (11oz) plain chocolate (at least 70% cocoa solids), broken into chunks
300ml (½ pint) double cream
250g (9oz) mascarpone cheese
3 tbsp cognac
1 tbsp vanilla extract
6 tbsp crème fraîche
chocolate curls to decorate (see page 273)

1 Melt the plain chocolate in a heatproof bowl over a pan of gently simmering water, making sure the base of the bowl doesn't touch the water. Remove from the heat and add the cream, mascarpone, cognac and vanilla extract. Mix well – the hot chocolate will melt into the cream and mascarpone.

2 Divide the mixture among six 150ml (¼ pint) glasses and chill for 20 minutes.

3 To serve, spoon some crème fraîche on top of each chocolate pot and decorate with the chocolate curls.

★ GET AHEAD
To prepare ahead *Make the chocolate curls and keep in a sealed container in the fridge for up to one day.*

Baked Chocolate and Coffee Custards

Preparation Time 15 minutes, plus chilling • Cooking Time 20–25 minutes, plus cooling • Serves 6 •
Per Serving 448 calories, 37g fat (of which 20g saturates), 28g carbohydrate, 0.3g salt • **Easy**

300ml (½ pint) semi-skimmed milk
140ml (4½fl oz) double cream
200g (7oz) plain chocolate (at least
    70% cocoa solids), broken into
    pieces
4 large egg yolks
1 tbsp golden caster sugar
3 tbsp very strong, cold black
    coffee
grated orange zest to decorate
    (optional)
thin shortbread biscuits to serve

FOR THE TOPPING
125g (4oz) mascarpone cheese
1 tsp icing sugar
grated zest and juice of ½ orange

1 Preheat the oven to 170°C (150°C
fan oven) mark 3. Put the milk,
cream and chocolate into a pan over
a very low heat until melted. Stir
until smooth.

2 Mix the egg yolks, sugar and
coffee together in a bowl, then pour
the warm chocolate milk on to
them. Briefly mix, then strain
through a sieve into a jug. Pour into
six 150ml (¼ pint) ramekins, then
stand them in a large roasting tin
containing enough hot water to
come halfway up their sides. Bake
for 20–25 minutes until just set and
still a little wobbly in the middle –
they will firm as they cool. Lift the
dishes out of the roasting tin and
leave to cool, then stand them on a
small tray and chill in the fridge for
at least 3 hours.

3 To make the topping, beat the
mascarpone, icing sugar, orange
zest and juice together until
smooth. Cover and chill for 1–2
hours. To serve, put a spoonful of
the mascarpone mixture on top of
each custard and decorate with
grated orange zest, if you like. Serve
with thin shortbread biscuits.

★ GET AHEAD
To prepare ahead *Bake the custards*
and leave to cool. Make the topping and
cover the bowl. Cover the ramekins with
clingfilm and chill, with the topping, for
up to 24 hours.
To use *Complete the recipe.*

Cheat's Chocolate Pots

Preparation Time 5 minutes, plus chilling • Cooking Time 5 minutes • Serves 4 • Per Serving 380 calories, 17g fat (of which 0g saturates), 53g carbohydrate, 0.0g salt • Easy

500g carton fresh custard
200g (7oz) plain chocolate (at least 50% cocoa solids), broken into pieces

1 Pour the custard into a small pan and add the chocolate pieces. Heat gently, stirring all the time, until the chocolate has melted.

2 Pour the mixture into four small coffee cups and chill in the fridge for 30 minutes–1 hour before serving.

★ TRY SOMETHING DIFFERENT
Serve the mixture warm as a sauce for Vanilla Ice Cream (see page 270).

Chocolate and Banana Crêpes

★

Preparation Time 15 minutes, plus chilling • Cooking Time 30–40 minutes • Serves 4 • Per Serving 656 calories, 30g fat (of which 12g saturates), 75g carbohydrate, 0.3g salt • **Easy**

150g (5oz) plain chocolate (at least 70% cocoa solids), chopped or grated
100g (3½oz) plain flour
1 large egg
a pinch of salt
300ml (½ pint) semi-skimmed milk
25g (1oz) butter
1 tbsp light muscovado sugar
4 bananas, thickly sliced
125ml (4fl oz) brandy
sunflower oil to fry
icing sugar to dust

1 Put half the chocolate to one side and put the remainder into a food processor or blender with the flour, egg, salt and milk. Whiz until smooth. Pour the batter into a jug, cover and chill for 30 minutes.

2 Melt the butter and sugar in a frying pan. Add the sliced bananas and stir-fry over a medium heat for 3 minutes. Carefully add the brandy and simmer for 2 minutes or until the bananas soften and the liquid is syrupy. Put to one side.

3 Brush an 18cm (7in) non-stick crêpe pan or small frying pan with oil and heat up. Stir the batter, then pour about 4 tbsp into the pan to thinly coat the base. Cook for 2 minutes or until golden brown. Cook the other side for 1 minute. Transfer to a plate and keep warm. Repeat with the remaining batter.

4 Put two spoonfuls of banana filling on one half of each crêpe and scatter the reserved chocolate on top. Fold in half, then in half again; keep warm while filling the remaining crêpes. Dust with icing sugar and serve.

Profiteroles

Preparation Time 25 minutes, plus chilling • **Cooking Time** 30 minutes, plus cooling • **Serves 6** • **Per Serving** 652 calories, 59g fat (of which 33g saturates), 35g carbohydrate, 0.3g salt • **A Little Effort**

65g (2½oz) plain flour
a pinch of salt
50g (2oz) butter, diced
2 large eggs, lightly beaten
300ml (½ pint) double cream
a few drops of vanilla extract
1 tsp caster sugar

FOR THE CHOCOLATE SAUCE
225g (8oz) plain chocolate (at least
    70% cocoa solids), broken into
    pieces
140ml (4½fl oz) double cream
1–2 tbsp Grand Marnier to taste
    (optional)
1–2 tsp golden caster sugar to taste
    (optional)

1 Preheat the oven to 220°C (200°C fan oven) mark 7. Sift the flour with the salt on to a sheet of greaseproof paper. Put the butter into a medium heavy-based pan with 150ml (¼ pint) water. Heat gently until the butter melts, then bring to a rapid boil. Remove from the heat and immediately tip in all the flour and beat thoroughly with a wooden spoon until the mixture is smooth and forms a ball. Turn into a bowl and leave to cool for 10 minutes.

2 Gradually add the eggs to the mixture, beating well after each addition. Ensure that the mixture becomes thick and shiny before adding any more egg – if it's added too quickly, the choux paste will become runny and the cooked buns will be flat.

3 Sprinkle a large baking sheet with a little water. Using two damp teaspoons, spoon about 18 small mounds of the choux paste on to the baking sheet, spacing well apart to allow room for them to expand. (Alternatively, spoon the choux paste into a piping bag fitted with a 1cm/½in plain nozzle and pipe mounds on to the baking sheet.)

4 Bake for about 25 minutes or until well risen, crisp and golden brown. Make a small hole in the side of each bun to allow the steam to escape and then put back in the oven for a further 5 minutes or until thoroughly dried out. Slide on to a large wire rack and leave to cool.

5 To make the sauce, put the chocolate and cream in a medium pan with 4 tbsp water. Heat gently, stirring occasionally, until the chocolate melts to a smooth sauce; do not boil. Remove from the heat.

6 To assemble, lightly whip the cream with the vanilla extract and sugar until it just holds its shape. Pipe into the hole in each choux bun, or split the buns open and spoon in the cream. Chill for up to 2 hours.

7 Just before serving, gently reheat the chocolate sauce. Add Grand Marnier and sugar to taste, if you like. Divide the choux buns among bowls and pour the warm chocolate sauce over them. Serve immediately.

★ FREEZING TIP
To freeze Complete the recipe to the end of step 4, then cool, wrap, seal, label and freeze.
To use Preheat the oven to 220°C (200°C fan oven) mark 7. Put the frozen buns on a baking sheet and bake in the oven for 5 minutes. Cool, then complete the recipe.

Chocolate Crêpes with a Boozy Sauce

Preparation Time 5 minutes, plus standing • Cooking Time 10–15 minutes • Serves 4 • Per Serving 594 calories, 35g fat (of which 17g saturates), 57g carbohydrate, 0.5g salt • **Easy**

100g (3½oz) plain flour, sifted

a pinch of salt

1 medium egg

300ml (½ pint) milk

sunflower oil to fry

50g (2oz) plain chocolate (at least 70% cocoa solids), roughly chopped

100g (3½oz) unsalted butter

100g (3½oz) light muscovado sugar, plus extra to sprinkle

4 tbsp brandy

1 Put the flour and salt into a bowl, make a well in the centre and add the egg. Use a balloon whisk to mix the egg with a little of the flour, then gradually add the milk to make a smooth batter. Cover and leave to stand for about 20 minutes.

2 Pour the batter into a jug. Heat 1 tsp oil in a 23cm (9in) frying pan, then pour in 100ml (3½fl oz) batter, tilting the pan so that the mixture coats the base, and fry for 1–2 minutes until golden underneath. Turn carefully and fry the other side. Tip on to a plate, cover with greaseproof paper and repeat with the remaining batter, using more oil as needed.

3 Divide the chocolate among the crêpes. Fold each crêpe in half, then in half again.

4 Put the butter and sugar into a heavy-based frying pan over a low heat. Add the brandy and stir. Slide the crêpes into the pan and cook for 3–4 minutes to melt the chocolate. Serve drizzled with sauce and sprinkled with sugar.

★ TRY SOMETHING DIFFERENT
Replace the brandy with Grand Marnier and use orange-flavoured plain chocolate.

White Chocolate and Berry Crêpes

Preparation Time 2 minutes • Cooking Time 10 minutes • Serves 4 • Per Serving 476 calories, 37g fat (of which 15g saturates), 37g carbohydrate, 0.2g salt • Easy

500g bag frozen mixed berries, thawed
100g (3½oz) white chocolate, broken into pieces
142ml carton double cream
4 thin ready-made crêpes

1 Put the thawed berries into a large pan and cook over a medium heat for 5 minutes or until heated through.

2 Meanwhile, put the chocolate and cream into a heatproof bowl set over a pan of simmering water, making sure the base of the bowl doesn't touch the hot water. Heat gently, stirring, for 5 minutes or until the chocolate has just melted. Remove the bowl from the pan and mix the chocolate and cream to a smooth sauce. Alternatively, microwave the chocolate and the cream together on full power for 2–2½ minutes (based on a 900W oven), then stir until smooth.

3 Meanwhile, heat the crêpes according to the pack instructions.

4 To serve, put each crêpe on a warmed plate and fold in half. Spoon a quarter of the berries into the middle of each, then fold the crêpe over the filling and pour the hot chocolate sauce over the top.

★ COOK'S TIPS
● *Instead of mixed berries, try using just one type of berry.*
● *See Making batters, page 275.*

Chocolate Cherry Roll

★

Preparation Time 30 minutes • Cooking Time 30 minutes, plus cooling • Serves 8 • Per Serving 185 calories, 5g fat (of which 2g saturates), 30g carbohydrate, 0.3g salt • Gluten Free • A Little Effort

4 tbsp cocoa powder, plus extra
   to dust
100ml (3½fl oz) milk, plus
   3 tbsp extra
5 medium eggs, separated
125g (4oz) golden caster sugar
1–2 tbsp cherry jam
400g can pitted cherries, drained
   and chopped
icing sugar to dust

1 Preheat the oven to 180°C (160°C fan oven) mark 4. Line a 30.5 × 20.5cm (12 × 8in) Swiss roll tin with baking parchment. Mix the cocoa and 3 tbsp milk together in a bowl. Heat the 100ml (3½ fl oz) milk in a pan until almost boiling, then add to the bowl, stirring. Leave to cool for 10 minutes.

2 Whisk the egg whites in a clean grease-free bowl until soft peaks form. In a separate bowl, whisk together the egg yolks and caster sugar until pale and thick. Gradually whisk in the cooled milk, then fold in the egg whites. Spoon the mixture into the prepared tin and smooth the surface. Bake in the oven for 25 minutes or until just firm.

3 Turn out on to a board lined with baking parchment and peel off the lining parchment. Cover with a damp teatowel.

4 Spread the jam over the sponge and top with the cherries. Roll up from the shortest end, dust with cocoa powder and icing sugar, then cut into slices and serve.

★ TRY SOMETHING DIFFERENT
You can add whipped cream to the roll, but you will need to cool it first. To do this, turn out the sponge on to baking parchment. Do not remove the lining paper but roll the sponge around it while still warm. Leave to cool, unroll and peel off the paper. Spread with the jam and fruit, then the cream, and re-roll.

Chocolate Meringue Roulade

Preparation Time 30 minutes • Cooking Time 1 hour, plus cooling • Serves 6 • Per Serving 279 calories, 10g fat (of which 1g saturates), 47g carbohydrate, 0.1g salt • Easy

5 large egg whites
175g (6oz) golden caster sugar
1 tsp cornflour
125g (4oz) chocolate spread
4 tbsp half-fat crème fraîche
50g (2oz) cooked vacuum-packed
    chestnuts, roughly chopped
    (optional)
icing sugar and cocoa powder
    to dust
whipped cream or crème fraîche to
    serve (optional)

1 Preheat the oven to 110°C (90°C fan oven) mark ¼. Line a 30.5 × 21cm (12 × 8½in) Swiss roll tin with baking parchment.

2 Whisk the eggs whites in a large heatproof bowl until frothy, then whisk in the caster sugar. Stand the bowl over a pan of gently simmering water and whisk for 4–5 minutes at high speed until very thick and shiny. Remove the pan from the heat and whisk in the cornflour. Spoon into the tin and smooth the surface.

3 Bake for 1 hour or until just firm on top. Leave to cool for 1 hour; don't worry if the meringue weeps.

4 Put the chocolate spread into a bowl and beat in the crème fraîche. Fold in the chestnuts, if using.

5 Turn the meringue out on to a sheet of baking parchment dusted with icing sugar and carefully peel off the lining parchment. Make a shallow cut in the meringue, 2.5cm (1in) in from the edge of a short end. Spread the chocolate mixture over the meringue and roll it up, from the cut end. Dust with icing sugar and cocoa powder and serve with whipped cream or crème fraîche, if you like.

Chocolate Mousse Roulade

Preparation Time 45 minutes, plus chilling • Cooking Time 40 minutes, plus cooling • Cuts into 8 slices •
Per Slice 510 calories, 30g fat (of which 16g saturates), 53g carbohydrate, 0.4g salt • Gluten Free • For the Confident Cook

6 large eggs, separated
150g (5oz) caster sugar, plus extra
    to sprinkle
50g (2oz) cocoa powder
frosted fruit and leaves to decorate

FOR THE FILLING
225g (8oz) milk chocolate, roughly
    chopped
2 large eggs, separated
125g (4oz) fresh or frozen
    cranberries, halved
50g (2oz) granulated sugar
grated zest and juice of ½ medium
    orange
200ml (7fl oz) double cream

1 Preheat the oven to 180°C (160°C fan oven) mark 4. Line a 30.5 × 20.5cm (12 × 8in) Swiss roll tin with baking parchment – it needs to stick up around the edges of the tin by 5cm (2in) to allow the cake to rise.

2 First, make the filling. Put the chocolate into a large heatproof bowl and add 50ml (2fl oz) water. Place over a pan of gently simmering water, making sure the base of the bowl doesn't touch the water. Leave to melt for 15–20 minutes. Remove the bowl from the pan and, without stirring, add the egg yolks, then stir until smooth. Put the egg whites into a clean, grease-free bowl and whisk until soft peaks form, then fold into the chocolate. Cover and chill for at least 2 hours.

3 Put the cranberries into a pan with the sugar, orange zest and juice and 100ml (3½fl oz) water. Bring to a gentle simmer, then leave to barely simmer for 30 minutes, stirring occasionally until the cranberries are soft; there should be no liquid left in the pan. Remove from the heat and leave to cool.

4 To make the cake, put the egg yolks into a bowl and whisk with a hand-held electric whisk for 1–2 minutes until pale. Add the sugar and whisk until the mixture has the consistency of thick cream. Sift the cocoa powder over the mixture and fold in with a large metal spoon.

5 Put the egg whites into a clean, grease-free bowl and whisk until soft peaks form. Stir a spoonful of the egg whites into the chocolate mixture to loosen it, then fold in the remainder. Pour the mixture into the prepared tin.

6 Bake for about 25 minutes or until well risen and spongy. Leave to cool completely in the tin (it will sink dramatically).

7 Put a sheet of baking parchment on the worksurface and sprinkle with caster sugar. Turn the cold cake out on to the sugar and peel off the parchment. Spoon the chocolate filling on top and spread to within 2.5cm (1in) of the edge. Sprinkle on the glazed cranberries. Lightly whip the cream, spoon over the cranberries, then spread lightly to cover.

8 Holding a short edge of the baking parchment, gently lift and roll, pushing the edge down so it starts to curl. Keep lifting and rolling as the cake comes away from the paper. Don't worry if it cracks. Remove the paper. Chill for up to 8 hours. Decorate with frosted fruit and leaves to serve.

White Chocolate Mousse Cake

Preparation Time 30 minutes, plus freezing and thawing • Cooking Time 20–30 minutes • Cuts into 10 slices •
Per Slice 416 calories, 32g fat (of which 19g saturates), 27g carbohydrate, 0.2g salt • Easy

oil to oil
450g (1lb) white chocolate
285ml (9½fl oz) double cream
finely grated zest of 1 large orange
2 tsp orange liqueur, such as Grand
   Marnier
300g (11oz) Greek yogurt

1 Lightly oil a shallow 20.5cm (8in) round cake tin and line with baking parchment.

2 Break the chocolate into pieces, put into a large heatproof bowl with half the cream and melt over a pan of gently simmering water, making sure the base of the bowl doesn't touch the water. Leave for 20–30 minutes until the chocolate has melted. Don't stir – just leave it to melt.

3 Meanwhile, put the orange zest and liqueur into a small bowl. Leave to soak. Whip the remaining cream until it just holds its shape.

4 Remove the bowl of melted chocolate from the pan and beat in the yogurt. Fold in the cream with the zest and liqueur mixture.

5 Spoon the mixture into the prepared tin, cover with clingfilm and freeze overnight. One hour before serving, transfer from the freezer to the fridge. Unwrap and put on a serving plate. Decorate, if you like (see Cook's Tip).

 COOK'S TIP
If you like, you can decorate the mousse cake with a few halved strawberries, some blueberries and a handful of unsprayed rose petals, then dust with icing sugar.

 FREEZING TIP
To freeze *Freeze as in step 5. It will keep, frozen, for up to one month.*
To use *Thaw as described in step 5.*

Chocolate Panettone Pudding

Preparation Time 30 minutes, plus soaking and resting • Cooking Time 1–1¼ hours • Serves 8 •
Per Serving 685 calories, 25g fat (of which 10g saturates), 97g carbohydrate, 0.9g salt • A Little Effort

125g (4oz) raisins
100ml (3½fl oz) brandy
75g (3oz) softened butter, plus extra
   to grease
700g (1½lb) panettone
2 × 500g cartons fresh custard, or
   750ml (1¼ pints) home-made
   (see page 269)
600ml (1 pint) semi-skimmed milk
200g (7oz) plain chocolate (at least
   70% cocoa solids), roughly
   chopped
icing sugar to dust

1 Put the raisins into a bowl, pour the brandy over them, cover and leave to soak overnight.

2 Preheat the oven to 180°C (160°C fan oven) mark 4. Grease a 3.4 litre (6 pint) ovenproof dish. Slice the panettone into slices about 5mm (¼in) thick. Spread with the butter and cut into quarters. Stir the custard and milk together and pour a thin layer over the base of the prepared dish. Arrange a layer of panettone on top and scatter some of the raisins and chocolate on top.

Pour on another thin layer of custard. Continue to layer up the panettone, raisins, chocolate and custard, finishing with a layer of custard. Leave to rest for 1 hour.

3 Stand the dish in a roasting tin and pour hot water around the dish to come halfway up the sides. Bake in the oven for 1–1¼ hours until the custard is set and the top has turned a deep brown, covering lightly with foil after 40 minutes to prevent over-browning. Dust the surface lightly with icing sugar to serve.

Chocolate and Prune Pudding

★

Preparation Time 10 minutes • Cooking Time 30–40 minutes • Serves 6 • Per Serving 195 calories, 8g fat
(of which 4g saturates), 24g carbohydrate, 0.3g salt • Gluten Free • Easy

600ml (1 pint) skimmed milk
50g (2oz) plain chocolate (at least
    70% cocoa solids), broken into
    tiny pieces, or chocolate chips
2 large eggs, plus 2 large egg yolks
40g (1½oz) light brown sugar
½ tsp cornflour
2 tbsp unsweetened cocoa powder,
    plus extra to dust
100g (3½oz) ready-to-eat prunes,
    chopped

1 Preheat the oven to 170°C (150°C fan oven) mark 3. Heat the milk in a pan to simmering point, then remove from the heat. Add the chocolate and stir until it has melted completely.

2 Whisk the eggs, egg yolks, sugar, cornflour and cocoa powder together in a heatproof bowl until smooth. Gradually pour in the hot chocolate milk, stirring until it is combined.

3 Put the prunes into the base of a serving dish or individual dishes, then strain in the milk mixture through a sieve. Put the dish(es) in a roasting tin and fill the tin with boiling water so it comes halfway up the sides of the dish(es). Bake for 30–40 minutes until just set.

4 Remove the dish(es) from the roasting tin and serve warm. Alternatively, leave to cool, then chill until ready to serve. Dust with cocoa before serving.

Chocolate Crumb Pudding

Preparation Time 20 minutes • **Cooking Time** 1¼–1½ hours • **Serves** 4 • **Per Serving** 776 calories, 49g fat (of which 29g saturates), 84g carbohydrate, 1.4g salt • **A Little Effort**

75g (3oz) butter, plus extra
   to grease
75g (3oz) golden caster sugar
50g (2oz) plain chocolate (at least
   70% cocoa solids), broken into
   pieces, melted (see page 273) and
   cooled for 5 minutes
1 medium egg, separated
½–1 tsp vanilla extract
125g (4oz) breadcrumbs
50g (2oz) self-raising flour, sifted
4–5 tbsp semi-skimmed milk

**FOR THE CHOCOLATE
FUDGE SAUCE**
50g (2oz) unsalted butter
50g (2oz) light muscovado sugar
50g (2oz) plain chocolate (at least
   70% cocoa solids), broken into
   pieces
100ml (3½fl oz) double cream

1 Half-fill a steamer or large pan with water and put it on to boil. Grease a 900ml (1½ pint) pudding basin. Cream the butter with the sugar in a bowl until pale and fluffy. Beat in the chocolate, egg yolk and vanilla extract. Combine the breadcrumbs and flour. Fold half into the mixture with 2 tbsp milk, then fold in the rest with enough milk to give a soft dropping consistency. Put the egg white into a clean, grease-free bowl and whisk until soft peaks form. Fold into the mixture, then spoon into the basin and cover (see Cook's Tip). Lower into the pan, cover tightly and steam for 1¼–1½ hours, topping up with boiling water as necessary.

2 To make the sauce, put the butter, sugar and chocolate into a small heavy-based pan and heat gently until the chocolate is melted. Pour in the cream, slowly bring to the boil and let it bubble for 3 minutes or until the sauce is glossy and thickened. Leave the sauce to cool slightly. Lift the basin out of the pan and remove the foil or greaseproof paper. Turn out the pudding on to a warmed plate. Serve with the hot chocolate fudge sauce.

★ **COOK'S TIP**
Lay a greased and pleated sheet of foil or a double thickness of greaseproof paper over the top of the bowl and secure under the rim with string.

Chocolate Steamed Sponge Pudding

Preparation Time 20 minutes • Cooking Time 1½ hours • Serves 4 • Per Serving 584 calories, 32g fat (of which 20g saturates), 68g carbohydrate, 1.4g salt • **Easy**

125g (4oz) butter, plus extra
   to grease
4 tbsp cocoa powder
125g (4oz) golden caster sugar
a few drops of vanilla extract
2 large eggs, beaten
175g (6oz) self-raising flour, sifted
2–4 tbsp semi-skimmed milk
custard to serve

1 Half-fill a steamer or large pan with water and put on to boil. Grease a 900ml (1½ pint) pudding basin. Blend the cocoa powder with 2 tbsp hot water to a smooth cream. Leave to cool. Cream the butter and sugar together in a bowl until pale and fluffy. Stir in the vanilla extract, then the cooled blended cocoa.

2 Add the eggs, a little at a time, beating well after each addition. Using a metal spoon, fold in half the flour, then fold in the remainder, with enough milk to give a soft, dropping consistency.

3 Spoon the mixture into the prepared basin and cover (see Cook's Tip, page 165). Lower into the pan, cover tightly and steam for 1½ hours, topping up with boiling water as necessary.

4 Lift out the basin and remove the foil or greaseproof paper. Turn out the pudding on to a warmed plate and serve with custard.

Quick Gooey Chocolate Puddings

Preparation Time 15 minutes • Cooking Time 12–15 minutes • Serves 4 • Per Serving 468 calories, 31g fat
(of which 19g saturates), 46g carbohydrate, 0.6g salt • **Easy**

100g (3½oz) unsalted butter, plus
   extra to grease
100g (3½oz) golden caster sugar,
   plus extra to dust
100g (3½oz) plain chocolate (at
   least 70% cocoa solids), broken
   into pieces
2 large eggs
20g (¾oz) plain flour
icing sugar to dust

1 Preheat the oven to 200°C
(180°C fan oven) mark 6. Grease
four 200ml (7fl oz) ramekins and
dust with caster sugar. Melt the
chocolate and butter in a heatproof
bowl over a pan of gently simmering
water, making sure the base of the
bowl doesn't touch the water. Take
the bowl off the pan and leave to
cool for 5 minutes.

2 Whisk the eggs, caster sugar and
flour together in a bowl until
smooth. Fold in the chocolate
mixture and pour into the ramekins.

3 Stand the dishes on a baking tray
and bake for 12–15 minutes until
the puddings are puffed and set on
the outside, but still runny inside.

4 Turn out, dust with icing sugar
and serve immediately.

Chocolate Puddings with White Chocolate Custard

★

Preparation Time 20 minutes • **Cooking Time** 20–25 minutes, plus cooling • **Serves 6** • **Per Serving** 347 calories, 20g fat (of which 10g saturates), 37g carbohydrate, 0.6g salt • **Easy**

- 125g (4oz) half-fat butter, plus extra to grease
- 75g (3oz) light muscovado sugar
- 75g (3oz) self-raising flour
- ½ tsp baking powder
- 2 tbsp cocoa powder, plus extra to dust
- 25g (1oz) hazelnuts, lightly toasted, skinned and roughly chopped
- 25g (1oz) plain chocolate (at least 70% cocoa solids), roughly chopped
- 2 large eggs, beaten
- White Chocolate Custard (see Cook's Tip) to serve

1 Preheat the oven to 180°C (160°C fan oven) mark 4. Grease six 150ml (¼ pint) ramekins and line the bases with non-stick baking parchment.

2 Put the butter and sugar into a pan and heat gently until combined. Leave to cool.

3 Sift the flour, baking powder and cocoa into a bowl. Stir in the nuts and chocolate. Make a well in the centre, pour in the butter mixture and eggs and beat well. Pour the mixture into the prepared ramekins and bake for 20–25 minutes until just firm to the touch. Leave to cool slightly and turn out; keep warm.

4 Trim the top from each pudding and place upside down on six plates. Dust with cocoa powder, pour the White Chocolate Custard around and serve immediately.

★ COOK'S TIP

White Chocolate Custard
Put 4 tbsp custard powder and 4 tsp sugar into a bowl; add enough of 450ml (¾ pint) skimmed milk to make a smooth paste. Heat the remaining milk until almost boiling, pour into the custard powder, then put back into the pan. Add 40g (1½oz) white chocolate drops and stir until the chocolate has melted and the custard thickened.

Warm Chocolate Fondants

Preparation Time 25 minutes • Cooking Time 10–12 minutes • Serves 6 • Per Serving 502 calories, 37g fat (of which 21g saturates), 39g carbohydrate, 0.5g salt • **Easy**

150g (5oz) unsalted butter, plus extra to grease
3 medium eggs, plus 3 medium egg yolks
50g (2oz) golden caster sugar
175g (6oz) plain chocolate (at least 70% cocoa solids), broken into pieces
50g (2oz) plain flour, sifted
6 chocolate truffles

1 Preheat the oven to 200°C (180°C fan oven) mark 6. Lightly grease six 200ml (7fl oz) ramekins. Put the whole eggs, egg yolks and sugar into a large bowl and beat with a hand-held electric whisk for 8–10 minutes until pale and fluffy.

2 Meanwhile, melt the chocolate and butter in a heatproof bowl set over a pan of gently simmering water, making sure the base of the bowl doesn't touch the water, stirring occasionally.

3 Stir a spoonful of the melted chocolate into the egg mixture, then gently fold the remaining chocolate mixture into the egg mixture. Fold in the flour.

4 Put a large spoonful of mixture into each ramekin. Put a chocolate truffle in the centre of each, taking care not to push it down. Divide the remainder of the mixture among the ramekins to cover the truffle; they should be about three-quarters full. Bake for 10–12 minutes until the top is firm and starting to rise and crack. Serve warm.

Cold Chocolate Soufflé

⭐

Preparation Time 20 minutes, plus soaking, cooling and chilling • **Serves 4** • **Per Serving** 585 calories, 50g fat (of which 27g saturates), 34g carbohydrate, 0.2g salt • **Gluten Free** • **Easy**

3 large eggs, separated
75g (3oz) golden caster sugar
75g (3oz) plain chocolate (at least 70% cocoa solids), broken into pieces
1 tbsp powdered gelatine (see Cook's Tips, page 142)
1 tbsp brandy
300ml (½ pint) double cream
chocolate curls (see page 273), or coarsely grated chocolate

1 Prepare a 600ml (1 pint) soufflé dish, 12.5cm (5in) in diameter (see Cook's Tips). Whisk the egg yolks and sugar together in a heatproof bowl set over a pan of hot water, until thick and creamy. Remove from the heat and whisk from time to time until cool. Melt the chocolate in a heatproof bowl over a pan of gently simmering water, making sure the base of the bowl doesn't touch the water. Cool slightly.

2 Put 2 tbsp water into a small heatproof bowl, sprinkle on the gelatine and leave to soak for 10 minutes. Stand this bowl over a pan of simmering water until the gelatine has dissolved. Cool slightly, then pour it into the egg mixture in a steady stream, stirring. Stir the melted chocolate and the brandy into the egg mixture. Leave to cool until it is almost at the point of setting.

3 Lightly whip half the cream and fold it into the chocolate mixture. Whisk the egg whites in a clean, grease-free bowl until stiff but not dry. Lightly fold them into the mixture. Pour into the prepared soufflé dish and chill in the fridge for 2–3 hours until set. To decorate, see Cook's Tips.

⭐ COOK'S TIPS

● *To line the soufflé dish, cut a double strip of greaseproof paper long enough to go around the soufflé dish with the ends overlapping slightly, and deep enough to reach from the base of the dish to about 7cm (2¾in) above the rim. Wrap the paper around the dish and secure under the rim with string or an elastic band, so that it fits closely to the top of the dish.*

● *Once the soufflé has set, remove the string or elastic band and ease the paper away with a knife dipped in hot water. Whip the remaining cream until thick and pipe it around the top edge of the soufflé. Top with chocolate curls or grated chocolate and serve.*

Chocolate Bread Pudding

Preparation Time 20 minutes, plus chilling • **Cooking Time** 50 minutes–1¼ hours • **Serves 6** • **Per Serving** 390 calories, 17g fat (of which 6g saturates), 51g carbohydrate, 0.7g salt • **Easy**

200g (7oz) baguette

100g (3½oz) milk chocolate, roughly chopped, plus 50g (2oz) plain or milk chocolate, in chunks

500g carton fresh custard

150ml (¼ pint) milk

1 large egg, beaten

butter to grease

1 tbsp demerara sugar

50g (2oz) walnuts, finely chopped

single cream to serve (optional)

1 Roughly chop the baguette and put it into a large bowl. Put the chopped milk chocolate into a pan with the custard and milk over a low heat. Stir gently until the chocolate has melted. Beat in the egg.

2 Pour the chocolate mixture over the bread, stir well to coat, then cover and chill for at least 4 hours.

3 Preheat the oven to 180°C (160°C fan oven) mark 4. Spoon the bread into a greased 1.4 litre (2½ pint), 7.5cm (3in) deep ovenproof dish. Bake for 30–40 minutes.

4 Sprinkle the demerara sugar, walnuts and chocolate chunks over the bread and put back into the oven for 20–30 minutes until lightly set. Serve the pudding warm, with single cream, if you like.

★ TRY SOMETHING DIFFERENT

Instead of baguette, use croissants or brioche for a richer pudding.

Double Chocolate Baked Alaskas

Preparation Time 20 minutes, plus freezing • Cooking Time 5 minutes • Serves 6 • Per Serving 630 calories, 30g fat (of which 0g saturates), 84g carbohydrate, 0g salt • A Little Effort

50g (2oz) hot melted butter, plus extra to grease
200g (7oz) plain chocolate digestive biscuits
600ml (1 pint) chocolate ice cream
2 chocolate flake bars, roughly chopped
4 large egg whites
225g (8oz) golden caster sugar
50g (2oz) desiccated coconut
cocoa powder, to dust
toasted coconut shavings (optional)

1 Lightly grease a baking sheet. Crush the biscuits to a fine powder in a food processor. (Alternatively, put them in a plastic bag and crush with a rolling pin, then transfer to a bowl.) Stir in the hot, melted butter. Using a 6.5cm (2½in) pastry cutter as a template, press the mixture into six rounds on the baking sheet and freeze for 30 minutes.

2 Beat the ice cream to soften it slightly and pile it into mounds on the biscuit bases. Make a shallow hollow in the centre of each ice cream mound and fill with the chopped chocolate flakes. Put back in the freezer for at least 1 hour or until firm.

3 Put the egg whites and sugar into a large bowl set over a pan of barely simmering water. Using an electric whisk, beat for 10 minutes or until the mixture is thick and glossy. Fold in the desiccated coconut. Leave to cool for 5 minutes.

4 Cover the ice cream mounds completely with a thick layer of meringue. Put back in the freezer for at least 4 hours or overnight.

5 To serve, preheat the oven to 220°C (200°C fan oven) mark 7, then bake the puddings for about 5 minutes or until golden. Dust with cocoa powder, top with toasted coconut shavings, if you like, and serve immediately.

Dark Chocolate Soufflés

Preparation Time 20 minutes • **Cooking Time** 20 minutes • **Serves 6** • **Per Serving** 134 calories, 4g fat (of which 2g saturates), 22g carbohydrate, 0.1g salt • **Gluten Free** • **Easy**

- 50g (2oz) plain chocolate (at least 70% cocoa solids), broken into pieces
- 2 tbsp cornflour
- 1 tbsp cocoa powder
- 1 tsp instant coffee granules
- 4 tbsp golden caster sugar
- 150ml (¼ pint) skimmed milk
- 2 medium eggs, separated, plus 1 medium egg white

1 Preheat the oven to 190°C (170°C fan oven) mark 5 and put a baking sheet inside to heat up. Put the chocolate in a pan with the cornflour, cocoa powder, coffee, 1 tbsp sugar and the milk. Warm gently to melt the chocolate. Increase the heat and stir until the mixture thickens. Cool slightly, then stir in the egg yolks. Cover with damp greaseproof paper.

2 Put the egg whites into a clean, grease-free bowl and whisk until soft peaks form. Gradually whisk in the remaining sugar until the mixture is stiff.

3 Stir one-third of the egg whites into the chocolate mixture. Fold in the remaining whites and divide among six 150ml (¼ pint) ramekins. Put the ramekins on a baking sheet and bake for 12 minutes or until well risen. Serve immediately.

★ TRY SOMETHING DIFFERENT

For an unusual twist, use flavoured plain chocolate such as ginger, mint or even chilli.

Mocha Soufflés

Preparation Time 15 minutes • Cooking Time 12 minutes, plus cooling • Serves 6 • Per Serving 132 calories, 5g fat (of which 2g saturates), 20g carbohydrate, 0.2g salt • Easy

50g (2oz) plain chocolate (at least 70% cocoa solids), roughly chopped
1 tbsp cornflour
1 tbsp cocoa powder
1–1½ tsp instant coffee granules
4 tbsp golden caster sugar
150ml (¼ pint) skimmed milk
2 medium egg yolks
3 medium egg whites
icing sugar or cocoa powder to dust

1 Preheat the oven to 190°C (170°C fan oven) mark 5 and put a baking sheet inside to heat up.

2 Put the chocolate into a non-stick pan with the cornflour, cocoa powder, coffee granules, 1 tbsp caster sugar and the milk. Warm gently, stirring over a low heat, until the chocolate has melted. Increase the heat and cook, stirring continuously, until the mixture just thickens. Leave to cool a little, then stir in the egg yolks. Cover the surface with a piece of damp greaseproof paper and leave to cool.

3 Put the egg whites into a clean, grease-free bowl and whisk until soft peaks form. Gradually whisk in the remaining caster sugar, a spoonful at a time, until the meringue is stiff but not dry.

4 Stir one-third of the meringue into the cooled chocolate mixture to lighten it, then gently fold in the remainder, using a large metal spoon. Divide the mixture among six 150ml (¼ pint) ramekins or ovenproof tea or coffee cups. Stand them on the hot baking sheet and bake for about 12 minutes or until puffed up.

5 Dust the soufflés with a little icing sugar or cocoa powder and serve immediately.

Rich Chocolate Terrine with Vanilla Sauce

Preparation Time 45 minutes, plus chilling • Cooking Time 1¾ hours, plus cooling • Serves 12 • Per Serving
356 calories, 25g fat (of which 13g saturates), 34g carbohydrate, 0.2g salt • Gluten Free • A Little Effort

oil to oil
350g (12oz) plain chocolate (at least
　70% cocoa solids), broken into
　pieces
40g (1½oz) cocoa powder, plus
　extra to dust
6 large eggs, beaten
125g (4oz) light muscovado sugar
300ml (½ pint) double cream
5 tbsp brandy (optional)
1 quantity Vanilla Sauce to serve
　(see Cook's Tip)

1 Preheat the oven to 150°C (130°C fan oven) mark 2. Oil and baseline a 900g (2lb) loaf tin. Melt the chocolate and cocoa powder in a heatproof bowl set over a pan of simmering water, making sure the base of the bowl doesn't touch the water, stirring from time to time. Leave to cool slightly.

2 Whisk the eggs with the sugar until smooth and creamy. In another bowl, whip the cream until soft peaks form. Gradually fold the melted chocolate and cream into the egg mixture, then add the brandy, if you like. Pour into the prepared tin and tap to level the mixture. Stand the tin in a roasting tray. Fill the tray with hot water to come halfway up the side and cover with baking parchment. Bake for 1¾ hours or until the terrine is just set in the centre – it will firm up as it cools. Leave the tin in the tray of water for 30 minutes, then lift out, cool and chill overnight.

3 To serve, dip the loaf tin in a bowl of warm water for 10 seconds. Invert on to a board and shake to unmould. Using a warm, sharp knife, cut the terrine into slices. Dust with cocoa powder and serve with Vanilla Sauce.

★ COOK'S TIP
Vanilla Sauce
Put 600ml (1 pint) double cream into a heavy-based pan. Scrape the seeds from a vanilla pod into the cream. Heat gently just to the boil, then leave to cool and infuse for about 15 minutes. Whisk 4 large egg yolks with 75g (3oz) golden caster sugar and ½ tsp cornflour in a bowl, add a little of the cooled cream and whisk until smooth. Add the remaining cream and stir well. Pour the sauce back into the rinsed-out pan and stir over a medium heat for 5 minutes or until thickened enough to lightly coat the back of the spoon. Strain, cool, cover and chill.

Chocolate and Chestnut Roulade

Preparation Time 20 minutes • Cooking Time 20–25 minutes, plus cooling • Cuts into 10 slices • Per Slice 409 calories, 28g fat (of which 17g saturates), 36g carbohydrate, 0.3g salt • Gluten Free • Easy

a little vegetable oil to oil
6 medium eggs, separated
200g (7oz) caster sugar, plus extra to dust
2–3 drops of vanilla extract
50g (2oz) cocoa powder, sifted

FOR THE FILLING
125g (4oz) plain chocolate (at least 50% cocoa solids), broken into pieces
300ml (½ pint) double cream
225g (8oz) unsweetened chestnut purée
200ml (7fl oz) full-fat crème fraîche
50g (2oz) icing sugar

1 Preheat the oven to 180°C (160°C fan oven) mark 4. Lightly oil a 33 × 20.5cm (13 × 8in) Swiss roll tin, then line with greaseproof paper.

2 Put the egg yolks, caster sugar and vanilla into a large bowl and whisk until pale and thick. Using a large metal spoon, fold in the cocoa powder. Put the egg whites into a clean, grease-free bowl and whisk until stiff peaks form. Fold into the cocoa mixture, then spoon the mixture into the prepared tin.

3 Bake for 20–25 minutes until just cooked – the top should be springy to the touch. Leave to cool in the tin for 10–15 minutes. Dust a sheet of baking parchment with caster sugar. Carefully turn out the roulade on to the parchment, then leave to cool. Peel away the lining paper.

4 Meanwhile, make the filling. Put the chocolate into a heatproof bowl set over a pan of gently simmering water, making sure the base of the bowl doesn't touch the water. Leave to melt. In a separate bowl, lightly whip the cream. Beat the chestnut

purée into the chocolate until smooth – the mixture will be quite thick. Whisk in the crème fraîche and icing sugar. Beat 1 tbsp of the whipped cream into the chocolate mixture, then use a metal spoon to fold in half the remaining cream.

5 Spread the filling over the roulade, then spread the remaining cream on top. Roll the roulade up from one of the narrow ends, using the baking parchment to help. Lift on to a serving plate and dust with caster sugar. Serve immediately.

Chocolate and Cherry Gâteau

Preparation Time 1 hour, plus soaking and chilling • Cooking Time 45 minutes, plus cooling • Serves 12 •
Per Serving 537 calories, 41g fat (of which 23g saturates), 38g carbohydrate, 0.2g salt • Easy

350g (12oz) fresh cherries, pitted,
    or 400g can pitted cherries,
    drained, plus extra fresh cherries
    to serve
3 tbsp dark rum
50g (2oz) almonds, toasted
50g (2oz) plain flour, sifted
125g (4oz) butter, softened, plus
    extra to grease
350g (12oz) plain chocolate (at least
    70% cocoa solids), roughly
    chopped
3 large eggs, separated
125g (4oz) caster sugar
450ml (¾ pint) double cream
chocolate curls (see page 273) and
    cocoa powder to decorate
single cream to serve (optional)

1 Put the cherries into a bowl with
2 tbsp rum. Cover and leave to soak
for at least 6 hours.

2 Whiz the almonds and flour in a
food processor until finely ground.
Preheat the oven to 180°C (160°C
fan oven) mark 4. Grease a 23cm
(9in) round deep cake tin and line
the base with greaseproof paper.

3 Melt 150g (5oz) chocolate with
3 tbsp water in a bowl over a pan of
gently simmering water, making
sure the base of the bowl doesn't
touch the water. Remove from the
heat, add the remaining rum and
the egg yolks and beat until smooth.
Beat the butter and sugar together
until pale and fluffy. Stir in the
chocolate mixture and fold in the
flour and almonds.

4 Whisk the egg whites in a clean,
grease-free bowl until soft peaks
form, then fold into the chocolate
mixture. Pour into the tin and bake
for 30–35 minutes until a skewer
comes out clean with a few crumbs
on it. Leave to cool in the tin for
10 minutes, then turn out on to a
wire rack to cool.

5 Put the remaining chocolate into a
large bowl. Bring the cream to the
boil, pour over the chocolate, leave
for 5 minutes, then stir until melted.
Leave to cool, then, using an electric
whisk, beat the mixture until thick
and pale. Clean the cake tin and put
the cake back into the tin. Spoon
the soaked cherries and any juice
over the cake. Spread the chocolate
cream on top, smooth the surface,
cover and chill for at least 2 hours.

6 Decorate with chocolate curls,
dust with cocoa and serve with fresh
cherries, and cream, if you like.

★ FREEZING TIP
To freeze Complete the recipe to the end
of step 4, wrap, label and freeze.
To use Thaw overnight at cool room
temperature. Complete the recipe.

White Chocolate Fruit Tarts

★

Preparation Time 40 minutes, plus chilling • Cooking Time 40–45 minutes, plus cooling • Serves 8 •
Per Serving 688 calories, 48g fat (of which 29g saturates), 58g carbohydrate, 0.5g salt • Easy

Sweet Shortcrust Pastry (see page
    268), made with 225g (8oz) plain
    flour, 150g (5oz) butter, 50g (2oz)
    icing sugar, 1 large egg and
    2–3 drops vanilla extract
flour to dust
450g (1lb) fresh mango, peeled,
    stoned and sliced
fresh mint sprigs to decorate
icing sugar to dust

FOR THE FILLING
275g (10oz) white chocolate,
    chopped
300ml (½ pint) double cream
1 vanilla pod, split lengthways
2 large eggs, separated
2 tbsp Kirsch

1 Roll out the pastry thinly on a
lightly floured worksurface and use
to line eight 9cm (3½in), 3cm (1¼in)
deep, loose-based tartlet tins (see
Cook's Tips). Prick with a fork and
chill for 30 minutes. Preheat the
oven to 200°C (180°C fan oven)
mark 6. Bake blind (see step 2, page
44). Leave to cool slightly.

2 To make the filling, put the
chocolate into a heatproof bowl.
Pour the cream into a small heavy-
based pan with the vanilla pod and
bring to the boil. Remove from the
heat, lift out the vanilla pod and add
the hot cream to the chocolate. Stir
until the chocolate is completely
melted. Leave to cool.

3 Preheat the oven to 190°C (170°C
fan oven) mark 5. Mix the egg yolks
and the Kirsch into the cooled
chocolate and cream mixture. Whisk
the egg whites in a clean, grease-
free bowl until soft peaks form, then
fold carefully into the chocolate
mixture until well incorporated. Pour
the mixture into the pastry cases and
bake for 10–15 minutes until just set
(see Cook's Tips).

4 Leave to cool in the tins and chill
for 5 hours or overnight. Don't
worry if the filling seems very soft –
it will become firmer as it chills.

5 Remove the tarts from the fridge
30 minutes before serving. Unmould
the tarts and arrange the mango
slices on top. Decorate with mint
sprigs and dust with icing sugar just
before serving.

★ COOK'S TIPS
● *Don't worry if the pastry cracks when
you're lining the tins – it's easy to patch
together.*
● *If the filling starts to get too dark
during cooking, cover it with foil.*
● *Try other fresh fruits as the topping for
these tarts, such as raspberries, halved
strawberries and sliced ripe pears.*

White Chocolate and Raspberry Tart

★

Preparation Time 35 minutes, plus chilling • Cooking Time 30 minutes, plus cooling • Serves 12 •
Per Serving 391 calories, 32g fat (of which 16g saturates), 24g carbohydrate, 0.3g salt • Easy

150g (5oz) plain flour, plus extra
   to dust
a pinch of salt
65g (2½oz) cold, unsalted butter,
   diced
100g (3½oz) ground hazelnuts
25g (1oz) sugar
1 large egg, beaten
250g tub mascarpone cheese
200g (7oz) white chocolate
142ml carton double cream
400g (14oz) fresh raspberries
golden icing sugar to dust

1 Sift the flour and salt into a food processor. Add the butter and whiz until the mixture resembles fine breadcrumbs. (Alternatively, rub the butter into the flour in a large bowl by hand or using a pastry cutter to resemble fine crumbs.) Add the hazelnuts, sugar and just enough egg and pulse, or stir, to bring the mixture together. Shape the pastry into a disc, wrap in clingfilm and chill for 30 minutes.

2 Roll out the pastry on a lightly floured worksurface, then press into the base and sides of a 20.5cm (8in) fluted pastry tin. Prick all over. Cover with a large round of baking parchment and top with baking beans. Chill until firm. Preheat the oven to 190°C (170°C fan oven) mark 5.

3 Bake for 12–15 minutes until the pastry has set. Remove the beans and parchment and continue baking for 5–10 minutes until the pastry is dry and slightly sandy to the touch. Cool in the tin on a wire rack.

4 Melt the mascarpone and chocolate together in a heatproof bowl over a pan of gently simmering water, making sure the base of the bowl doesn't touch the water. Don't stir, otherwise the mixture will thicken into a sticky mess.

5 Remove the bowl from the pan and leave to cool completely. Meanwhile, lightly whip the cream. Fold the chocolate into the cream. Spoon the filling into the pastry case and chill. To serve, top with fresh raspberries and dust with icing sugar.

Chocolate Orange Tart

Preparation Time 30 minutes, plus chilling • Cooking Time about 1 hour, plus cooling • Cuts into 8 slices •
Per Slice 441 calories, 28g fat (of which 17g saturates), 42g carbohydrate, 0.2g salt • **Easy**

Sweet Shortcrust Pastry (see page
   268), made with 150g (5oz) plain
   flour, a pinch of salt, 75g (3oz)
   unsalted butter, 25g (1oz) golden
   icing sugar, grated zest of
   1 orange and 2 large egg yolks
flour to dust
icing sugar to dust

FOR THE FILLING
175g (6oz) plain chocolate (at least
   50% cocoa solids), chopped
175ml (6fl oz) double cream
75g (3oz) light muscovado sugar
2 medium eggs
1 tbsp Grand Marnier or Cointreau

1 Roll out the pastry on a lightly
floured worksurface and use to line
a 20.5cm (8in) loose-based tart tin.
Prick the base all over with a fork,
put the tin on a baking sheet and
chill for 30 minutes. Preheat the
oven to 190°C (170°C fan oven)
mark 5.

2 Bake the pastry case blind (see
step 2, page 44). Remove from the
oven and put to one side. Reduce
the oven temperature to 170°C
(150°C fan oven) mark 3.

3 To make the filling, melt the
chocolate in a heatproof bowl set
over a pan of gently simmering
water, making sure the base of the
bowl doesn't touch the water.
Remove the bowl from the pan and
leave to cool for 10 minutes.

4 Put the cream, muscovado sugar,
eggs and liqueur into a bowl and
stir, using a wooden spoon to mix
thoroughly. Gradually stir in the
chocolate, then pour into the pastry
case and bake for 20 minutes or
until just set.

5 Serve warm or cold, dusted
liberally with icing sugar.

★ TRY SOMETHING
DIFFERENT
*Omit the orange zest and replace the
Grand Marnier with crème de menthe.*

Chocolate and Cherry Amaretti Tart

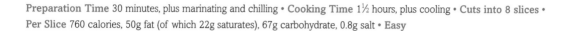

Preparation Time 30 minutes, plus marinating and chilling • Cooking Time 1½ hours, plus cooling • Cuts into 8 slices •
Per Slice 760 calories, 50g fat (of which 22g saturates), 67g carbohydrate, 0.8g salt • **Easy**

400g (14oz) pitted bottled or
    canned morello cherries, drained
3 tbsp brandy, sloe gin or almond-
    flavoured liqueur
150g (5oz) unsalted butter, softened
50g (2oz) icing sugar, plus extra
    to dust
1 small egg, beaten
225g (8oz) plain flour, plus extra
    to dust

FOR THE FILLING
100g (3½oz) plain chocolate,
    broken into pieces
125g (4oz) unsalted butter, softened
125g (4oz) caster sugar
3 large eggs, beaten
125g (4oz) ground almonds
25g (1oz) self-raising flour, sifted
50g (2oz) amaretti biscuits, finely
    crushed (see page 225)
75g (3oz) slivered or flaked
    almonds

1 Put the cherries into a bowl with
the brandy, gin or liqueur and leave
for 30 minutes or overnight. Put the
butter, icing sugar and egg into a
food processor and whiz until
almost smooth. Add the plain flour
and whiz until the mixture begins to
form a dough. (Alternatively, rub the
fat into the flour by hand or using a
pastry cutter to resemble fine
crumbs, then stir in the icing sugar
and egg.) Knead the pastry lightly,
then wrap and chill for 30 minutes.
Roll out the pastry on a lightly
floured worksurface and use to line
a 23cm (9in) loose-based fluted tart
tin. Chill for 20 minutes.

2 Preheat the oven to 200°C (180°C
fan oven) mark 6. Bake the pastry
case blind (see step 2, page 44).
Remove from the oven. Reduce the
oven temperature to 150°C (130°C
fan oven) mark 2.

3 To make the filling, melt the
chocolate in a heatproof bowl set
over a pan of gently simmering
water, making sure the base of
the bowl doesn't touch the water.
Stir once or twice until smooth.
Leave to cool.

4 Beat the butter with the sugar until
pale and fluffy. Gradually beat in the
eggs, alternating with the ground
almonds and self-raising flour. Fold in
the melted chocolate and biscuits.
Spoon one-third of the mixture into
the pastry case. Spoon the cherries
and juice over it. Spread the
remaining filling over the cherries.
Sprinkle on the slivered or flaked
almonds and bake for about 1 hour.
The tart will have a thin top crust but
will be soft underneath. Leave in the
tin for 10–15 minutes to firm up,
then unmould, dust with icing sugar
and serve warm.

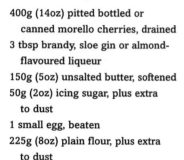 FREEZING TIP

To freeze Complete the recipe but
do not dust with icing sugar. Cool
completely, wrap, seal, label and freeze
for up to one month.
To use Thaw at a cool room
temperature overnight. Warm through at
200°C (180°C fan oven) mark 6 for
10 minutes and dust with icing sugar
before serving.

Black Forest Roulade

★

Preparation Time 35 minutes, plus chilling • Cooking Time 20 minutes, plus cooling • Cuts into 10 slices •
Per Slice 248 calories, 12g fat (of which 7g saturates), 33g carbohydrate, 0.1g salt • Easy

4 large eggs, separated
125g (4oz) golden caster sugar, plus
   extra to dust
125g (4oz) plain chocolate (at least
   70% cocoa solids), broken into
   pieces, melted and cooled a little
cocoa powder and icing sugar
   to dust

FOR THE FILLING
140ml (4½fl oz) whipping cream
1 tsp icing sugar
75g (3oz) Greek yogurt
2 × 425g cans morello cherries,
   drained, pitted and halved

1 Preheat the oven to 180°C (160°C
fan oven) mark 4. Line a 33 × 23cm
(13 × 9in) Swiss roll tin with baking
parchment.

2 Whisk the egg yolks with the
caster sugar in a large bowl until
thick and creamy. Whisk in the
melted chocolate. Whisk the egg
whites in a clean, grease-free bowl
until stiff peaks form. Fold into the
chocolate mixture. Pour into the tin,
smooth the surface and bake for
20 minutes or until firm to the
touch. Leave to cool in the tin for
10–15 minutes.

3 Put a sheet of baking parchment
on the worksurface and dust with
caster sugar. Carefully turn out the
roulade on to the parchment and
peel off the lining parchment. Cover
with a damp cloth and leave to cool
for 30 minutes.

4 To make the filling, lightly whip
the cream with the icing sugar, then
fold in the yogurt. Spread over the
cold roulade and scatter the cherries
on top. Roll up from one of the
narrow ends, using the baking
parchment to help. Chill for
30 minutes. Slice the roulade and
serve dusted with cocoa powder
and icing sugar.

Chocolate-dipped Strawberries

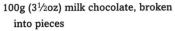

Preparation Time 20 minutes • Serves 6 • Per Serving 291 calories, 15g fat (of which 9g saturates), 37g carbohydrate, 0.1g salt • Vegetarian • Gluten Free • Easy

100g (3½oz) milk chocolate, broken
   into pieces
100g (3½oz) white chocolate,
   broken into pieces
100g (3½oz) plain chocolate (at
   least 70% cocoa solids), broken
   into pieces
700g (1½lb) strawberries

1 Put each type of chocolate side by side in a single heatproof serving bowl, keeping each type as separate as you can.

2 Melt the chocolate in a heatproof bowl set over a pan of gently simmering water, making sure the base of the bowl doesn't touch the water. Do not stir – keep the three types of chocolate separate. Holding each strawberry by its stalk, dip it into the chocolate. Arrange the strawberries in a shallow bowl to serve. Or let everyone dunk their own berries in the melted chocolate.

⭐ TRY SOMETHING DIFFERENT
Turn this into a fun chocolate fondue by offering different fruits for dunking, such as mango, pineapple chunks and raspberries, or even marshmallows. Provide a pile of cocktail sticks for spearing the fruit.

Ice Creams, Sorbets and Granitas

Instant Banana Ice Cream

Preparation Time 5 minutes, plus freezing • Serves 4 • Per Serving 173 calories, 1g fat (of which 0g saturates), 42g carbohydrate, 0g salt • Gluten Free • Easy

6 ripe bananas, about 700g (1½lb), peeled, cut into thin slices and frozen (see Cook's Tip)
1–2 tbsp virtually fat-free fromage frais
1–2 tbsp orange juice
1 tsp vanilla extract
splash of rum or Cointreau (optional)
a few drops of lime juice to taste

1 Leave the frozen banana slices to stand at room temperature for 2–3 minutes. Put the still frozen pieces in a food processor or blender with 1 tbsp fromage frais, 1 tbsp orange juice, the vanilla extract and the rum or Cointreau, if using.

2 Whiz until smooth, scraping down the sides of the bowl and adding more fromage frais and orange juice as necessary to give a creamy consistency. Add lime juice to taste and serve at once or turn into a freezerproof container and freeze for up to one month.

★ COOK'S TIP
To freeze bananas, peel them and slice thinly, then put the banana slices on to a large non-stick baking tray and put into the freezer for 30 minutes or until frozen. Transfer to a plastic bag and store in the freezer until needed.

Cheat's Raspberry Ice Cream

Preparation Time 5 minutes • Serves 6 • Per Serving 306 calories, 26g fat (of which 16g saturates), 19g carbohydrate, 0g salt • Gluten Free • Easy

300g (11oz) frozen raspberries
5–6 tbsp golden icing sugar
300ml (½ pint) extra-thick
 double cream
summer fruit or wafers to serve

1 Put six ramekins or freezerproof glasses into the freezer to chill. Put the frozen raspberries (don't allow them to thaw first) into a food processor with the icing sugar. Whiz for 3–4 seconds until the raspberries look like large crumbs. Add the cream and whiz again for 10 seconds.

2 Spoon into the ice-cold dishes and serve immediately, or spoon into a small freezerproof container and freeze for 20–30 minutes. Serve with summer fruit or wafers, if you like.

★ COOK'S TIP
Depending on the sweetness of the raspberries, you may need to add a little more icing sugar – taste the mixture before you spoon the ice cream into the dishes.

Easy Vanilla Ice Cream

Preparation Time 15 minutes, plus freezing • **Serves 6** • **Per Serving** 389 calories, 30g fat (of which 18g saturates), 26g carbohydrate, 0.2g salt • **Gluten Free** • **Easy**

300ml (½ pint) double cream
218g can condensed milk
200g carton fresh custard
2 tbsp vanilla extract
crisp sweet biscuits or wafers
  to serve

1 Line a 900g (2lb) loaf tin or plastic box with clingfilm. Pour the cream into a bowl and whip until soft peaks form. Stir in the condensed milk, custard and vanilla extract. Pour the mixture into the lined tin and freeze for 6 hours.

2 To serve, invert the ice cream on to a plate and remove the clingfilm. Slice and serve with sweet biscuits or wafers.

★ COOK'S TIP

If you make the ice cream in the morning and eat it later on that day, it will have the perfect 'soft scoop' texture. If it's been in the freezer for longer, you'll need to take it out 20 minutes before slicing to allow it to soften.

Chocolate Ice Cream

Preparation Time 20 minutes, plus infusing and freezing • Cooking Time 15 minutes, plus cooling • Serves 4 •
Per Serving 629 calories, 55g fat (of which 30g saturates), 39g carbohydrate, 0.2g salt • Gluten Free • Easy

300ml (½ pint) semi-skimmed milk
1 vanilla pod, split
125g (4oz) plain chocolate (at least
    70% cocoa solids), broken into
    pieces
3 large egg yolks
50–75g (2–3oz) golden caster sugar
300ml (½ pint) double cream

1 Pour the milk into a heavy-based pan, add the vanilla pod and chocolate and heat gently until the chocolate has melted. Bring almost to the boil, then remove the pan from the heat and leave to infuse for 20 minutes.

2 Whisk the egg yolks and sugar together in a bowl until thick and creamy. Gradually whisk in the hot milk, then strain back into the pan. Cook over a low heat, stirring constantly with a wooden spoon, until the custard has thickened enough to lightly coat the back of the spoon; do not allow it to boil or it will curdle. Pour into a chilled bowl and leave to cool.

3 Add the cream to the cold chocolate custard and whisk until evenly blended.

4 Pour into an ice-cream maker and churn for about 30 minutes or until frozen. (Alternatively, freeze in a shallow freezerproof container until firmly frozen, beating two or three times during freezing to break down the ice crystals and ensure an even texture.) Leave to soften at cool room temperature for about 20–30 minutes before serving.

Rum and Raisin Ice Cream

★

Preparation Time 40 minutes, plus freezing • Cooking Time 5 minutes • Serves 8 • Per Serving 517 calories, 41g fat (of which 25g saturates), 29g carbohydrate, 0.1g salt • Gluten Free • Easy

250g (9oz) large muscatel or Lexia
    raisins
100ml (3½fl oz) dark rum
600ml (1 pint) double cream
4 large egg yolks
3 tbsp golden syrup
1 tbsp black treacle
ice cream cones to serve (optional)

1 Put the raisins into a pan, add the rum and bring to the boil. Turn off the heat and leave to soak while you're making the ice cream.

2 Whip the cream until it just holds its shape. Put the egg yolks, golden syrup and treacle in another bowl. Whisk with a hand-held electric whisk for 2–3 minutes until it has a mousse-like consistency. Pour into the cream and whisk for a further 3–4 minutes until thick.

3 Set the freezer to fast-freeze (or turn to coldest setting). Pour the ice cream mixture into a 2 litre (3½ pint) roasting tin and freeze for 45 minutes–1 hour until it begins to harden around the edges.

4 Add the soaked fruit and any remaining liquid to the ice cream and mix well. Put back in the freezer for 45 minutes. Spoon into a 1.7 litre (3 pint) sealable container and freeze for at least 2 hours. Serve in ice cream cones, if you like.

Spicy Ginger Ice Cream

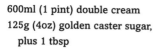

Preparation Time 30 minutes, plus chilling and freezing • **Cooking Time** 10 minutes, plus cooling • **Serves 8** •
Per Serving 541 calories, 46g fat (of which 28g saturates), 27g carbohydrate, 0.2g salt • **Easy**

600ml (1 pint) double cream
125g (4oz) golden caster sugar,
    plus 1 tbsp
4 medium eggs, separated
2 tsp ground ginger
4 pieces preserved stem ginger,
    roughly chopped
brandy snaps to serve

FOR THE SAUCE
50g (2oz) unsalted butter
50g (2oz) golden caster sugar
2 tbsp whisky
2 tbsp ginger syrup (from the jar of
    preserved stem ginger)

1 Whip the cream until just thick, then chill. Whisk 125g (4oz) sugar with the egg yolks in another bowl until pale and creamy.

2 Put the egg whites into a clean, grease-free bowl and whisk until stiff. Beat in the 1 tbsp sugar.

3 Fold the cream into the egg yolk mixture with the ground ginger, then fold in the egg whites. Pour into a freezerproof container and freeze for 4 hours.

4 To make the sauce, put the butter, sugar, whisky and ginger syrup into a pan and heat gently. Bring to the boil, then reduce the heat and simmer for 5 minutes or until thick. Leave to cool.

5 Fold the preserved stem ginger through the ice cream and drizzle the sauce over. Stir once or twice to create a ripple effect. Freeze for a further 4 hours or overnight. Serve with brandy snaps.

Italian Ice Cream Cake

Preparation Time 30 minutes, plus freezing and softening • **Cuts into 10 slices** • **Per Slice** 522 calories, 33g fat (of which 15g saturates), 46g carbohydrate, 0.2g salt • **Easy**

400g (14oz) fresh cherries, pitted
   and quartered
4 tbsp Amaretto liqueur
10 tbsp crème de cacao liqueur
200g (7oz) Savoiardi biscuits or
   sponge fingers
5 medium egg yolks
150g (5oz) golden caster sugar
450ml (¾ pint) double cream,
   lightly whipped
1 tbsp vanilla extract
75g (3oz) pistachio nuts or
   hazelnuts, roughly chopped
75g (3oz) plain chocolate (at least
   70% cocoa solids), roughly
   chopped
2–3 tbsp cocoa powder
2–3 tbsp golden icing sugar

1 Put the cherries and Amaretto into a bowl, stir, cover with clingfilm and put to one side. Pour the crème de cacao into a shallow dish. Quickly dip a sponge finger into the liqueur on one side only, then cut in half lengthways to separate the sugary side from the base. Repeat with each biscuit.

2 Double-line a deep 24 × 4cm (9½ × 1½ in) round tin with clingfilm. Arrange the sugar-coated sponge finger halves, sugar side down, on the base of the tin. Drizzle with any remaining crème de cacao.

3 Put the egg yolks and caster sugar into a bowl and whisk until pale, light and fluffy. Fold in the cream, vanilla extract, nuts, chocolate and cherries with Amaretto. Spoon on top of the sponge fingers in the tin and cover with the remaining sponge finger halves, cut side down. Cover with clingfilm and freeze for at least 5 hours.

4 Upturn the cake on to a serving plate and remove the clingfilm. Sift cocoa powder and icing sugar over the cake and cut into wedges. Before serving, leave at room temperature for 20 minutes if the weather is warm, 40 minutes at cool room temperature, or 1 hour in the fridge, to allow the cherries to thaw and the ice cream to become mousse-like.

★ COOK'S TIP
For a decorative top, use the tin to cut a template circle of greaseproof paper, then fold to make eight triangles. Cut these out. Put four on the cake and dust the uncovered cake with cocoa powder. Remove the triangles. Cover the cocoa with four triangles and dust the uncovered cake with icing sugar.

Mocha Ice Cream

Preparation Time 20 minutes, plus freezing • Cooking Time 10–15 minutes, plus cooling • Serves 8 •
Per Serving 510 calories, 46g fat (of which 0g saturates), 21g carbohydrate, 0g salt • Gluten Free • Easy

600ml (1 pint) double cream
300ml (½ pint) semi-skimmed milk
6 large egg yolks
50g (2oz) golden caster sugar
150ml (¼ pint) strong espresso
    coffee, cooled
50g (2oz) plain chocolate chips

FOR THE SAUCE
75g (3oz) plain chocolate (at least
    70% cocoa solids), broken into
    pieces
a few drops of vanilla extract

1 Pour the cream and milk into a heavy-based pan and bring just to the boil. Meanwhile, whisk the egg yolks and sugar together in a bowl until pale and creamy. Slowly pour the hot cream mixture into the bowl, whisking all the time. Put back into the pan and heat gently, stirring with a wooden spoon until the custard thickens enough to lightly coat the back of the spoon.

2 Strain the custard into a bowl, stir in the coffee and leave to cool completely. When cold, stir in the chocolate chips.

3 Pour into an ice-cream maker and churn for about 30 minutes, or according to the manufacturer's instructions until frozen. (Alternatively, freeze the mixture in a freezerproof container, beating at hourly intervals to break down the ice crystals and ensure an even texture, until the ice cream is firmly frozen.)

4 About 30 minutes before serving, transfer the ice cream to the fridge to soften. Meanwhile, make the sauce. Put the chocolate, vanilla extract and 50ml (2fl oz) water into a pan and heat gently until the chocolate has melted. Bring to the boil and let it bubble for a few minutes until thickened. Leave to cool slightly.

5 Scoop the ice cream into serving bowls and pour the chocolate sauce over it. Serve at once.

Pistachio and Date Ice Cream

Preparation Time 15 minutes, plus freezing • Cooking Time 8 minutes • Serves 6 • Per Serving 516 calories, 38g fat (of which 19g saturates), 38g carbohydrate, 0.4g salt • Gluten Free • A Little Effort

100g (3½oz) shelled pistachio nuts
218g can condensed milk
300ml (½ pint) double cream
1 tbsp orange flower water
125g (4oz) Medjool dates, stoned
   and roughly chopped
3 pomegranates

1 Keep 15g (½oz) pistachios to one side and put the rest into a food processor. Add the condensed milk and whiz for 1–2 minutes to roughly chop the nuts and flavour the milk.

2 Pour the cream into a bowl and whip until soft peaks form. Stir in the chopped pistachios and condensed milk, orange flower water and dates.

3 Line six 150ml (¼ pint) dariole moulds or clean yogurt pots with clingfilm, leaving some clingfilm hanging over the edges. Spoon in the cream mixture and freeze for at least 5 hours.

4 Cut the pomegranates in half, scoop out the seeds and discard any pith. Push the seeds through a sieve to extract the juice. Put the juice into a pan and bring to the boil, then reduce the heat and simmer for about 8 minutes until reduced to a syrup. Cool, put into a small airtight container and chill until needed.

5 To serve, ease the ice cream out of the moulds and remove the clingfilm. Cut each in half vertically and arrange on plates. Chop the remaining pistachios and sprinkle them over, then drizzle with some pomegranate sauce.

★ TRY SOMETHING DIFFERENT
Replace the pistachios with hazelnuts and the dates with dried cherries.

Nougat Ice Cream

Preparation Time 20 minutes, plus chilling and freezing • Cooking Time 20 minutes, plus cooling • Serves 6 •
Per Serving 520 calories, 32g fat (of which 15g saturates), 48g carbohydrate, 0.5g salt • Gluten Free • Easy

900ml (1½ pints) full-fat milk
300ml (½ pint) single cream
200g (7oz) white nougat, broken or
    chopped into chunks
8 medium egg yolks
125g (4oz) golden caster sugar
chopped pistachio nuts and
    almonds to decorate

1 Pour the milk into a pan and add the cream. Gently bring to the boil. Remove the pan from the heat and add the nougat. Put to one side until the nougat has melted, stirring occasionally.

2 Whisk the egg yolks with the sugar in a large bowl. Pour the milk and nougat mixture into the bowl, stir well, then pour back into the pan. Cook over a low heat, stirring constantly, for about 15 minutes or until the mixture coats the back of a wooden spoon. Pour into a bowl, cool and chill until cold.

3 When cold, tip the mixture into an ice-cream maker and churn according to the manufacturer's instructions until thick. Spoon into a chilled 2 litre (3½ pint) freezerproof container, smooth the surface and cover with a piece of greaseproof paper. (Alternatively, transfer the mixture to the freezerproof container and freeze for 4 hours. Whisk to break up the ice crystals and freeze for a further 4 hours, then whisk again. Cover with greaseproof paper.) Cover and freeze until ready to serve.

4 Put the ice cream in the fridge for 20 minutes before serving to soften slightly. Scoop into balls and scatter with chopped pistachios and almonds to serve.

Toffee Crunch Ice Cream

Preparation Time 20 minutes, plus freezing • Cooking Time 5 minutes, plus cooling • Serves 8 • Per Serving 535 calories, 33g fat (of which 19g saturates), 60g carbohydrate, 0.4g salt • **Easy**

3 chocolate-covered fudge finger
  bars, about 100g (3½oz) total
  weight
284ml carton double cream
2 medium eggs, separated
50g (2oz) icing sugar
500g carton chilled ready-made
  custard
5 chocolate bars with a butter
  almond centre, 175g (6oz) total
  weight, broken into pieces

1 Break the fudge bars into a heatproof bowl. Add 2 tbsp cream and heat slowly over a pan of simmering water. Leave to cool until tepid but still liquid.

2 Whisk together the egg yolks and sugar until pale, fairly thick and mousse-like.

3 Whip the remaining cream and egg whites in separate bowls until they both form soft peaks.

4 Fold together the whipped cream, custard, egg yolk mixture, fudge bar mixture and most of the chocolate bar pieces. Finally, fold in the whisked egg whites.

5 Pour the mixture into a shallow freezerproof container to a depth of about 5cm (2in) and freeze overnight. Before serving, leave to soften for about 40 minutes in the fridge, then stamp out into shapes, if you like. Decorate with the remaining chocolate bar pieces to serve.

Iced Raspberry Soufflés

Preparation Time 1¼ hours, plus freezing • Serves 8 • Per Serving 683 calories, 45g fat (of which 27g saturates), 69g carbohydrate, 0.1g salt • Gluten Free • A Little Effort

juice of 1 orange
juice of 1 lemon
700g (1½lb) raspberries
225g (8oz) caster sugar
450ml (¾ pint) double cream, lightly whipped
2 large egg whites
225g (8oz) plain chocolate (at least 70% cocoa solids), broken into pieces
350g (12oz) mixed berries, such as redcurrants, blueberries and blackberries
chocolate curls (see page 273) to decorate

1 Wrap eight 100ml (3½fl oz) glasses with non-stick baking parchment to come 2.5cm (1in) above the glass. Put 2 tbsp each of the citrus juices into a food processor with the raspberries and sugar. Whiz until smooth, then sieve. Keep 150ml (¼ pint) to one side, cover and chill. Put the remaining sauce into a large bowl, then fold in the cream. Whisk the egg whites in a clean, grease-free bowl until soft peaks form, then fold into the raspberry cream. Spoon into the glasses so the mixture reaches the top of the paper. Freeze overnight.

2 Cut eight strips of baking parchment. Melt the chocolate in a heatproof bowl over a pan of gently simmering water, making sure the base of the bowl doesn't touch the water. Cool slightly, then brush over the parchment. Remove the soufflés from the freezer and peel off the parchment. Wrap the chocolate-covered strips around the soufflés and freeze for 5 minutes. Peel away the parchment and put back into the freezer.

3 Put the soufflés in the fridge for 20 minutes before serving. Decorate with berries and chocolate curls and serve with the reserved sauce.

★ COOK'S TIPS

● *Don't over-whip the cream, as the acidity of the raspberries will help to thicken it – aim for a soft, dropping consistency.*

● *To make one large soufflé, line the outside of a 1.3 litre (2¼ pint) soufflé dish with a collar of non-stick baking parchment, deep enough to come about 5cm (2in) above the rim of the dish. Omit the chocolate collar (step 2) and don't turn the soufflé out of its dish for serving.*

Cinnamon and Nutmeg Ice Cream

★

Preparation Time 10 minutes, plus freezing • Cooking Time 5 minutes, plus cooling • Serves 8 • Per Serving 221 calories, 15g fat (of which 9g saturates), 16g carbohydrate, 0.1g salt • **Gluten Free** • **Easy**

½ tsp ground cinnamon, plus extra to dust
½ tsp freshly grated nutmeg
50g (2oz) golden caster sugar
150ml (¼ pint) double cream
250g (9oz) mascarpone cheese
400g carton fresh custard

1 Put the cinnamon, nutmeg, sugar and cream into a small pan, bring slowly to the boil, then put to one side to cool.

2 Put the mascarpone into a large bowl and beat until smooth. Stir in the custard and the cooled spiced cream. Pour the mixture into a shallow freezerproof container and freeze for 2–3 hours.

3 Whisk to break up the ice crystals and freeze for a further 2–3 hours. To serve, scoop into balls and dust with cinnamon.

Cognac and Crème Fraîche Ice Cream

Preparation Time 5 minutes, plus freezing • **Serves 8** • **Per Serving** 339 calories, 25g fat (of which 17g saturates), 24g carbohydrate, 0g salt • **Gluten Free** • **Easy**

500g carton crème fraîche
175g (6oz) golden icing sugar, sifted
4 tbsp cognac

1 Line a 450g (1lb) loaf tin with clingfilm. Put the crème fraîche, icing sugar and cognac into a bowl and whisk well – the mixture will become thin, but continue whisking until it thickens slightly.

2 Pour the mixture into the lined tin, then cover and freeze for 6 hours.

3 To shape the ice-cream balls, dip an ice-cream scoop in a jug of boiling water before using.

⭐ GET AHEAD
To prepare ahead *Make this up to a month in advance and store in the freezer.*

Baked Alaska

★

Preparation Time 30 minutes, plus freezing • Cooking Time 3–4 minutes • Serves 8 • Per Serving 659 calories, 30g fat (of which 17g saturates), 1g carbohydrate, 0.5g salt • Easy

1 large sponge flan case, 25.5cm
  (10in) diameter
5 tbsp orange juice
7 tbsp jam – any kind
1.5 litre tub vanilla ice cream
6 large egg whites
a pinch of cream of tartar
a pinch of salt
275g (10oz) golden caster sugar

1 Put the flan case on an ovenproof plate. Spoon the orange juice over the sponge, then spread over the jam. Scoop the ice cream on top of the jam, then freeze for at least 30 minutes.

2 Put the egg whites into a large, clean, grease-free bowl and whisk until stiff. Beat in the cream of tartar and salt. Use a large spoon to fold in the sugar, 1 tbsp at a time, then whisk until very thick and shiny.

3 Spoon the meringue over the ice cream to cover, making sure that the meringue is sealed to the flan case edge all the way round. Freeze for at least 1 hour or overnight.

4 Preheat the oven to 230°C (210°C fan oven) mark 8. Bake for about 3–4 minutes until the meringue is tinged golden brown. Serve immediately. If the Baked Alaska has been in the freezer overnight, bake and leave to stand for 15 minutes before serving.

★ TRY SOMETHING DIFFERENT
Replace the jam with ginger conserve and use ginger ice cream instead of vanilla.

Iced Lemon Meringue

Preparation Time 30 minutes, plus freezing • **Cooking Time** 1 hour 35 minutes, plus drying • **Serves 8** •
Per Serving 420 calories, 24g fat (of which 13g saturates), 49g carbohydrate, 0.1g salt • **Gluten Free** • **A Little Effort**

**4 large egg whites, at room
  temperature**
1 tsp lemon juice
100g (3½oz) golden caster sugar
100g (3½oz) light muscovado sugar
1 tbsp cornflour, sifted
½ tsp almond extract
25g (1oz) flaked almonds
Lemon Filling (see Cook's Tip)
fresh raspberries to decorate
**Raspberry Coulis (see page 269)
  to serve**

1 Preheat the oven to 140°C (120°C
fan oven) mark 1. Cut out three
35.5 × 20.5cm (14 × 8in) rectangles
of baking parchment and put on a
baking sheet.

2 Whisk the egg whites in a clean,
grease-free bowl until soft peaks
form. Add the lemon juice and
whisk until stiff. Whisk in the sugars,
1 tbsp at a time, until glossy. Beat in
1 tbsp boiling water, then fold in the
cornflour and almond extract.
Divide among the rectangles,
leaving a 10cm (4in) border. Keep
1 tbsp almonds to one side and
sprinkle the rest over the meringues.

3 Bake for 20 minutes, then reduce
the oven temperature to 110°C
(90°C fan oven) mark ¼ and bake
for 1¼ hours. Turn off the oven and
leave for 30 minutes–1 hour to dry.

4 Sandwich the meringues with the
Lemon Filling. Put on a baking sheet
and open-freeze until firm. Wrap
and refreeze.

5 To serve, transfer the meringue to
the fridge for 5 minutes. Toast the
reserved almonds and sprinkle over
the top. Slice, decorate with
raspberries and serve with the
Raspberry Coulis.

★ COOK'S TIP
Lemon Filling
*Mix 2 tbsp cornflour with 1 tbsp water,
then stir in 4 large egg yolks, 100g (3½oz)
golden caster sugar, the grated zest and
juice of 1 lemon and 1 lime. Bring 125ml
(4fl oz) milk to the boil, stir in the
cornflour and stir over a low heat until
thick. Tip into a bowl, cover with wet
greaseproof paper and cool. Whip
300ml (½ pint) double cream until
soft peaks form, then gently fold into
the filling.*

Banana and Chocolate Ice Cream Pie

Preparation Time 15 minutes, plus freezing • **Cuts into 8 slices** • **Per Slice** 406 calories, 26g fat (of which 15g saturates), 42g carbohydrate, 0.6g salt • **Easy**

500ml tub chocolate ice cream
75g (3oz) butter, plus extra to
　grease
200g (7oz) plain chocolate digestive
　biscuits, crushed (see page 225)
2 large bananas, sliced
juice of ½ lemon
1 king-size Mars Bar, cut into thin
　slivers and chilled

1 Remove the ice cream from the freezer to let it soften. Grease a 20.5cm (8in) loose-based fluted flan tin and baseline with greaseproof paper. Put the butter into a small pan and melt over a medium heat.

2 Put the crushed biscuits into a bowl, add the melted butter and mix until well combined. Tip the crumb mixture into the prepared tin and press evenly on to the base, using the back of a spoon to smooth the surface.

3 Toss the bananas in the lemon juice and scatter over the base. Upturn the ice cream tub on to the bananas and use a palette knife to spread the ice cream evenly, covering the fruit. Scatter the Mars Bar slices over the ice cream and freeze for at least 1 hour. Slice to serve.

Mango Ice Cream Terrine

★

Preparation Time 20–25 minutes, plus freezing • Serves 8 • Per Serving 306 calories, 21g fat (of which 13g saturates), 26g carbohydrate, 0.1g salt • **Easy**

oil to oil
2 small mangoes, peeled, stoned and chopped
2 medium eggs
125g (4oz) golden caster sugar
300ml (½ pint) double cream, whipped
1½ tsp coconut rum liqueur, such as Malibu
4 ratafia biscuits, roughly crushed

1 Lightly oil a 900g (2lb) loaf tin, then line with clingfilm, leaving some clingfilm hanging over the edges and smoothing any creases.

2 Whiz the mangoes in a food processor or blender until smooth. Keep to one side. Put the eggs and sugar into a large bowl and, using a hand-held electric whisk, whisk together for about 5 minutes or until thick.

3 Add the whipped cream to the mixture and fold together with a large metal spoon. Fold in three-quarters of the puréed mango and the coconut liqueur. Spoon the remaining mango purée into the lined tin to cover the base, then pour in the ice cream mixture. Cover with the overhanging clingfilm and freeze overnight or for up to one month.

4 Remove the ice cream from the freezer 5 minutes before serving. Unwrap the clingfilm. Turn out on to a serving dish, sprinkle with the crushed biscuits, slice and serve.

★ TRY SOMETHING DIFFERENT
Replace the mangoes with 1 small pineapple, and the ratafia with gingernut biscuits.

Strawberry and Black Pepper Granita

★

Preparation Time 10 minutes, plus freezing • Serves 6 • Per Serving 67 calories, trace fat (of which 0g saturates), 17g carbohydrate, 0g salt • Gluten Free • Dairy Free • Easy

400g (14oz) strawberries, hulled
75g (3oz) golden caster sugar
juice of ½ lemon
ground black pepper

1 Whiz the strawberries to a purée in a food processor or blender. Add the sugar, lemon juice and a good grinding of black pepper and stir in 450ml (¾ pint) water. Pulse to mix, then pour into a freezerproof container.

2 Freeze for 2 hours. Use a fork to stir in the frozen edges then freeze again for 1 hour. Fork through, then freeze for a further 1 hour or overnight. Use a fork to break up the granita, then serve in tall glasses.

Orange Sorbet

Preparation Time 20 minutes, plus chilling and freezing • Cooking Time 10 minutes, plus cooling • Serves 6 •
Per Serving 169 calories, trace fat, 44g carbohydrate, 0.1g salt • **Dairy Free** • **Gluten Free** • **Easy**

**grated zest of 3 oranges and juice
 of 6 oranges (about 600ml/
 1 pint)**
200g (7oz) golden granulated sugar
1 tbsp orange flower water
1 medium egg white
**Medjool dates, sliced, and 1 orange,
 cut into segments, to decorate**

1 Pour 300ml (½ pint) water into a large pan, add the orange zest and sugar and bring slowly to the boil. Stir occasionally with a wooden spoon to dissolve the sugar. Reduce the heat and simmer for 5 minutes. Leave to cool for 1–2 minutes, then strain the syrup into a clean bowl.

2 Strain the orange juice into the cooled syrup and stir in the orange flower water. Chill for 30 minutes.

3 For best results, freeze in an ice-cream maker (see Cook's Tip). Otherwise, pour into a shallow 18cm (7in) square freezerproof container and freeze for 3 hours until slushy. Mash well with a fork and freeze until solid. Whisk the egg white until stiff, then fold into the mixture. Put the sorbet back into the freezer and freeze for 2 hours or overnight until solid.

4 Put the sorbet in the fridge for 15–20 minutes before serving to soften slightly. Decorate with dates and orange segments.

★ COOK'S TIP
If you're using an ice-cream maker, add the whisked egg white halfway through churning, which will give the sorbet a creamier texture.

Cranberry Christmas Bombe

★

Preparation Time 30 minutes, plus chilling and freezing • **Cooking Time** 15 minutes, plus cooling • **Serves 8** •
Per Serving 236 calories, 6g fat (of which 4g saturates), 44g carbohydrate, 0.1g salt • **Gluten Free** • **A Little Effort**

125g (4oz) granulated sugar
300ml (½ pint) cranberry juice
225g (8oz) each cranberries and
    raspberries, fresh or frozen
2 large egg whites
75g (3oz) caster sugar
oil to oil
500ml tub vanilla ice cream
Sugared Redcurrants (see Cook's
    Tips) to decorate

1 Put the granulated sugar and cranberry juice into a pan and heat gently until the sugar dissolves. Bring to the boil, then add the cranberries. Reduce the heat, cover and simmer for 15 minutes until very soft. Leave to cool. Blend with the raspberries in a food processor or blender, press through a nylon sieve, then chill.

2 Whisk the egg whites in a clean, grease-free bowl until soft peaks form. Whisk in the caster sugar, a spoonful at a time, and continue whisking until stiff and glossy. Fold into the fruit purée. Pour into an ice-cream maker and churn until stiff.

3 Meanwhile, lightly oil a 1.4 litre (2½ pint) pudding basin, then put a disc of foil in the base. Put the basin into the freezer for 30 minutes. Spoon the cranberry sorbet into the basin, creating a hollow in the centre, and put back into the freezer. Leave the vanilla ice cream at room temperature for 10 minutes. Spoon the ice cream into the centre of the sorbet and press down well. Freeze for 4 hours or until firm.

4 To unmould the bombe, dip the basin in hot water for 10 seconds, then loosen the edges with a round-bladed knife, invert on to a plate, shake firmly and remove the foil. Decorate with Sugared Redcurrants. Use a warm knife to cut the bombe into wedges.

★ **COOK'S TIPS**

● *Sugared Redcurrants*
Dip a few sprigs of redcurrants in 1 large egg white, lightly beaten, then dip them in a little caster sugar. Shake off any excess sugar, then leave the redcurrants to harden on a baking sheet lined with greaseproof paper.
● *For an even more indulgent Christmas dessert, use clotted cream or Bailey's ice cream instead of vanilla.*
● *Make this up to two weeks in advance and store in the freezer.*

Frozen Yogurt Sorbet

Preparation Time 15 minutes, plus freezing • **Serves 8** • **Per Serving** 120 calories, 6g fat (of which 3g saturates), 14g carbohydrate, 0.2g salt • **Gluten Free** • **Easy**

450g (1lb) frozen mixed fruit, thawed, plus extra to serve
100g (3½oz) clear honey
3 medium egg whites
450g (1lb) low-fat Greek yogurt

1 Line a 750ml (1¼ pint) loaf tin with clingfilm. Whiz the thawed fruit in a food processor or blender to make a purée. Sieve into a bowl, pressing all the juice through with the back of a spoon. Stir the honey into the juice.

2 Put the egg whites into a clean, grease-free bowl and whisk until soft peaks form, then fold into the fruit with the yogurt. Pour the mixture into the lined tin and freeze for 4 hours. Stir to break up the ice crystals, then freeze again for 4 hours. Stir again, then freeze for a further 4 hours or until firm.

3 Put the sorbet in the fridge for 20 minutes before serving. Turn out on to a serving plate and remove the clingfilm. Slice and serve with a spoonful of thawed fruit.

★ COOK'S TIP
Use any selection of frozen mixed fruit. Summer berries and forest fruits also work well.

Lemon Sorbet

Preparation Time 10 minutes, plus chilling and freezing • **Cooking Time** 15 minutes • **Serves 4** • **Per Serving** 130 calories, 0g fat, 33g carbohydrate, 0g salt • **Gluten Free** • **Dairy Free** • **Easy**

3 juicy lemons
125g (4oz) golden caster sugar
1 large egg white

1 Finely pare the lemon zest, using a zester, then squeeze the juice. Put the zest into a pan with the sugar and 350ml (12fl oz) water and heat gently until the sugar has dissolved. Increase the heat and boil for 10 minutes. Leave to cool.

2 Stir the lemon juice into the cooled sugar syrup. Cover and chill in the fridge for 30 minutes.

3 Strain the syrup through a fine sieve into a bowl. In another bowl, beat the egg white until just frothy, then whisk into the lemon mixture.

4 For best results, freeze in an ice-cream maker. Otherwise, pour into a shallow freezerproof container and freeze until almost frozen; mash well with a fork and freeze until solid. Transfer the sorbet to the fridge 30 minutes before serving to soften slightly.

⭐ TRY SOMETHING DIFFERENT
Orange Sorbet
Replace two of the lemons with oranges.
Lime Sorbet
Replace two of the lemons with four limes.

Chocolate Cinnamon Sorbet

Preparation Time 10 minutes, plus chilling and freezing • Cooking Time 15 minutes, plus cooling • Serves 8 •
Per Serving 118 calories, 1g fat (of which 1g saturates), 27g carbohydrate, 0.2g salt • Gluten Free • Dairy Free • Easy

200g (7oz) golden granulated sugar
50g (2oz) unsweetened cocoa
   powder
1 tsp instant espresso coffee
   powder
1 cinnamon stick
8 tsp crème de cacao (chocolate
   liqueur) to serve (optional)

1 Put the sugar, cocoa powder, coffee and cinnamon stick into a large pan with 600ml (1 pint) water. Bring to the boil, stirring until the sugar has completely dissolved. Boil for 5 minutes, then remove from the heat and leave to cool. Remove the cinnamon stick, then chill.

2 If you have an ice-cream maker, put the mixture into it and churn for about 30 minutes until firm. Otherwise, pour into a freezerproof container and put in the coldest part of the freezer until firmly frozen, then transfer the frozen mixture to a blender or food processor and blend until smooth. Quickly put the mixture back in the container and freeze for at least 1 hour.

3 To serve, scoop the sorbet into individual cups and, if you like, drizzle 1 tsp chocolate liqueur over each portion. Serve immediately.

Peach and Black Cherry Granita

Preparation Time 15 minutes, plus freezing • Serves 6 • Per Serving 150 calories, trace fat, 39g carbohydrate, 0g salt •
Dairy Free • Gluten Free • Easy

400g can peach slices in syrup
100g (3½oz) golden caster sugar
4 tbsp lemon juice
**400g can pitted black cherries
in syrup**

1 Drain the peaches and keep the syrup in a measuring jug. Add cold water to the fruit syrup to make it up to 300ml (½ pint).

2 Whiz the peaches in a food processor or blender until smooth. Add half the sugar and half the lemon juice and whiz for a few more seconds. Add the reserved syrup and whiz again to combine.

3 Pour the mixture into a shallow freezerproof container and cover with a tight-fitting lid, then freeze for 2 hours.

4 Repeat steps 1 to 3 with the cherries and the remaining sugar and lemon juice.

5 The mixtures should have started to freeze around the sides and base after 2 hours, so take a large fork and mash the unfrozen mixture into the frozen. Cover and put back in the freezer for a further 1 hour, then mash once more.

6 Spoon alternate layers of peach and cherry granita into six sundae glasses and serve immediately. Alternatively, cover and store the granitas in the freezer for up to three months. To serve, put the granitas in the fridge for 30 minutes before serving to soften slightly.

⭐ TRY SOMETHING
DIFFERENT
Use canned apricots and canned raspberries instead of peaches and cherries.

Cheesecakes, Gâteaux, Meringues and Trifles

Blueberry Cheesecake

Preparation Time 15 minutes, plus chilling • **Cooking Time** 45 minutes, plus cooling • **Cuts into 8 slices** •
Per Slice 376 calories, 24g fat (of which 14g saturates), 36g carbohydrate, 0.4g salt • **Easy**

1 large sponge flan case, 23–25.5cm
   (9–10in) diameter
butter to grease
300g (11oz) cream cheese
1 tsp vanilla extract
100g (3½oz) golden caster sugar
150ml (¼ pint) soured cream
2 medium eggs
2 tbsp cornflour

FOR THE TOPPING
150g (5oz) blueberries
2 tbsp redcurrant jelly

1 Preheat the oven to 180°C (160°C fan oven) mark 4. Use the base of a 20.5cm (8in) springform cake tin to cut out a round from the flan case, discarding the edges. Grease the tin and baseline with greaseproof paper, then put the flan base into it. Press down with your fingers.

2 Put the cream cheese, vanilla extract, sugar, soured cream, eggs and cornflour into a food processor and whiz until evenly combined. Pour the mixture over the flan base and shake gently to level the surface. Bake for 45 minutes or until just set and pale golden. Turn off the oven and leave the cheesecake inside, with the door ajar, for about 30 minutes. Leave to cool, then chill for at least 2 hours.

3 To serve, put the blueberries into a pan with the redcurrant jelly and heat through until the jelly has melted and the blueberries have softened slightly – or place in a heatproof bowl and cook on full power in a 900W microwave for 1 minute. Spoon them over the top of the cheesecake. Cool and chill for 15 minutes before serving.

 TRY SOMETHING DIFFERENT
Use raspberries or other soft berries instead of blueberries.

Warm Ginger Ricotta Cake

Preparation Time 25 minutes • Cooking Time 1¼ hours, plus cooling • Cuts into 8 slices • Per Slice 494 calories, 36g fat (of which 21g saturates), 38g carbohydrate, 0.8g salt • Easy

75g (3oz) unsalted butter, melted, plus extra to grease

225g (8oz) digestive biscuits, finely crushed (see page 225)

200g (7oz) cream cheese

225g (8oz) ricotta cheese

4 tbsp double cream

3 medium eggs, separated

1 tbsp cornflour

1 piece of preserved stem ginger in syrup, finely chopped, plus 1 tbsp syrup

125g (4oz) icing sugar

Ginger and Whisky Sauce to serve (optional, see Cook's Tips)

4 Bake for 30 minutes. Reduce the oven temperature to 180°C (160°C fan oven) mark 4, cover the cake loosely with foil and bake for a further 45 minutes. The cake should be just set in the centre. Cool for 15 minutes on a wire rack.

5 Serve warm, with Ginger and Whisky Sauce, if you like.

⭐ COOK'S TIPS
● *Ginger and Whisky Sauce*
Gently heat 300ml (½ pint) single cream with 2 tsp preserved stem ginger syrup and 1 tsp whisky. Serve just warm, with the cake.
● *The cake may also be served with sliced oranges soaked in ginger syrup and Cointreau.*

1 Preheat the oven to 200°C (180°C fan oven) mark 6. Grease a 20.5cm (8in) springform cake tin. Put the biscuits into a bowl, add the melted butter and mix to combine. Tip just over half the crumb mixture into the prepared tin and press evenly into the base and up the sides. Put to one side while you make the filling.

2 Beat together, or whiz in a food processor, the cheeses, cream, egg yolks, cornflour, ginger and syrup. Transfer to a bowl.

3 Put the egg whites into a clean, grease-free bowl and whisk until soft peaks form. Gradually whisk in the icing sugar, keeping the mixture stiff and shiny. Fold into the ginger mixture. Spoon on to the biscuit base. Smooth the surface. Sprinkle the top with the remaining crumbs.

Orange and Chocolate Cheesecake

★

Preparation Time 45 minutes • Cooking Time 2–2¼ hours, plus cooling • Cuts into 12 slices • Per Slice 767 calories, 60g fat (of which 37g saturates), 53g carbohydrate, 1.2g salt • **Easy**

225g (8oz) chilled unsalted butter, plus extra to grease
250g (9oz) plain flour, sifted
150g (5oz) light muscovado sugar
3 tbsp cocoa powder
dark chocolate curls to decorate (see page 273, optional)

FOR THE TOPPING
2 oranges
800g (1lb 12oz) cream cheese
250g (9oz) mascarpone cheese
4 large eggs
225g (8oz) golden caster sugar
2 tbsp cornflour
½ tsp vanilla extract
1 vanilla pod

1 Preheat the oven to 180°C (160°C fan oven) mark 4. Grease a 23cm (9in) springform cake tin and baseline with baking parchment.

2 Cut 175g (6oz) butter into cubes. Melt the remaining butter and put to one side. Put the flour and cubed butter into a food processor with the sugar and cocoa powder. Whiz until the texture of fine breadcrumbs. (Alternatively, rub the butter into the flour in a large bowl by hand or using a pastry cutter. Stir in the sugar and cocoa.) Pour in the melted butter and pulse, or stir with a fork, until the mixture comes together.

3 Spoon the crumb mixture into the prepared tin and press evenly on to the base, using the back of a metal spoon to smooth the surface. Bake for 35–40 minutes until lightly puffed; avoid over-browning or the base will have a bitter flavour. Remove from the oven and leave to cool. Reduce the oven temperature to 150°C (130°C fan oven) mark 2.

4 Meanwhile, make the topping. Grate the zest from the oranges, then squeeze the juice – you will need 150ml (¼ pint). Put the cream cheese, mascarpone, eggs, sugar, cornflour, grated orange zest and vanilla extract into a large bowl. Using a hand-held electric whisk, beat the ingredients together thoroughly until well combined.

5 Split the vanilla pod in half lengthways and, using the tip of a sharp knife, scrape out the seeds and add them to the cheese mixture. Beat in the orange juice and continue whisking until the mixture is smooth.

6 Pour the cheese mixture over the cooled biscuit base. Bake for about 1½ hours or until pale golden on top, slightly risen and just set around the edge. The cheesecake should still be slightly wobbly in the middle; it will set as it cools. Turn off the oven and leave the cheesecake inside, with the door ajar, to cool for 1 hour. Remove and leave to cool completely (about 3 hours), then chill.

7 Just before serving, unclip the tin and transfer the cheesecake to a plate. Scatter chocolate curls on top to decorate, if you like.

Raspberry Cheesecake

Preparation Time 30 minutes, plus chilling • **Serves 10** • **Per Serving** 270 calories, 19g fat (of which 10g saturates), 20g carbohydrate, 0.5g salt • **Easy**

100g (3½oz) unsalted butter, melted, plus extra to grease
25g (1oz) blanched almonds, lightly toasted, then finely chopped
225g (8oz) almond butter biscuits, crushed (see page 225)
a few drops of almond extract
450g (1lb) raspberries
300g (11oz) Greek yogurt
150g (5oz) low-fat soft cheese
1 tbsp powdered gelatine (see Cook's Tips, page 142)
2 medium egg whites
50g (2oz) icing sugar

1 Grease a 20.5cm (8in) round springform cake tin. Mix the almonds with the crushed biscuits and melted butter, then add the almond extract. Tip the crumb mixture into the prepared tin and press evenly on to the base, using the back of a spoon to smooth the surface. Chill for 1 hour or until firm.

2 To make the filling, purée 225g (8oz) raspberries in a blender, then press through a sieve. Put three-quarters of the purée to one side and return the rest to the blender. Add the yogurt and cheese, then

whiz to blend. Transfer to a bowl. Sprinkle the gelatine over 2 tbsp water in a heatproof bowl and leave to soak for 2–3 minutes. Put the bowl over a pan of simmering water until the gelatine has dissolved.

3 Whisk the egg whites with the icing sugar until thick and shiny. Fold into the cheese mixture. Arrange half the remaining berries over the biscuit base, then pour the cheese mixture over the berries. Add the reserved purée and swirl with a knife to marble. Top with the remaining berries and chill for 3–4 hours.

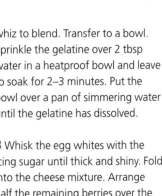

★ TRY SOMETHING DIFFERENT
● *Blueberry Cheesecake*
Replace the raspberries with blueberries.
● *Pineapple and Ginger Cheesecake*
Omit the almonds and replace the almond biscuits with 250g (9oz) crushed gingernut biscuits. Omit the almond extract. Replace the raspberries with fresh pineapple chunks.

Toffee Cheesecake

Preparation Time 15 minutes, plus chilling • Cooking Time 50 minutes–1 hour, plus cooling • Serves 10 •
Per Serving 379 calories, 24g fat (of which 13g saturates), 34g carbohydrate, 1.1g salt • **Easy**

300g pack digestive biscuits
125g (4oz) unsalted butter, melted

FOR THE FILLING
450g (1lb) curd cheese
140ml (4½fl oz) double cream
juice of ½ lemon
3 medium eggs, beaten
50g (2oz) golden caster sugar
6 tbsp dulce de leche toffee sauce,
    plus extra to drizzle

1 Put the biscuits into a food processor and whiz until they resemble fine crumbs. (Alternatively, put them in a plastic bag and crush with a rolling pin.) Transfer to a bowl. Add the butter and blend briefly, or stir in, to combine. Tip the crumb mixture into a 20.5cm (8in) springform cake tin and press evenly into the base and up the sides, then chill for about 1 hour or until firm.

2 Preheat the oven to 200°C (180°C fan oven) gas mark 6. To make the filling, put the curd cheese and cream into a food processor or blender and whiz until smooth. Add the lemon juice, eggs, sugar and toffee sauce, then blend again until smooth. Pour into the chilled biscuit case and bake for 10 minutes. Reduce the oven temperature to 180°C (160°C fan oven) mark 4, then bake for 45 minutes or until set and golden brown.

3 Turn off the oven and leave the cheesecake inside, with the door ajar, until it is cool. When completely cool, chill for at least 2 hours to firm up the crust.

4 To remove the cheesecake from the tin, run a knife around the edge of the cake. Open the tin carefully, then use a palette knife to ease the cheesecake out. Cut into wedges, put on a serving plate and drizzle with toffee sauce.

★ COOK'S TIP
To slice the cheesecake easily, use a sharp knife dipped into a jug of boiling water and then wiped dry.

Marbled Chocolate Cheesecake

Preparation Time 25 minutes, plus chilling • Cooking Time 45 minutes, plus cooling • Cuts into 18 squares •
Per Square 325 calories, 27g fat (of which 14g saturates), 18g carbohydrate, 0.5g salt • Easy

150g (5oz) digestive biscuits, finely
   crushed (see page 225)
100g (3½oz) ground almonds
75g (3oz) unsalted butter, melted
75g (3oz) plain chocolate (at least
   70% cocoa solids)
5 large eggs, separated
150g (5oz) golden caster sugar
600g (1lb 5oz) cream cheese
1½ tsp vanilla bean paste
golden icing sugar to dust (optional)

1 Line the base and sides of a 33 × 23 × 5cm (13 × 9 × 2in) roasting tin with greaseproof paper, leaving the excess hanging over the sides. Put the crushed biscuits into a bowl, add the almonds and butter and mix until well combined. Tip the crumb mixture into the prepared tin and press evenly on to the base, using the back of a spoon to smooth the surface. Chill for about 1 hour or until firm.

2 Preheat the oven to 170°C (150°C fan oven) mark 3. Melt the chocolate in a heatproof bowl over a pan of gently simmering water, making sure the base of the bowl doesn't touch the water. Don't stir, or it will congeal. Remove the bowl from the pan and leave to cool slightly.

3 Put the egg whites into a clean, grease-free bowl and whisk until soft peaks form. Add 25g (1oz) sugar and whisk until stiff peaks form. In a separate bowl, using the same whisk, mix the cream cheese, remaining sugar, yolks and vanilla. Using a metal spoon, stir a spoonful of egg white into the cheese mixture. Carefully fold in the remaining whites. Put a quarter of the mixture into the egg white bowl. Fold the chocolate into it. Pour the vanilla mixture over the biscuit base, dollop spoonfuls of chocolate mixture on top and marble using a knife.

4 Bake for 45 minutes or until set. Cool in the tin, then chill for 2 hours.

5 Remove from the tin and dust with icing sugar, if you like.

 TO STORE
Store in an airtight container. It will keep for up to one week.

White Chocolate and Ginger Cheesecake with Cranberry Sauce

Preparation Time 25 minutes, plus chilling • Cooking Time 1 hour 40 minutes, plus cooling • Cuts into 10 slices •
Per Slice 494 calories, 36g fat (of which 22g saturates), 36g carbohydrate, 0.7g salt • Easy

175g (6oz) gingernut biscuits, finely
    crushed (see page 225)
50g (2oz) unsalted butter, melted
150g (5oz) white chocolate
250g (9oz) mascarpone cheese
400g (14oz) cream cheese
4 medium eggs, beaten
100g (3½oz) golden caster sugar
75g (3oz) preserved stem ginger,
    finely chopped
icing sugar to dust

FOR THE SAUCE
175g (6oz) fresh cranberries
60g (2½oz) golden caster sugar
1 tsp ground ginger

1 Line the base and sides of a 23cm (9in) loose-bottomed cake tin with greaseproof paper. Pour the biscuits into a bowl and stir in the melted butter. Tip the crumb mixture into the prepared tin and press evenly on to the base, using the back of a spoon to smooth the surface. Chill for about 1 hour or until firm.

2 Preheat the oven to 150°C (130°C fan oven) mark 2. Put 100g (3½oz) chocolate into a heatproof bowl over a pan of gently simmering water, making sure the base of the bowl doesn't touch the water, and leave to melt. Leave to cool slightly. Put the mascarpone and cream cheese into a large bowl and beat together until smooth. Stir in the eggs, caster sugar, ginger and melted white chocolate.

3 Pour into the prepared tin and bake in the centre of the oven for 1½ hours or until the cheesecake just wobbles slightly when the tin is tapped. Leave in the tin, place on a wire rack and leave to cool. When cold, chill for at least 4 hours.

4 To make the sauce, heat the cranberries, sugar and ground ginger in a pan with 100ml (3½fl oz) water. Simmer for 5 minutes or until the cranberries burst. Blend until smooth, then push through a sieve into a bowl and leave to chill.

5 Remove the cake from the tin and transfer to a plate. Dust with icing sugar, grate the remaining chocolate over the top and serve with the cranberry sauce.

★ FREEZING TIP
To freeze Complete the recipe to the end of step 4. Wrap the whole tin in clingfilm; put the sauce in a freezerproof container. Freeze both. They will keep for up to one month.
To use Thaw in the fridge.

Lemon and Orange Cheesecake

Preparation Time 30 minutes, plus chilling • **Cooking Time** 1¼ hours, plus cooling • **Cuts into 12 slices** •
Per Slice 530 calories, 40g fat (of which 24g saturates), 36g carbohydrate, 0.8g salt • **Easy**

150g (5oz) digestive biscuits
50g (2oz) Bourbon biscuits
50g (2oz) unsalted butter, melted
700g (1½lb) cream cheese
250g tub mascarpone cheese
225g (8oz) caster sugar
5 tsp plain flour
zest of 1 large orange and 1 lemon
1 vanilla pod, split along its length
3 large eggs, plus 2 large egg yolks,
   beaten

TO DECORATE
a few unsprayed rose petals
golden icing sugar

1 Preheat the oven to 180°C (160°C
fan oven) mark 4. Line the base and
sides of a deep 20.5cm (8in)
springform tin with baking
parchment.

2 Put the biscuits and butter into
a food processor and whiz into
crumbs. (Alternatively, put the
biscuits in a plastic bag and crush
with a rolling pin then stir in the
butter.) Tip the crumb mixture into
the prepared tin and press evenly
on to the base, using the back of
a spoon to smooth the surface.

3 Bake for 15 minutes, then cool for
10 minutes. Reduce the oven
temperature to 140°C (120°C fan
oven) mark 1. Put the cream cheese
into a large bowl with the
mascarpone, sugar, flour and
orange and lemon zest. Scrape in
the vanilla seeds and beat until
smooth. Slowly add the beaten
eggs, keeping the mixture smooth.
Pour the mixture into the tin and
shake gently to level the surface.
Bake for 1 hour.

4 Remove the cheesecake from the
oven and leave to cool completely in
the tin. Chill for 2 hours. Arrange
rose petals on top and dust with
icing sugar to serve.

★ GET AHEAD
To prepare ahead *Complete the recipe
to the end of step 4, but don't decorate
it. Chill for up to three days or freeze for
up to one month.*
To use *Thaw overnight (if frozen) and
decorate with the rose petals and sugar.*

Lemon, Almond and Blueberry Gâteau

Preparation Time 25 minutes • Cooking Time 30–35 minutes, plus cooling • Cuts into 10–12 slices • Per Slice 189 calories, 5g fat (of which 1g saturates), 32g carbohydrate, 0.2g salt • Easy

4 large eggs
200g (7oz) golden caster sugar
1 tsp vanilla extract
75g (3oz) plain flour, sifted
50g (2oz) ground almonds
500g (1lb 2oz) fat-free Greek yogurt
3–4 tbsp maple syrup
zest of ½ lemon
225g (8oz) blueberries
15g (½oz) flaked almonds, toasted
icing sugar to dust (optional)

1 Preheat the oven to 180°C (160°C fan oven) mark 4. Line a 20.5cm (8in) cake tin with baking parchment.

2 Put the eggs, sugar and vanilla extract into a bowl and whisk with a hand-held electric whisk for 10 minutes or until the mixture is pale and mousse-like. Using a large metal spoon, fold in the flour and ground almonds, taking care not to over-mix and knock out the air. Pour into the prepared tin.

3 Bake for 30–35 minutes until golden and the cake is beginning to pull away from the sides of the paper. Turn the tin upside down on to a wire rack and leave to cool completely.

4 Beat the yogurt, syrup and lemon zest together. Cut the cake in half horizontally. Spread half the yogurt mixture over the base. Top with most of the blueberries. Replace the top, then spread the remaining mixture over it. Scatter the flaked almonds and remaining blueberries over the top. Dust with a little icing sugar, if you like.

★ GET AHEAD
To prepare ahead *Complete the recipe to the end of step 2. Wrap the tin in clingfilm and store in an airtight container. It will keep for up to two days.* **To use** *Complete the recipe.*

Black Forest Gâteau

Preparation Time 30 minutes • Cooking Time 45–50 minutes, plus cooling • Cuts into 12 slices • Per Slice 400 calories, 21g fat (of which 12g saturates), 53g carbohydrate, 0.4g salt • A Little Effort

125g (4oz) unsalted butter, melted
200g (7oz) plain flour
50g (2oz) cornflour
50g (2oz) cocoa powder, plus extra
    to dust
2 tsp espresso instant coffee
    powder
1 tsp baking powder
4 large eggs, separated
300g (11oz) golden caster sugar
2 × 300g jars morello cherries in
    syrup
2 tbsp Kirsch
200ml (7fl oz) double cream
2 tbsp icing sugar, sifted
fresh cherries and chocolate curls
    (see page 273) to decorate

1 Preheat the oven to 180°C (160°C fan oven) mark 4. Brush a little of the melted butter over the base and sides of a 20.5cm (8in), 9cm (3½in) deep cake tin. Line the base and sides of the tin with baking parchment.

2 Sift the flour, cornflour, cocoa powder, coffee powder and baking powder together three times – this helps to add air and makes sure all the ingredients are well mixed.

3 Put the egg yolks, sugar and 100ml (3½fl oz) cold water into a freestanding mixer and whisk for 8 minutes or until the mixture leaves a trail for 3 seconds.

4 Add the rest of the melted butter, pouring it around the edge of the bowl so the mixture doesn't lose any air, then quickly fold it in, followed by the sifted flour mixture in two batches.

5 Put the egg whites into a clean, grease-free bowl and whisk until stiff, then gently fold a spoonful into the cake mixture to loosen. Carefully fold in the rest of the egg whites, making sure there are no white blobs left. Pour into the prepared tin and bake in the oven for 45–50 minutes until a skewer inserted into the centre comes out clean. Leave to cool in the tin for 10 minutes, then turn out on to a wire rack to cool completely.

6 When the cake is cold, trim the top to make a flat surface. Turn the cake over so that the top becomes the base. Using a long serrated bread knife, carefully cut into three horizontally.

7 Drain the cherries, reserving 250ml (9fl oz) of the syrup. Put the syrup into a pan and simmer to reduce by half. Stir in the Kirsch. Brush the hot syrup on to each layer of the cake – including the top – using all the liquid.

8 Lightly whip the cream with the icing sugar. Spread one-third over the bottom layer and cover with half the cherries. Top with the next cake layer and repeat with another third of the cream and the remaining cherries. Top with the final cake layer and spread with the remaining cream. Decorate with fresh cherries, chocolate curls and a dusting of cocoa powder.

Chocolate and Hazelnut Meringues

Preparation Time 25 minutes, plus softening • Cooking Time 2 hours, plus cooling • Serves 6 • Per Serving 520 calories, 42g fat (of which 19g saturates), 32g carbohydrate, 0.1g salt • Gluten Free • Easy

125g (4oz) hazelnuts
125g (4oz) caster sugar
75g (3oz) plain chocolate (at least 70% cocoa solids)
2 medium egg whites
300ml (½ pint) double cream
redcurrants, blackberries and chocolate shavings to decorate
physalis (Cape gooseberries) dipped in caramel (see Cook's Tip) to serve (optional)

1 Preheat the oven to 110°C (90°C fan oven) mark ¼ and preheat the grill. Line two baking sheets with non-stick baking parchment. Spread the hazelnuts over a baking sheet. Toast under the hot grill until golden brown, turning them frequently. Put the hazelnuts in a clean teatowel and rub off the skins. Put the nuts in a food processor with 3 tbsp of the sugar and process to a fine powder. Add the chocolate and pulse until roughly chopped.

2 Put the egg whites into a clean, grease-free bowl and whisk until stiff. Whisk in the remaining sugar, a spoonful at a time, until the mixture is stiff and shiny. Fold in the nut mixture.

3 Spoon the mixture on to the prepared baking sheets, making small rough mounds about 9cm (3½in) in diameter. Bake for about 45 minutes until the meringues will just peel off the paper. Gently push in the base of each meringue to form a deep hollow, then put back in the oven for 1¼ hours or until crisp and dry. Leave to cool.

4 Whip the cream until it just holds its shape; spoon three-quarters on to the meringues. Leave in the fridge to soften for up to 2 hours.

5 Decorate the meringues with the remaining cream, fruit and chocolate shavings. Serve immediately, with caramel-dipped physalis, if you like.

 COOK'S TIP
To make the caramel, dissolve 125g (4oz) caster sugar in a small heavy-based pan over a low heat. Bring to the boil and bubble until a golden caramel colour. Dip each physalis into the caramel, then place on an oiled baking sheet and cool.

★ GET AHEAD
To prepare ahead Complete the recipe to the end of step 3, then store the meringues in an airtight container for up to one week.
To use Complete the recipe.

Toasted Hazelnut Meringue Cake

Preparation Time 10 minutes • Cooking Time about 30 minutes, plus cooling • Cuts into 8 slices • Per Slice 598 calories, 38g fat (of which 16g saturates), 57g carbohydrate, 0.1g salt • Easy

oil to oil
175g (6oz) skinned hazelnuts, toasted
3 large egg whites
175g (6oz) golden caster sugar
250g carton mascarpone cheese
285ml (9½fl oz) double cream
3 tbsp Bailey's Irish Cream liqueur, plus extra to serve
140g (4½oz) frozen raspberries
340g jar redcurrant jelly

1 Preheat the oven to 190°C (170°C fan oven) mark 5. Lightly oil two 18cm (7in) sandwich tins and baseline with baking parchment. Whiz the hazelnuts in a food processor until finely chopped.

2 Put the egg whites into a clean, grease-free bowl and whisk until stiff peaks form. Whisk in the sugar, a spoonful at a time. Using a metal spoon, fold in half the nuts. Divide the mixture between the tins and spread evenly. Bake in the middle of the oven for about 30 minutes, then leave to cool in the tins for 30 minutes.

3 To make the filling, put the mascarpone cheese into a bowl. Beat in the cream and liqueur until smooth. Put the raspberries and redcurrant jelly into a pan and heat gently until the jelly has melted. Sieve, then cool.

4 Use a palette knife to loosen the edges of the meringues, then turn out on to a wire rack. Peel off the baking parchment and discard. Put a large sheet of baking parchment on a board and sit one meringue on top, flat side down. Spread one-third of the mascarpone mixture over the meringue, then drizzle with raspberry purée. Top with the other meringue, then cover the whole cake with the rest of the mascarpone mixture. Sprinkle with the remaining hazelnuts. Carefully put the cake on to a serving plate and drizzle with more liqueur, if you like.

★ FREEZING TIP

To freeze Freezing the meringue makes it slightly softer but no less tasty. Complete the recipe to the end of step 4, but don't put on serving plate or drizzle with more liqueur. Using the paper, lift the cake into the freezer, then freeze until solid. Once solid, store in a sturdy container in the freezer for up to one month.
To use Thaw overnight in the fridge, then complete the recipe.

Lemon Meringue Pie

Preparation Time 40 minutes • Cooking Time about 50 minutes, plus standing • Serves 8 • Per Serving 692 calories, 36g fat (of which 21g saturates), 83g carbohydrate, 0.6g salt • **Easy**

23cm (9in) ready-made sweet
  pastry case

**FOR THE FILLING AND
  MERINGUE**
7 medium eggs, 4 separated, at
  room temperature
finely grated zest of 3 lemons
175ml (6fl oz) freshly squeezed
  lemon juice (about 4 lemons),
  strained
400g can condensed milk
150ml (¼ pint) double cream
225g (8oz) golden icing sugar

1 Preheat the oven to 180°C (160°C fan oven) mark 4. To make the filling, put 4 egg yolks into a bowl with the 3 whole eggs. Add the lemon zest and juice and whisk lightly. Mix in the condensed milk and cream.

2 Pour the filling into the pastry case and bake for 30 minutes or until just set in the centre. Put to one side to cool while you prepare the meringue. Increase the oven temperature to 200°C (180°C fan oven) mark 6.

3 For the meringue, whisk the egg whites and sugar together in a heatproof bowl over a pan of gently simmering water, using a hand-held electric whisk, for 10 minutes or until very shiny and thick. Remove from the heat and whisk at a low speed for a further 5–10 minutes until the bowl is cool.

4 Pile the meringue on top of the lemon filling and swirl with a palette knife to form peaks. Bake for 5–10 minutes until the meringue is tinged brown. Leave to stand for about 1 hour, then serve.

Baked Raspberry Meringue Pie

Preparation Time 15 minutes • **Cooking Time** 8 minutes • **Serves 8** • **Per Serving** 176 calories, 2g fat (of which 1g saturates), 37g carbohydrate, 0.1g salt • **Easy**

8 trifle sponges

450g (1lb) raspberries, lightly crushed

2–3 tbsp raspberry liqueur

3 medium egg whites

150g (5oz) golden caster sugar

1 Preheat the oven to 230°C (210°C fan oven) mark 8. Put the trifle sponges in the base of a 2 litre (3½ pint) ovenproof dish. Spread the raspberries on top and drizzle with the raspberry liqueur.

2 Put the egg whites into a clean, grease-free bowl and whisk until stiff peaks form. Gradually whisk in the sugar until the mixture is smooth and glossy. Spoon the meringue mixture over the raspberries and bake for 6–8 minutes until golden.

★ COOK'S TIP
If you don't have any raspberry liqueur, you can use another fruit-based liqueur such as Grand Marnier instead.

Marshmallow Meringue Cake

★

Preparation Time 45 minutes, plus chilling, freezing and softening • **Cooking Time** 2–2½ hours, plus cooling • **Serves 10** •
Per Serving 479 calories, 24g fat (of which 14g saturates), 62g carbohydrate, 0.2g salt • **Gluten Free** • **For the Confident Cook**

225g (8oz) golden caster sugar
125g (4oz) light muscovado sugar
6 large eggs, separated
1 tsp cornflour
½ tsp vinegar
50g (2oz) flaked almonds, toasted
    (optional)
chocolate shavings and icing sugar
    to dust

FOR THE FILLING
Marshmallow Ice Cream (see
    Cook's Tip)
4 bananas, about 450g (1lb)

1 Preheat the oven to 130°C (110°C fan oven) mark ½. Line two baking sheets with baking parchment. Using a felt-tip pen, mark out a 23cm (9in) diameter circle on each, then turn the paper over.

2 Sift the caster and muscovado sugars together. Put the egg whites into a clean, grease-free bowl and whisk until they're stiff and dry. Whisk in the sugars, 1 tbsp at a time, for about 5 minutes until the mixture is glossy and very stiff. Whisk in the cornflour and vinegar.

3 Spoon just over half the meringue on to one of the prepared baking sheets in a ring shape around the circumference of the circle and sprinkle with half the almonds, if using. Spread the remaining mixture evenly over the other circle to cover it completely. Sprinkle with the remaining almonds and bake for 2–2½ hours, then turn off the oven and leave the meringues inside, with the door ajar, to cool for 30 minutes.

4 About 30 minutes before serving, remove the ice cream from the freezer to soften. Put the meringue circle on a serving plate. Slice the bananas and scatter evenly over the base. Spoon the ice cream mixture over the bananas and put the meringue ring on top, pressing down gently. Decorate with chocolate shavings and a dusting of icing sugar, then serve immediately.

★ COOK'S TIP
Marshmallow Ice Cream
Bring 450ml (¾ pint) full-fat milk to scalding point in a small pan and add 1 tsp vanilla extract. Put 6 egg yolks into a bowl and pour the hot milk over them, whisking. Pour back into the cleaned pan and cook over a low heat, stirring until the mixture coats the back of a spoon. Put 200g (7oz) small white marshmallows in a bowl, strain the warm custard over them and stir until they have almost melted. Cool quickly, then cover and chill for 30 minutes. Fold 300ml (½ pint) lightly whipped double cream into the custard. Pour into a freezerproof container and freeze for 3–4 hours until just firm. (Alternatively, if you have an ice-cream maker, churn the custard until just firm.) Stir in 125g (4oz) chopped chocolate and freeze.

Strawberries with Chocolate Meringue

Preparation Time 15 minutes • Cooking Time 20–25 minutes • Serves 6 • Per Serving 132 calories, 2g fat (of which trace saturates), 27g carbohydrate, 0.1g salt • Gluten Free • Dairy Free • Easy

225g (8oz) strawberries, chopped
finely grated zest of ½ orange
125g (4oz) caster sugar, plus
   1 tbsp extra
3 large egg whites
1 tbsp cocoa powder, sifted
15g (½oz) hazelnuts, toasted and
   chopped

1 Preheat the oven to 150°C (130°C fan oven) mark 2. Mix the strawberries with the orange zest and 1 tbsp caster sugar. Divide among six ramekins.

2 Put the egg whites into a clean, grease-free bowl and whisk until soft peaks form. Add the remaining sugar and whisk until the whites are stiff and shiny. Fold in the cocoa.

3 Spoon the chocolate meringue over the fruit and sprinkle the hazelnuts on top.

4 Bake for 20–25 minutes until the meringue is crisp on the outside and soft in the middle. Serve at once.

★ TRY SOMETHING DIFFERENT
● *Use raspberries instead of strawberries, leaving them whole.*
● *Try lightly toasted flaked almonds instead of the hazelnuts.*

Almond Toffee Meringues

Preparation Time 35 minutes • Cooking Time 22–25 minutes, plus cooling and drying • Makes 4 •
Per Meringue 458 calories, 4g fat (of which trace saturates), 95g carbohydrate, 0.2g salt • Easy

oil to oil
25g (1oz) light muscovado sugar
100g (3½oz) egg whites (about
   3 medium eggs)
225g (8oz) caster sugar
25g (1oz) flaked almonds
lightly whipped cream to serve

**FOR THE MARINATED
   SUMMER FRUIT**
125ml (4fl oz) crème de cassis
juice of 1 orange
2 tbsp redcurrant jelly
200g (7oz) raspberries
4 nectarines, halved, stoned and
   sliced

1 To make the marinated fruit, put
the crème de cassis, orange juice
and redcurrant jelly into a small
pan. Heat gently to melt, then
bubble for 2–3 minutes until syrupy.
Pour into a large bowl to cool. Add
the raspberries and nectarines and
stir gently. Cover and chill.

2 Preheat the oven to 170°C
(150°C fan oven) mark 3 and
preheat the grill. Lightly oil a baking
sheet and sprinkle the muscovado
sugar over it. Grill for 2–3 minutes
until the sugar begins to bubble
and caramelise. Cool for about
15 minutes, then break the sugar
into a food processor and whiz to
a coarse powder.

3 Put the egg whites and caster
sugar into a large, clean bowl over a
pan of gently simmering water. Stir
until the sugar has dissolved and
the egg white is warm (about
10 minutes). Remove from the heat
and place on a teatowel. Beat with a
hand-held electric whisk for at least
15 minutes or until cold and glossy
and standing in stiff, shiny peaks
when the whisk is lifted. Cover two
baking sheets with baking
parchment. Fold half the powdered
sugar into the meringue mixture.
Spoon four oval mounds on to the
baking sheets, leaving plenty of

space between each. Sprinkle with
flaked almonds and the remaining
powdered sugar. Bake for
20 minutes, then turn off the heat
and leave in the oven to dry out
overnight. Serve with the marinated
fruit and lightly whipped cream.

★ COOK'S TIPS
● *Make sure the bowl does not touch the
hot water while you make the meringues.*
● *The flavour of the marinated fruit will
be even better if you chill it overnight. (If
the syrup thickens during chilling, stir in
1–2 tbsp orange juice.)*

Rhubarb and Raspberry Meringue

Preparation Time 15 minutes • Cooking Time 15–20 minutes • Serves 4 • Per Serving 94 calories, trace fat, 22g carbohydrate, 0.1g salt • Gluten Free • Dairy Free • Easy

450g (1lb) rhubarb, cut into 2.5cm (1in) pieces
75g (3oz) caster sugar
2.5cm (1in) piece preserved stem ginger, finely chopped (optional)
finely grated zest and juice of 1 orange (optional)
75g (3oz) frozen raspberries
1 large egg white

1 Preheat the oven to 180°C (160°C fan) mark 4. Put the rhubarb in a large saucepan with 25g (1oz) caster sugar, the chopped preserved stem ginger, if using, and the orange zest. Cover and cook gently for 2–3 minutes, adding a little orange juice if necessary. Add the raspberries then spoon the mixture into four 150ml (¼ pint) ramekins or ovenproof teacups.

2 Whisk the egg white and remaining sugar together in a heatproof bowl until foamy. Put the bowl over a saucepan of simmering water and continue to whisk for 5 minutes or until it is stiff and shiny.

3 Place a spoonful of meringue mixture on top of each ramekin and bake for 5–10 minutes or until lightly golden.

Tropical Fruit and Coconut Trifle

★

Preparation Time 30 minutes, plus chilling • Serves 16 • Per Serving 404 calories, 29g fat (of which 18g saturates), 33g carbohydrate, 0.2g salt • Easy

1 small pineapple, roughly chopped
2 bananas, thickly sliced
2 × 400g cans mango slices in
    syrup, drained, syrup reserved
2 passion fruits, halved
175g (6oz) plain sponge, such as
    Madeira cake, roughly chopped
3 tbsp dark rum (optional)
200ml (7fl oz) coconut cream
500g carton fresh custard
500g carton Greek yogurt
600ml (1 pint) double cream
6 tbsp dark muscovado sugar

1 Put the pineapple pieces into a large trifle bowl, add the banana and mango slices and spoon the passion fruit pulp over them. Top with the chopped sponge, then pour on the rum, if using, and 6 tbsp of the reserved mango syrup.

2 Mix together the coconut cream and custard and pour the mixture over the sponge.

3 Put the Greek yogurt and double cream into a bowl and whisk until thick. Spoon or pipe the mixture over the custard, then sprinkle with muscovado sugar. Cover and chill for at least 1 hour before serving.

★ GET AHEAD
To prepare ahead *Complete the recipe, cover and chill for up to two days.*

Apricot and Peach Trifle

Preparation Time 20 minutes, plus chilling • Serves 10 • Per Serving 672 calories, 50g fat (of which 24g saturates), 49g carbohydrate, 0.4g salt • Easy

2 packs trifle sponges, each
   containing 8 sponges, or
   1 ready-made Madeira cake –
   about 450g (1lb)
6 tbsp apricot jam
4 tbsp sherry
4 × 400g cans apricots in natural
   fruit juice, drained
2 × 400g cans peaches in natural
   fruit juice, drained
600ml (1 pint) double cream
500g carton fresh custard
250g (9oz) mascarpone cheese
50g (2oz) pecan nuts, toasted

1 Cut the trifle sponges in half horizontally and spread one half with the apricot jam. Cover with the other half to make mini sandwiches. If using cake, cut into slices first, then sandwich together in pairs with jam. Use to line a large glass serving bowl. Drizzle over the sherry, then add the apricots.

2 Put the peaches into a food processor or blender and whiz to a purée. Pour over the apricots.

3 Pour the cream into a large bowl and whip until soft peaks form. Chill. Put the whisk to one side – you needn't rinse it.

4 Put the custard and mascarpone into a large bowl and whisk together briefly to mix well. Pour over the fruit in an even layer.

5 Spoon the whipped cream over the custard mix and scatter the pecans over the top. Chill for at least 1 hour before serving.

★ GET AHEAD
*To **prepare ahead** Complete the recipe to the end of step 2 up to two days ahead.*
*To **use** When ready to serve, complete the recipe. If you'd rather make the whole thing two days ahead, that's fine, but the cream will be firmer, rather than soft and luscious. Don't scatter over the toasted pecans until just before serving.*

White Chocolate and Red Fruit Trifle

Preparation Time 45 minutes, plus chilling • Cooking Time 15 minutes, plus cooling • Serves 8 • Per Serving 943 calories, 68g fat (of which 41g saturates), 82g carbohydrate, 0.5g salt • **Easy**

3 × 500g bags frozen mixed berries

125g (4oz) golden caster sugar, plus 1 tsp

250g (9oz) biscotti or cantuccini biscuits, plus crushed biscuits (see page 225) to decorate

5 tbsp dessert wine or fruit juice (such as cranberry and orange)

FOR THE TOPPING

450ml (¾ pint) double cream, lightly whipped

200g (7oz) white chocolate, broken into pieces and melted (see page 273)

500g carton fresh custard (at room temperature)

500ml (18fl oz) crème fraîche, beaten until smooth

1 Put the berries into a large pan with 125g (4oz) caster sugar and heat gently for about 5 minutes or until the sugar has dissolved and the berries have thawed. Sieve the mixture over a bowl to catch the juices. Pour the juices back into the pan, then tip the berries into the bowl. Bring the juices to the boil, then reduce the heat and simmer for 10 minutes or until reduced to about 150ml (¼ pint). Pour over the berries and leave to cool.

2 Lay the biscuits over the bottom of a 3 litre (5¼ pint) trifle dish and sprinkle with the dessert wine or fruit juice. Scatter the cooled berries over the top.

3 To make the topping, transfer half the cream to a bowl, cover and chill; leave the rest of the cream at room temperature. Pour the melted chocolate into a cold bowl and gradually fold in the custard. Fold in the room-temperature whipped cream. Pour the chocolate custard over the fruit to cover it evenly. Fold the chilled cream into the crème fraîche with the 1 tsp sugar, then spoon over the custard. Chill for 2 hours. Remove from the fridge 20 minutes before serving. Scatter crushed biscuits over the top.

★ COOK'S TIP
Remember to remove the carton of custard from the fridge 20 minutes before you start to make the trifle, to bring it to room temperature.

Caramelised Orange Trifle

★

Preparation Time 40 minutes, plus chilling • Cooking Time about 20 minutes, plus cooling • Serves 16 •
Per Serving 376 calories, 16g fat (of which 10g saturates), 50g carbohydrate, 0.2g salt • Gluten Free • For the Confident Cook

125g (4oz) light muscovado sugar

2 × 135g packs orange jelly, broken
   into cubes

100ml (3½fl oz) brandy

10 oranges, peeled and all pith
   removed

150g (5oz) ratafia biscuits

4 tbsp sweet sherry

500g carton fresh custard

300ml (½ pint) double cream

2 × 250g cartons mascarpone
   cheese

¼ tsp vanilla extract

125g (4oz) granulated sugar

1 Put the muscovado sugar into a large heavy-based pan. Add 100ml (3½fl oz) water and dissolve the sugar over a low heat. Increase the heat and cook for 5 minutes or until the sugar is syrupy and thick. Remove from the heat and add 450ml (¾ pint) boiling water (the sugar will splutter). Add the jelly and stir until dissolved. Add the brandy and put to one side.

2 Slice the orange flesh into rounds, putting any juice to one side. Add the juice – about 125ml (4fl oz) – to the jelly and leave to cool. Tip the ratafia biscuits into the base of a 3.5 litre (6¼ pint) bowl and drizzle with sherry. Arrange the orange rounds on top, then pour the jelly over. Chill for 4 hours until set.

3 Pour the custard over the top and smooth over. Put the cream, mascarpone and vanilla extract into a bowl and combine with a hand-held electric mixer. Spoon three-quarters of the mixture on to the custard and smooth the surface. Put the remainder in a piping bag and pipe 10 swirls around the edge. Chill in the fridge.

4 Line a large baking sheet with baking parchment. Half-fill the sink with cold water. Heat the granulated sugar in a heavy-based pan until dissolved. Increase the heat and cook to a golden caramel, then plunge the base of the pan into a sink of cold water. Dip a fork into the pan and pick up the caramel, then flick it back and forth over the parchment to form fine strands. Put the sugar strands on top of the trifle and serve.

★ TRY SOMETHING
DIFFERENT
For an alternative decoration, try sprinkling some silver dragees, crystallised flowers, toasted flaked almonds or grated chocolate over instead of the sugar strands.

Tiramisu Torte

★

Preparation Time 40 minutes • Cooking Time 45 minutes, plus cooling and chilling • Serves 10 • Per Serving 682 calories, 50g fat (of which 30g saturates), 51g carbohydrate, 0.9g salt • Easy

275g (10oz) amaretti biscuits, ratafias or macaroons
75g (3oz) unsalted butter, melted
700g (1½lb) mascarpone or full-fat cream cheese (at room temperature)
150g (5oz) caster sugar
3 medium eggs, separated
25g (1oz) plain flour, sifted
3 tbsp dark rum
½ tsp vanilla extract
175g (6oz) plain chocolate (at least 50% cocoa solids)
1 tbsp finely ground coffee
3 tbsp Tia Maria or other coffee liqueur

1 Put the biscuits into a food processor and whiz until finely ground. (Alternatively, put them in a plastic bag and crush with a rolling pin.) Add the melted butter and stir until well mixed. Spoon into a 23cm (9in) springform cake tin. Using the back of a spoon, press evenly over the base and 4cm (1½in) up the sides to form a shell. Chill for at least 30 minutes or until firm.

2 Preheat the oven to 200°C (180°C fan oven) mark 6. Using a wooden spoon or an electric mixer, beat the cheese until smooth. Add the sugar and beat again until smooth, then beat in the egg yolks. Transfer half of the mixture to another bowl and stir in the flour, rum and vanilla.

3 Melt the chocolate in a heatproof bowl over a pan of gently simmering water, making sure the base of the bowl doesn't touch the water. Cool slightly, then stir in the coffee and coffee liqueur. Stir into the remaining half of the cheese mixture.

4 Put the egg whites into a clean, grease-free bowl and whisk until soft peaks form, then fold half the egg whites into each flavoured cheese mixture. Spoon alternate mounds of the two mixtures into the biscuit case until full. Using a knife, swirl them together for a marbled effect.

5 Bake for 45 minutes, covering with foil if it seems to be over-browning. At this stage the torte will be soft in the middle. Leave in the switched-off oven with the door slightly ajar, to cool; it will firm up during this time. Chill for several hours before serving.

Dessert Cakes and Strudels

Strawberry and Chocolate Muffins

Preparation Time 5 minutes • Serves 4 • Per Serving 420 calories, 20g fat (of which 12g saturates), 55g carbohydrate, 0.6g salt • Easy

2 chocolate muffins, halved
4 tbsp mascarpone cheese, softened
600g (1lb 5oz) strawberries, hulled
  and roughly chopped
plain chocolate (at least 70% cocoa
  solids), grated, to decorate

1 Divide the muffin halves among four plates. Top each half with a tablespoon of the mascarpone and a good spoonful of the chopped strawberries.

2 Sprinkle with the grated chocolate and serve immediately.

Apple and Blueberry Cake

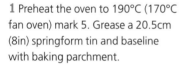

Preparation Time 30 minutes • Cooking Time 45–55 minutes, plus cooling • Cuts into 8 slices • Per Slice 396 calories, 15g fat (of which 9g saturates), 65g carbohydrate, 0.6g salt • **Easy**

125g (4oz) unsalted butter, diced,
  plus extra to grease
225g (8oz) self-raising flour, sifted
½ tsp salt
175g (6oz) granulated sugar, golden
  if possible
2 large eggs, beaten
2 large Granny Smith apples,
  peeled, cored and sliced
140g (4½oz) fresh blueberries
175g (6oz) apricot jam
1 tbsp lemon juice

1 Preheat the oven to 190°C (170°C fan oven) mark 5. Grease a 20.5cm (8in) springform tin and baseline with baking parchment.

2 Put the flour and salt into a large mixing bowl, add the diced butter and rub in the flour until the mixture looks like fine breadcrumbs. Add 140g (4½oz) sugar and the beaten eggs and stir well.

3 Spread half the mixture in a thin layer in the tin, then layer the sliced apples and the blueberries evenly over the surface, setting aside a little of the fruit for the top of the cake. Sprinkle with the remaining sugar, then spoon in the rest of the cake mixture. Add the remaining apple slices and blueberries, pressing them down slightly into the mixture.

4 Bake for 45–55 minutes until risen and firm to the touch and a skewer inserted into the centre comes out clean. Cool in the tin for 10 minutes, then turn out on to a wire rack to cool completely.

5 Warm the jam and lemon juice in a small pan until evenly combined. Sieve the mixture and, while it's still warm, brush it over the top of the cake. Serve immediately.

★ FREEZING TIP
To freeze Complete the recipe to the end of step 4. Wrap the cake in a freezer bag and freeze for up to one month.
To use Thaw for 3 hours at cool room temperature, then complete the recipe. To serve warm, heat individual cake slices in the microwave on full power for 1 minute per slice.

Rhubarb Crumble Cake

Preparation Time 25 minutes • **Cooking Time** 1 hour–1 hour 20 minutes, plus cooling • **Cuts into 10 slices** •
Per Slice 394 calories, 25g fat (of which 11g saturates), 37g carbohydrate, 0.5g salt • **Easy**

150g (5oz) unsalted butter,
   softened, plus extra to grease
400g (14oz) rhubarb, trimmed and
   cut into 2.5cm (1in) pieces
175g (6oz) golden caster sugar
2 large eggs, beaten
100g (3½oz) ground almonds
3 tbsp milk
125g (4oz) self-raising flour
1 tsp cinnamon
½ tsp ground ginger
50g (2oz) flaked almonds
icing sugar to dust
custard and Poached Rhubarb to
   serve (see Cook's Tip)

FOR THE CRUMBLE TOPPING
40g (1½oz) cold unsalted butter,
   diced
50g (2oz) plain flour
40g (1½oz) demerara sugar

1 Preheat the oven to 180°C (160°C fan oven) mark 4. Grease a 20.5cm (8in) springform tin and line with greaseproof paper.

2 Put the rhubarb into a pan with 25g (1oz) caster sugar and 100ml (3½fl oz) water and simmer for about 5 minutes. Strain and put to one side.

3 To make the topping, rub the chilled diced butter into the plain flour until the mixture resembles breadcrumbs. Stir in the demerara sugar and put to one side.

4 Beat the softened butter and remaining caster sugar together until pale and fluffy. Gradually add the eggs, beating well after each addition. Using a large metal spoon, fold in the ground almonds, milk, self-raising flour and spices, then fold in the flaked almonds. Turn into the prepared tin, smooth the surface and top with rhubarb, then sprinkle with the crumble topping.

5 Bake for 1–1¼ hours until a skewer inserted into the centre comes out clean. Leave to cool in the tin for 5 minutes, then remove from the tin. Dust with icing sugar and serve warm with custard and poached rhubarb, or cool on a wire rack and serve cold.

★ COOK'S TIP
Poached Rhubarb
Chop 250g (9oz) rhubarb into 6.5cm (2½in) pieces. Put into a pan with 50g (2oz) caster sugar, 25g (1oz) preserved stem ginger, cut into slivers, and 75ml (3fl oz) water. Cover and simmer gently for 5 minutes.

★ GET AHEAD
To prepare ahead *Complete the recipe without icing sugar up to one day in advance. Store in an airtight container.*
To use *Dust with icing sugar to serve.*

Lemon and Berry Crunch Cake

Preparation Time 40 minutes, plus setting • Cooking Time 50 minutes–1 hour, plus cooling • Serves 8 •
Per Serving 428 calories, 18g fat (of which 10g saturates), 67g carbohydrate, 0.5g salt • **Easy**

150g (5oz) unsalted butter,
    softened, plus extra to grease
2 medium eggs, plus 1 medium
    egg yolk
a pinch of salt
150g (5oz) caster sugar
150g (5oz) self-raising flour, sifted
grated zest and juice of 1 lemon
125g (4oz) raspberries and
    blueberries
white currants, blackcurrants, wild
    strawberries and crème fraîche
    or Greek yogurt to serve

**FOR THE LEMON CRUNCH
    TOPPING**
25ml (1fl oz) bottled lemon juice
    (see Cook's Tips)
225g (8oz) caster sugar
25g (1oz) rough white sugar cubes,
    lightly crushed

1 Preheat the oven to 170°C (150°C
fan oven) mark 3. Grease and
baseline a 1.1 litre (2 pint) loaf tin.

2 Lightly beat the eggs and egg yolk
with the salt. Put the butter and
sugar in a bowl and cream together
until light and fluffy. Gradually beat
in the eggs, beating for 10 minutes.

3 Fold in the flour with the lemon
zest and 2 tbsp of the juice (put
the rest to one side). Fold in the
raspberries and blueberries. Spoon
the mixture into the prepared tin
and bake for 50 minutes–1 hour.
Leave in the tin for 5 minutes, then
turn out on to a wire rack to cool.

4 To make the topping, mix the
reserved fresh lemon juice, bottled
lemon juice and caster sugar
together in a bowl. Spoon over the
cake and sprinkle the top with
crushed sugar. Put to one side for
1 hour. Slice and serve with berries
and crème fraîche or yogurt.

⭐ COOK'S TIPS
● *We used bottled lemon juice, as it
gives a more intense lemony flavour than
fresh juice.*
● *The weight of the fruit may make it
sink towards the bottom of the cake.
Don't worry if this happens – it will still
taste just as wonderful.*
● *Other summer berries such as
blackberries, loganberries and
blackcurrants can be used, if you like.*

Raspberry and Peach Cake

Preparation Time 15 minutes • Cooking Time 1–1¼ hours, plus cooling • Cuts into 8 slices • Per Slice 405 calories, 24g fat (of which 14g saturates), 44g carbohydrate, 0.8g salt • Easy

200g (7oz) unsalted butter, melted, plus extra to grease
250g (9oz) self-raising flour, sifted
100g (3½oz) golden caster sugar
4 medium eggs, beaten
125g (4oz) raspberries
2 large, almost-ripe peaches or nectarines, halved, stoned and sliced
4 tbsp apricot jam
juice of ½ lemon

1 Preheat the oven to 190°C (170°C fan oven) mark 5. Grease a 20.5cm (8in) springform cake tin and baseline with baking parchment.

2 Put the flour and sugar into a large bowl. Make a well in the centre and add the melted butter and the eggs. Mix well.

3 Spread half the mixture over the base of the cake tin and add half the raspberries and sliced peaches or nectarines. Spoon on the remaining cake mixture, smooth over, then add the remaining raspberries and peaches or nectarines, pressing them down into the mixture slightly.

4 Bake for 1–1¼ hours until risen and golden and a skewer inserted into the centre comes out clean. Remove from the oven and leave in the tin to cool for 10 minutes.

5 Warm the jam and the lemon juice together in a small pan and brush over the cake to glaze. Serve warm or at room temperature.

★ TO STORE
Store in an airtight container. It will keep for up to one week.

Tropical Fruit Cake

Preparation Time 40 minutes • **Cooking Time** 1 hour 20 minutes, plus cooling • **Cuts into 8 slices** • **Per Slice** 857 calories, 60g fat (of which 32g saturates), 74g carbohydrate, 0.3g salt • **For the Confident Cook**

125g (4oz) unsalted butter,
softened, plus extra to grease
125g (4oz) caster sugar
grated zest of 1 orange and
3 tbsp juice
2 large eggs, lightly beaten
a pinch of salt
125g (4oz) semolina
125g (4oz) desiccated coconut
200g (7oz) ground almonds
1 tsp baking powder
300ml (½ pint) double cream
icing sugar to taste
vanilla extract to taste
1 mango, 1 papaya or pineapple,
1 star fruit and 1 banana, peeled
and sliced
6 lychees, peeled and stoned
50g (2oz) coconut slices (see
Cook's Tip)
125g (4oz) granulated sugar

FOR THE CITRUS SYRUP
pared zest of 1 orange and juice of
2 oranges
pared zest of 1 lemon and juice of
3 lemons
125g (4oz) caster sugar

1 Preheat the oven to 170°C (150°C fan oven) mark 3. Grease a 23cm (9in) springform cake tin and baseline with baking parchment.

2 To make the cake, whisk the butter and 125g (4oz) caster sugar together in a food processor (or use a hand-held electric whisk) until pale and fluffy. Beat the orange zest, eggs and salt together, then beat into the butter mixture, a spoonful at a time. Using a large metal spoon, fold in the semolina, desiccated coconut, ground almonds, baking powder and orange juice. Spoon the mixture into the prepared tin and smooth the surface.

3 Bake for 45–50 minutes until a skewer inserted into the centre comes out clean. Leave to cool in the tin for 15 minutes, then turn out on to a wire rack to cool completely.

4 Meanwhile, make the citrus syrup. Put the orange and lemon zests and juice, caster sugar and 450ml (¾ pint) water into a pan. Bring to the boil and bubble for 15–20 minutes until syrupy. Put to one side to cool.

5 Cut about 1cm (½ in) from the centre of the cake, crumble and keep the crumbs to one side. Prick the cake with a fine skewer – without piercing right through, or the syrup will run through – and spoon the syrup over it. Set aside 3 tbsp of the syrup.

6 Whip the cream until soft peaks form, then add the icing sugar and vanilla extract to taste. Carefully fold in the reserved cake crumbs, one-third of the prepared fruit and the reserved syrup. Stir gently to combine, taking care not to mash the fruit. Spoon on to the cake. Decorate with the remaining fruit and coconut slices.

7 For the decoration, line a large baking sheet with baking parchment. Half-fill the sink with cold water. Heat the granulated sugar in a heavy-based pan until dissolved. Increase the heat and cook to a golden caramel, then plunge the base of the pan into a sink of cold water. Dip a fork into the pan and pick up the caramel, then flick it back and forth over the parchment to form fine strands. Put the sugar strands on top of the cake and serve.

⭐ COOK'S TIP
For fresh coconut slices, use a vegetable peeler to pare off thin slices, sprinkle with a little caster sugar and grill until lightly browned.

⭐ GET AHEAD
To prepare ahead *Complete the recipe to the end of step 3. Wrap the tin well in clingfilm and greaseproof paper and store in a cool place. It will keep for two to three days.*
To use *Complete the recipe.*

Warm Lemon Syrup Cake

★

Preparation Time 15 minutes • Cooking Time 1 hour, plus cooling and soaking • Cuts into 12 slices •
Per Slice 360 calories, 18g fat (of which 10g saturates), 49g carbohydrate, 0.5g salt • Easy

225g (8oz) unsalted butter,
    softened, plus extra to grease
grated zest of 2 lemons and 2 tbsp
    lemon juice
225g (8oz) caster sugar
4 large eggs, beaten
225g (8oz) self-raising flour, sifted
75g (3oz) candied lemon peel, finely
    chopped (optional)

**FOR THE SYRUP AND
    DECORATION**
175g (6oz) caster sugar
finely sliced zest and strained juice
    of 3 lemons

1 Preheat the oven to 180°C (160°C
fan oven) mark 4. Grease a 20.5cm
(8in) round deep cake tin and
baseline with baking parchment.

2 Cream the butter and lemon zest
together. Gradually beat in the
sugar, followed by the eggs; the
mixture should be stiff. Fold in the
flour, candied peel, if using, and
lemon juice. Spoon the mixture
into the prepared tin, smooth the
surface and bake for about
1 hour or until golden.

3 Meanwhile, prepare the syrup and
topping. Put the sugar, lemon juice
and 75ml (2½fl oz) water into a pan.
Warm gently until the sugar
dissolves, then bring to the boil and
bubble for 1 minute. Leave to cool.

4 As soon as the cake is cooked,
turn out into a shallow dish and
immediately spoon the syrup over
it. Leave for about 30 minutes for
the syrup to soak in. Serve warm,
topped with the sliced lemon zest.

Mincemeat Streusel

Preparation Time 15 minutes • Cooking Time 45 minutes, plus cooling • Serves 8 • Per Serving 429 calories, 21g fat (of which 3g saturates), 61g carbohydrate, 0.3g salt • Easy

50g (2oz) unsalted butter, chilled and cut into cubes, plus extra to grease

340g pack sweet shortcrust pastry

75g (3oz) self-raising flour, sifted, plus extra to dust

finely grated zest of ½ lemon

50g (2oz) light muscovado sugar

25g (1oz) ground almonds

350g jar mincemeat

Brandy Butter (see Cook's Tip, page 26) or thick cream to serve

1 Preheat the oven to 180°C (160°C fan oven) mark 4. Grease a 33 × 10cm (13 × 4in) fluted rectangular tin and baseline with greaseproof paper.

2 Roll out the pastry on a lightly floured worksurface and use to line the prepared tin. Prick the pastry with a fork, cover with baking parchment and baking beans and bake for 15 minutes. Remove the parchment and beans and bake for a further 15 minutes, then leave to cool for 5 minutes. Do not turn off the oven.

3 Meanwhile, to make the streusel topping, put the flour and lemon zest in a bowl. Add the butter and rub it in until the mixture resembles crumbs. Stir in the sugar and ground almonds.

4 Spread the mincemeat evenly over the pastry and sprinkle the streusel on top. Bake for 15 minutes until the topping is golden. Leave to cool for 30 minutes, then remove from the tin. Slice and serve warm with Brandy Butter or cream.

Apple and Cranberry Strudel

Preparation Time 20 minutes • Cooking Time 40 minutes • Serves 6 • Per Serving 178 calories, 2g fat (of which trace saturates), 40g carbohydrate, 0g salt • **Dairy Free** • **Easy**

700g (1½lb) red apples, quartered, cored and thickly sliced

1 tbsp lemon juice

2 tbsp golden caster sugar

100g (3½oz) dried cranberries

6 sheets of filo pastry

1 tbsp olive oil

crème fraîche or Greek yogurt to serve

1 Preheat the oven to 190°C (170°C fan oven) mark 5. Put the apples into a bowl and mix with the lemon juice, 1 tbsp sugar and the cranberries.

2 Lay three sheets of filo pastry side by side, overlapping the long edges. Brush with a little oil. Cover with three more sheets of filo and brush again. Tip the apple mixture on to the pastry, leaving a 2cm (¾in)

border all round. Brush the border with a little water, then roll up the strudel from a long edge. Put on to a non-stick baking sheet, brush with the remaining oil and sprinkle with the remaining sugar.

3 Bake for 40 minutes or until the pastry is golden and the apples are soft. Serve with crème fraîche or Greek yogurt.

Spiced Nut Strudel

Preparation Time 30 minutes • Cooking Time 30 minutes • Serves 8 • Per Serving 405 calories, 26g fat
(of which 7g saturates), 38g carbohydrate, 0.4g salt • Easy

50g (2oz) glacé cherries, chopped
200g (7oz) mixed chopped nuts,
  such as walnuts, hazelnuts and
  almonds
50g (2oz) raisins
50g (2oz) fresh white breadcrumbs
25g (1oz) dark muscovado sugar
25g (1oz) chopped candied peel
1 tsp each ground cinnamon and
  ground ginger
75g (3oz) unsalted butter
6 tbsp maple syrup, plus extra
  to drizzle
1 large egg, beaten
8 large sheets filo pastry, thawed
  if frozen

1 Preheat the oven to 190°C (170°C fan oven) mark 5. Put the cherries into a bowl with the nuts, raisins, breadcrumbs, sugar, candied peel, cinnamon and ginger. Melt 50g (2oz) butter and add to the mixture with the maple syrup and egg. Mix well.

2 Melt the remaining butter. Lay one sheet of filo pastry on a worksurface, then brush it lightly with melted butter. Take a second sheet of filo pastry and position it so that it overlaps the first sheet by 5cm (2in), then brush lightly with melted butter.

3 Spoon half of the strudel filling over the filo pastry, leaving a 5cm (2in) border all round. Lay another two sheets of filo pastry over the filling, brushing them with butter. Spoon the remaining filling on top. Fold the two long edges of the pastry over the edge of the filling. Loosely roll up like a Swiss roll to enclose the filling. Carefully transfer the strudel to a baking sheet, placing it seam side down. Brush lightly with melted butter.

4 Cut the remaining filo pastry into strips. Crumple the filo strips and arrange them on top of the strudel. Brush with the remaining melted butter and bake for 30 minutes or until the pastry is a deep golden brown. Drizzle a little maple syrup over and serve warm.

★ GET AHEAD
To prepare ahead *Complete the recipe, cool and store in an airtight container in a cool place for up to two days.*
To use *Preheat the oven to 180°C (160°C fan oven) mark 4 and heat the pie for 15–20 minutes.*

Pear and Cranberry Strudel

Preparation Time 20 minutes • **Cooking Time** 40–45 minutes • **Serves** 8 • **Per Serving** 190 calories, 12g fat (of which 6g saturates), 9g carbohydrate, 0.2g salt • **Easy**

75g (3oz) butter, melted, plus extra
  to grease
125g (4oz) fresh cranberries
550g (1¼lb) Williams or Comice
  pears, cored and sliced
50g (2oz) Brazil nuts, chopped
  and toasted
grated zest and juice of 1 lemon
25g (1oz) golden caster sugar
1 tbsp fresh white breadcrumbs
1 tsp ground cinnamon
7 sheets filo pastry, thawed if
  frozen
icing sugar to dust

1 Preheat the oven to 190°C (170°C fan oven) mark 5. Grease a large baking sheet. Toss the cranberries with the pears, nuts and lemon juice. Mix the lemon zest with 1 tbsp caster sugar, the breadcrumbs and cinnamon, then combine with the cranberry mixture.

2 Lay a clean teatowel on a board and put three sheets of filo pastry on it, each overlapping the other by 12.5cm (5in) to make a 56 × 48cm (22 × 19in) rectangle. Brush with melted butter, then put three more sheets on top and brush again.

3 Spoon the pear mixture on to the pastry and roll up from a long edge. Carefully lift on to the baking sheet, placing it seam side down. Cut the remaining filo pastry into strips, crumple and place on the strudel; brush with melted butter. Sprinkle the strudel with the remaining caster sugar and bake for 40–45 minutes, covering with foil if the top browns too quickly. Dust the strudel with icing sugar. Serve warm.

★ TRY SOMETHING
DIFFERENT
Replace the lemon zest and juice with orange, the cranberries with blueberries and the Brazil nuts with hazelnuts.

Apple and Blueberry Strudel

★

Preparation Time 15 minutes • Cooking Time 40 minutes • Serves 6 • Per Serving 178 calories, 2g fat
(of which trace saturates), 40g carbohydrate, 0g salt • Dairy Free • Easy

700g (1½lb) red apples, quartered,
    cored and thickly sliced
1 tbsp lemon juice
2 tbsp golden caster sugar
100g (3½oz) dried blueberries
1 tbsp olive oil
6 sheets of filo pastry, thawed
    if frozen
crème fraîche to serve

1 Preheat the oven to 190°C (170°C
fan oven) mark 5. Put the apples
into a large bowl and mix with the
lemon juice, 1 tbsp sugar and the
dried blueberries.

2 Warm the oil. Lay three sheets of
filo pastry side by side, overlapping
the long edges. Brush with the oil.
Cover with three more sheets of filo
and brush again.

3 Tip the apple mixture on to the
pastry and roll up from a long edge.
Put on to a non-stick baking sheet.
Brush with the remaining oil and
sprinkle with the remaining sugar.
Bake for 40 minutes or until the
pastry is golden and the apples soft.
Serve with crème fraîche.

Grilled Coconut Cake

Preparation Time 5 minutes • Cooking Time 5 minutes • Serves 4 • Per Serving 434 calories, 24g fat
(of which 0g saturates), 51g carbohydrate, 1g salt • Easy

4 thick slices coconut or
    Madeira cake
icing sugar to dust
Greek yogurt or crème fraîche and
    fresh fruit to serve

1 Preheat the grill. Cook the cake
under the hot grill until lightly
charred on both sides. Dust with
icing sugar and serve with thick
Greek yogurt and fresh fruit, cut
into bite-size pieces.

★ TRY SOMETHING
DIFFERENT
Passion Fruit Sauce
Scoop the pulp from 8 ripe passion fruits
into a food processor and briefly whiz to
loosen the seeds and pulp. Transfer to a
small pan with 1 tbsp sugar and 2 tbsp
coconut rum liqueur, such as Malibu,
and simmer for 2–3 minutes, until syrupy.
Cool. Drizzle over the grilled cake and
serve with fresh tropical fruits.

Orange and White Chocolate Cake

★

Preparation Time 35 minutes, plus chilling • Cooking Time 40 minutes, plus cooling and soaking • Cuts into 14 slices •
Per Slice 544 calories, 35g fat (of which 18g saturates), 48g carbohydrate, 0.3g salt • For the Confident Cook

butter to grease

6 large eggs, separated

250g (9oz) golden caster sugar

150g (5oz) self-raising flour, sifted

150g (5oz) ground almonds

grated zest of 2 oranges and juice
    of 3 large oranges

100g (3½oz) golden granulated
    sugar

225ml (8fl oz) sweet white wine

350g (12oz) strawberries, thinly
    sliced

FOR THE WHITE
    CHOCOLATE GANACHE

225g (8oz) white chocolate,
    chopped

600ml (1 pint) double cream

1 Preheat the oven to 180°C (160°C fan oven) mark 4. Grease a 23cm (9in) round deep cake tin and line with baking parchment.

2 Put the egg whites into a clean, grease-free bowl and whisk until soft peaks form. Gradually beat in 50g (2oz) caster sugar and whisk until the mixture is stiff and glossy. Put the egg yolks and remaining sugar into another bowl and whisk until soft and mousse-like. Carefully stir in the flour, fold in one-third of the egg whites, then fold in the remaining egg whites, the ground almonds and orange zest. Pour the mixture into the prepared tin.

3 Bake for 35 minutes or until a skewer inserted into the centre comes out clean. Leave to cool in the tin for 10 minutes, then turn out on to a wire rack and leave to cool completely.

4 Put the orange juice, granulated sugar and wine into a small pan and stir over a low heat until the sugar has dissolved. Bring to the boil and bubble for 5 minutes or until syrupy. Cool and put to one side.

5 To make the ganache, put the chocolate into a heatproof bowl with half the cream. Put the bowl over a pan of gently simmering water, making sure the base of the bowl doesn't touch the water, and leave until the chocolate melts, then stir to combine. Remove the bowl from the pan and cool, then beat with a wooden spoon until cold and thick. Whip the remaining cream lightly and beat a large spoonful into the chocolate cream to loosen it. Fold in the remainder. Chill for 2 hours.

6 Cut the cake in half horizontally, pierce all over with a skewer and put it, cut sides up, on a baking sheet. Drizzle the orange syrup over the cake and leave to soak in. Spread a quarter of the ganache over the base cake and scatter with 225g (8oz) strawberries. Cover with the top half of the cake and press down lightly. Using a palette knife, smooth the remaining ganache over the top and sides of the cake. Chill for up to 4 hours.

7 Decorate with the remaining strawberries and serve.

Basics

Sweet Shortcrust Pastry

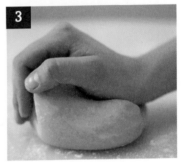

To make 125g (4oz) pastry, you will need:

125g (4oz) plain flour, a pinch of salt, 50g (2oz) unsalted butter, cut into small pieces, 2 medium egg yolks and 50g (2oz) caster sugar.

1 Sift the flour and salt into a bowl and add the butter. Using your fingertips or a pastry cutter, rub or cut the butter into the flour until the mixture resembles fine breadcrumbs.

2 Using a fork, mix in the egg yolks, sugar and 1½ tsp water until the mixture holds together; add a little more water if necessary.

3 Gather the dough in your hands and knead lightly. Form into a ball, wrap tightly in clingfilm and chill for at least 30 minutes before using. (This 'relaxes' the pastry and prevents the pastry shrinking when it is baked.)

DOS AND DON'TS OF BAKING

★ Weigh out all the ingredients carefully before starting the recipe, so that you have everything to hand when you begin to make the cake.

★ Always work in metric or imperial – never mix the two measurements.
★ Allow the oven to preheat to the correct temperature.

★ Try not to be heavy-handed – when folding in flour, use light strokes so the air doesn't get knocked out.

Accompaniments

Vanilla Custard

Perfect as an accompaniment to many desserts, a simple vanilla custard can be served hot or cold.

To serve eight, you will need:
600ml (1 pint) full-fat milk, 1 vanilla pod or 1 tbsp vanilla extract, 6 large egg yolks, 2 tbsp golden caster sugar, 2 tbsp cornflour.

1 Put the milk into a pan. Split the vanilla pod and scrape the seeds into the pan, then drop in the pod. If using vanilla extract, pour it in. Bring to the boil, then turn off the heat and leave to cool for 5 minutes.

2 Put the egg yolks, sugar and cornflour into a bowl and whisk to blend. Remove the vanilla pod from the milk and gradually whisk the warm milk into the egg mixture.

3 Rinse out the pan. Pour the custard back in and heat gently, stirring constantly, for 2–3 minutes.

The mixture should thicken enough to coat the back of a wooden spoon in a thin layer. Remove the pan from the heat.

★ COOK'S TIP
Make custard up to four hours in advance. If you are not serving the custard immediately, pour it into a jug. Cover the surface with a circle of wet greaseproof paper to prevent a skin from forming, then cover with clingfilm and chill. To serve hot, reheat very gently.

Raspberry Coulis

Chilled fruit purées are great with ice cream and meringues.

To serve four to six, you will need:
225g (8oz) raspberries, 2 tbsp Kirsch or framboise eau de vie (optional), icing sugar to taste.

1 Put the raspberries into a blender or food processor with the Kirsch or eau de vie, if using. Whiz until they are completely puréed.

2 Transfer the purée to a fine sieve, and press and scrape it through the sieve until nothing is left but the pips.

3 Sweeten with icing sugar to taste and chill until needed.

★ TRY SOMETHING DIFFERENT
Use different soft fruits and liqueurs. For example, try crème de cassis with blackcurrants or Amaretto with apricots.

Making ice cream

Rich and creamy, fresh and fruity or sweet and indulgent, ice creams and iced desserts are easy to make. Good ice cream should have a smooth, creamy texture. Using an ice-cream maker is the best way to achieve it, but freezing and breaking up the ice crystals by hand works well, too.

Vanilla Ice Cream

To serve four to six, you will need:
300ml (½ pint) milk, 1 vanilla pod, split lengthways, 3 medium egg yolks, 75g (3oz) golden caster sugar, 300ml (½ pint) double cream.

1 Put the milk and vanilla pod into a pan. Heat slowly until almost boiling. Cool for 20 minutes, then remove the vanilla pod. Whisk the egg yolks and sugar together in a large bowl until thick and creamy. Gradually whisk in the milk, then strain back into the pan.

2 Cook over a low heat, stirring with a wooden spoon, until thick enough to coat the back of the spoon – do not boil. Pour into a chilled bowl and leave to cool.

3 Whisk the cream into the custard. Pour into an ice-cream maker and freeze or churn according to the manufacturer's instructions or make by hand (see opposite). Store in a covered freezerproof container for up to two months. Put the ice cream in the fridge for 15–20 minutes before serving to soften slightly.

★ TRY SOMETHING DIFFERENT

Fruit Ice Cream
Sweeten 300ml (½ pint) fruit purée (such as rhubarb, gooseberry, raspberry or strawberry) to taste, then stir into the cooked custard and churn.

Chocolate Ice Cream
Omit the vanilla and add 125g (4oz) plain chocolate to the milk. Heat gently until melted, then bring almost to the boil and proceed as above.

Coffee Ice Cream
Omit the vanilla and add 150ml (¼ pint) cooled strong coffee to the cooked custard.

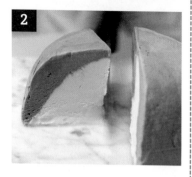

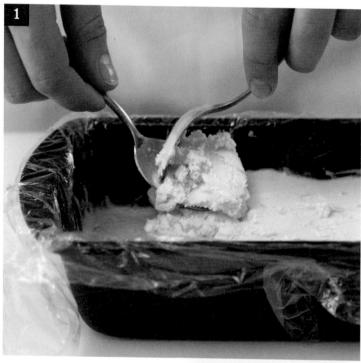

Ice cream bombes

1 Make two flavoured ice creams of distinct colours. While the first ice cream is still soft, press it against the sides and base of a large mould or bowl lined with clingfilm, making a hollow in the centre. Put into the freezer until firm.

2 Fill the hollow with the soft second ice cream and cover with clingfilm. Freeze until firm, then unmould and serve in slices.

Layering

1 For a layered effect, make two or more flavoured ice creams of distinct colours. While the first ice cream is still soft, pack it into a mould lined with clingfilm. Freeze until firm, then layer the second ice cream on top and freeze until firm.

2 Continue in the same way with the remaining flavour(s). Serve cut into slices.

Making ice cream by hand

1 If possible, set the freezer to fast-freeze 1 hour ahead. Pour the ice-cream mixture into a shallow freezerproof container, cover and freeze until partially frozen.

2 Spoon into a bowl and mash with a fork to break up the ice crystals. Return to the container and freeze for a further 2 hours. Repeat and freeze for another 3 hours.

Rippling

1 Make Vanilla Ice Cream (see page 270) and churn in an ice-cream maker (or make by hand) until thick, but soft. Spoon some of the ice cream into a bowl, or directly into a freezerproof container, then drizzle with fruit purée. Top with more ice cream and fruit purée.

2 Pass a wooden spoon handle through the ice cream five or six times to ripple the ice cream. Freeze for 4–5 hours until firm.

THREE QUICK SAUCES FOR ICE CREAM

The Best Chocolate Sauce

1 Put 75g (3oz) chopped plain chocolate into a heatproof bowl set over a pan of simmering water, making sure the base of the bowl doesn't touch the water. Pour in 150ml (¼ pint) double cream, then leave over a low heat for 10 minutes or until the chocolate has melted. Don't stir.

2 Once melted, stir until smooth. Serve with Vanilla Ice Cream (see page 270) or poached pears.

★ TRY SOMETHING DIFFERENT
● *Add a shot of espresso coffee to the cream and chocolate while they are melting together.*
● *Use mint-flavoured chocolate instead of plain.*
● *Pour a little orange or coffee-flavoured liqueur into the bowl while the chocolate and cream are melting.*

Butterscotch Sauce

Heat 50g (2oz) butter, 50g (2oz) golden caster sugar, 75g (3oz) light muscovado sugar and 150g (5oz) golden syrup together gently, stirring, until melted. Cook for 5 minutes, then remove from the heat. Stir in 125ml (4fl oz) double cream, a few drops of vanilla extract and the juice of ½ lemon and stir over a low heat for 1–2 minutes.

Strawberry Sauce

Put 225g (8oz) hulled strawberries and 2–3 tbsp icing sugar into a food processor and whiz well to combine. Sieve the sauce and chill in the fridge until needed.

Using chocolate

As well as being a delicious ingredient in many sweet pies and tarts, chocolate can also be used to make attractive decorations for desserts.

Melting

For cooking or making decorations, chocolate is usually melted first.

1 Break the chocolate into pieces and put into a heatproof bowl or in the top of a double boiler.

2 Set over a pan of gently simmering water, making sure the base of the bowl is not touching the water. Heat very gently until the chocolate starts to melt, then stir only once or twice until it is completely melted.

Shaving

This is very easy to do because the chocolate doesn't need melting.

1 Hold a chocolate bar upright on the worksurface and shave pieces off the edge with a swivel peeler.

2 Alternatively, grate the chocolate against a coarse or medium-coarse grater, to make very fine shavings.

Chocolate curls

1 Melt the chocolate (see above) and spread it out in a thin layer on a marble slab or clean worksurface. Leave to firm up.

2 Use a sharp blade (such as a pastry scraper, a cook's knife or a very stiff spatula) to scrape through the chocolate at a 45-degree angle. The size of the curls will be determined by the width of the blade.

Making cheesecakes

There are many ways to make this perennial favourite, which can be baked or simply chilled and set with gelatine. When baking cheesecakes, watch the temperature – too high a heat can cause the top to crack.

Chilled cheesecake

An uncooked cheesecake is usually set with gelatine and made with a mixture of cream cheese and perhaps some cottage cheese flavoured with lemon zest. The mixture is poured on to a biscuit crumb base (usually made with crushed biscuits mixed with melted butter) that has been pressed into a flan tin then chilled until firm. The whole cheesecake is then chilled to set. Fresh fruit or a fruit coulis can be added as a topping.

★COOK'S TIPS

● *Use a springform cake tin to make the cheesecake easier to unmould.*
● *To slice the cheesecake easily, use a sharp knife dipped into a jug of boiling water and then wiped dry.*
● *You can prepare, cook and chill these cheesecakes up to one day ahead. Keep chilled but bring back to room temperature before serving.*

Baked Chocolate Cheesecake

To serve 12, you will need:
200g (7oz) pack Bourbon biscuits, 50g (2oz) melted butter, 200g (7oz) chopped milk chocolate, 2 × 250g (9oz) tubs mascarpone cheese, 2 × 200g (7oz) tubs ricotta cheese, 4 large eggs, 100g (3½oz) caster sugar, 2–3 drops vanilla extract, cocoa-dusted almonds, cocoa for dusting, crème fraîche to serve.

1 Line a 20.5cm (8in) springform tin with non-stick baking parchment. Whiz the biscuits in a processor to crumbs, then mix in the melted butter. Tip into the tin and press down using the back of a spoon. Chill for 1 hour.

2 Preheat the oven to 180°C (fan 160°C) mark 4. Melt the chocolate in a heatproof bowl over a pan of gently simmering water, making sure the base of the bowl doesn't touch the water. Remove from the heat and leave to cool a little.

3 Beat the mascarpone and ricotta cheeses, eggs, sugar, vanilla extract and melted chocolate together in a bowl. Spoon over the biscuit base and bake for 1–1¼ hours or until golden on top but slightly wobbly in the centre. Turn off the oven, leave the door ajar and leave the cheesecake inside to cool.

4 When cooled, decorate with cocoa-dusted almonds, dust with cocoa and serve with crème fraîche. Cut into slices to serve.

Making batters

Batters can serve a number of purposes and are remarkably versatile for something so simple. All you need to remember when working with them is to mix quickly and lightly.

Pancakes

To make 8 pancakes, you will need:
125g (4oz) plain flour, a pinch of salt,
1 medium egg, 300ml (½ pint) milk, oil
and butter to fry.

1 Sift the flour and salt, make a well in the middle and whisk in the egg. Work in the milk, then leave to stand for 20 minutes. Heat a pan and coat lightly with oil and butter. Coat thinly with batter.

2 Cook the pancake for about 1½–2 minutes until golden, turning carefully turning once.

SWEET PANCAKE FILLINGS

★ Sprinkle with caster sugar and squeeze lemon juice over.

★ Spread with 1 tbsp chocolate spread and top with sliced bananas.

★ Spread with chopped strawberries, drizzle with cream and fold in half.

★ TRY SOMETHING DIFFERENT

● *Orange, Lemon or Lime Pancakes*
Add the finely grated zest of 1 lemon, ½ orange or 1 lime with the milk.

● *Chocolate Pancakes*
Replace 15g (½oz) flour with sifted cocoa powder.

White Chocolate and Berry Crêpes

To serve 4, you will need:
1 quantity of basic pancake mixture (see left), 500g bag frozen mixed berries, thawed, 150g (5oz) white chocolate, broken into pieces, 150ml (¼ pint) carton double cream.

1 Make the pancake mixture as left and leave to stand for 20 minutes.

2 Put the berries into a large pan, place over a medium heat and cook for 5 minutes until heated through.

3 Put the chocolate and cream into a heatproof bowl set over a pan of simmering water, making sure the base of the bowl doesn't touch the water. Heat gently, stirring, for 5 minutes or until the chocolate is just melted. Remove the bowl from the pan and mix the chocolate and cream to a smooth sauce.

4 Meanwhile, cook the pancakes as left and keep warm, interleaved with greaseproof paper. To serve, put two pancakes on each warmed plate and fold each in half. Spoon an eighth of the berries into the middle of each crêpe. Fold over the filling and pour the hot chocolate sauce over the top. Serve at once.

Making meringues

Sweet and simple to make, meringues have two ingredients: egg whites and sugar. Home-made meringues have a lovely freshness that's often lacking in store-bought ones. Stored in a container, they will keep for several weeks.

Simple meringues

For 12 meringues, you will need:

3 medium egg whites, 175g (6oz) caster sugar.

1 Preheat the oven to 170°C (150°C fan oven) mark 3. Cover a baking sheet with baking parchment.

2 Put the egg whites into a large, clean, grease-free bowl. Whisk until soft peaks form. Add a spoonful of sugar and whisk until glossy.

3 Keep adding the sugar a spoonful at a time, whisking thoroughly after each addition, until you have used half the sugar. The mixture should be thick and glossy.

4 Sprinkle the remaining sugar over the mixture and then gently fold in using a metal spoon.

5 Hold a dessertspoon in each hand and pick up a spoonful of mixture in one spoon, then scrape the other one against it to lift the mixture off. Repeat the process a few times, to form a rough oval shape. Using the empty spoon, push the oval on to the baking sheet; hold it just over the sheet so that it doesn't drop from a great height. Continue this process with the remaining mixture to make 12 meringues.

6 Put the meringues in the oven and bake for 15 minutes, then turn the oven off and leave them in the oven to dry out overnight.

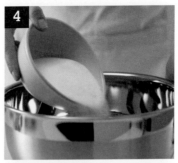

★ TRY SOMETHING DIFFERENT

● *For a richer flavour, add 1 tsp vanilla extract or 50g (2oz) ground almonds or toasted hazelnuts.*

● *You can add a tiny amount of food colouring to make them a pale pink, lilac, and so on.*

● *Shape the meringues using a pastry bag instead of dessertspoons, if you like.*

● *Poaching the meringues keeps them soft throughout, perfect for serving on a pool of custard to make floating islands. To poach meringues, form them into ovals using two soup spoons and poach in a pan of simmering water for about 3 minutes.*

PERFECT MERINGUES

★ Meringues are best baked in the evening, or whenever you know you won't be needing your oven for a good few hours, as they must be left to dry in the turned-off oven for several hours.

★ Get a pan of water simmering gently before you start making the meringues, and line a large baking sheet with greaseproof paper or a silicone baking mat.

★ Make sure the mixing bowl is spotlessly clean, as the tiniest trace of grease can keep the whites from whisking up properly. Also, check that your electric whisk is absolutely clean.

★ If using a freestanding mixer with a whisk attachment, rather than a hand-held whisk, put the bowl of the mixer over the pan of simmering water. Dry it off and return it to the mixer stand.

★ Don't rush the whisking process. If the egg whites are not beaten for long enough, they won't hold their shape when baked.

Pistachio Praline Floating Islands

To serve 4–6, you will need:
vegetable oil, 50g (2oz) unskinned pistachio nuts, 200g (7oz) golden caster sugar, 2 large eggs, separated, 300ml (½ pint) single cream, 300ml (½ pint) milk

1 To make the praline, oil a baking sheet. Put the pistachios and 50g (2oz) sugar into a small heavy-based pan over a low heat. Stir until the sugar dissolves and begins to caramelise. Cook until deep brown, then immediately pour on to the prepared baking sheet. Leave to cool completely, then whiz to a coarse powder in a food processor.

2 To make the meringue, whisk the egg whites in a clean, grease-free bowl until soft peaks form.

Gradually whisk in 75g (3oz) caster sugar until the mixture is very stiff and shiny. Quickly and lightly fold in all but 2 tbsp of the praline.

3 Put the cream, milk and remaining sugar into a medium pan and bring to a gentle simmer. Spoon 5–6 small rounds of meringue mixture into the pan and cook gently for 2–3 minutes or until doubled in size and firm to the touch. Carefully remove the meringues with a slotted spoon and drain on kitchen paper. Repeat with the remaining mixture to make 12–18 poached meringues depending on size.

4 Whisk the egg yolks into the poaching liquid. Heat gently, stirring all the time, until the custard thickens slightly to the consistency of double cream; don't boil.

5 Strain the custard into a serving dish, or individual dishes, and position the meringues on top. Leave to cool, then chill for 30 minutes, or up to 2–3 hours.

6 Serve sprinkled with the reserved pistachio praline.

Fruit basics

All kinds of fruit appears in tarts and pies. A few simple techniques will make it easy to prepare both familiar and not-so-familiar fruit.

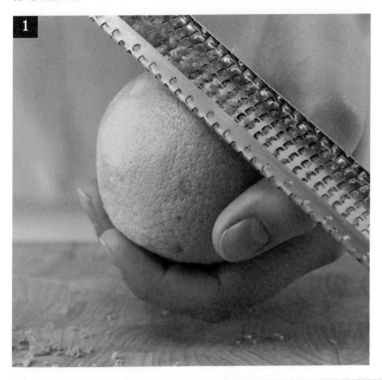

Zesting citrus fruit

Orange and lemon zest are important flavourings in many recipes. Most citrus fruit is sprayed with wax and fungicides or pesticides. Unless you buy unwaxed fruit, wash it with a tiny drop of washing-up liquid and warm water, then rinse with clean water and dry thoroughly on kitchen paper.

1 To use a grater, rub the fruit over the grater, using a medium pressure to remove the zest without removing the white pith.

2 To use a zester, press the blade into the citrus skin and run it along the surface to take off long strips of zest.

Segmenting citrus fruit

Segments of orange make a good topping for sweet tarts and can also be served alongside the dessert; they need to be prepared so that no skin, pith or membrane remains.

1 Cut off a slice at both ends of the fruit, then cut off the peel, just inside the white pith.

2 Hold the fruit over a bowl to catch the juice and cut between the segments, just inside the membrane, to release the flesh. Continue until all the segments are removed. Squeeze the juice from the membrane into the bowl and use as required.

Preparing apples

1 To core an apple, push an apple corer straight through the apple from the stem to the base. Remove the core and use a small sharp knife to pick out any stray seeds or seed casings.

2 To peel, hold the fruit in one hand and run a swivel peeler under the skin, starting from the stem end and moving around the fruit, taking off the skin until you reach the base.

3 To slice, halve the cored apple. For crescent-shaped slices, stand the fruit on its end and cut slices into the hollow as if you were slicing a pie. For flat slices, hold the apple cut-side down and slice with the knife blade at right angles to the hollow left by the core.

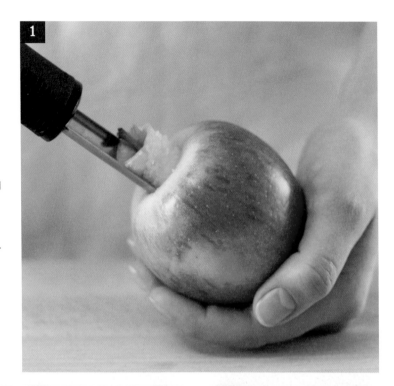

Preparing pears

1 To core, use a teaspoon to scoop out the seeds and core through the base of the pear. Trim away any remaining hard pieces with a small knife. If you halve or quarter the pear, remove any remaining seeds.

2 To peel, cut off the stem. Peel off the skin in even strips from the tip to the base.

3 To slice, halve the cored, peeled pear lengthways, then slice with the pear halves lying cut side down on the chopping board.

4 To make pear fans, slice at closely spaced intervals from the base to about 2.5cm (1in) from the tip, making sure you don't cut all the way through. Press gently to fan the

slices, then use a palette knife to lift the pear gently on to your pie or plate.

★ COOKS' TIP

Preserving colour

The flesh of apples and pears starts to turn brown when exposed to air. If you are not going to use the prepared fruit immediately, toss with lemon juice.

Pitting cherries

A cherry stoner will remove the stones neatly, but it is important to position the fruit correctly.

1 First, remove the stems from the cherries, then wash the fruit and pat dry on kitchen paper. Put each cherry on the stoner with the stem end facing up. Close the stoner and gently press the handles together so that the metal rod pushes through the fruit, pressing out the stone.

2 Alternatively, if you do not have a cherry stoner, cut the cherries in half and remove the stones with the tip of a small pointed knife.

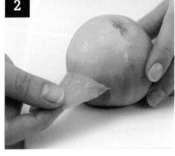

Peeling peaches

Peaches may be peeled for use in pies and tarts.

1 Put the peach into a bowl of boiling water for 15–60 seconds (depending on ripeness). Don't leave in the water for too long, as the heat will soften the flesh. Put into a bowl of cold water.

2 Work a knife between the skin and flesh to loosen the skin, then gently pull to remove. Rub the flesh with lemon juice.

Stoning larger fruits

Peaches, nectarines, plums, greengages and apricots can all be prepared in the same way.

1 Following the cleft along one side of the fruit, cut through to the stone all around the fruit.

2 Twist gently to separate the halves. Ease out the stone with a small knife. Rub the flesh with lemon juice to prevent discoloration.

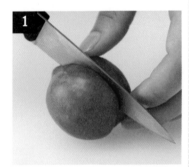

Preparing pineapples

1 Cut off the base and crown of the pineapple and stand the fruit on a chopping board. Using a knife, peel away a section of skin, going just deep enough to remove the hard, inedible 'eyes'. Repeat all the way around.

2 Use a small knife to cut out any remaining traces of the eyes.

3 Cut the peeled pineapple into slices.

4 You can buy special tools for coring pineapples but a 7.5cm (3in) biscuit cutter or an apple corer works just as well. Place the biscuit cutter over the core and press firmly down to remove the core. If using an apple corer, cut out in pieces, as it will be too wide to remove in one piece.

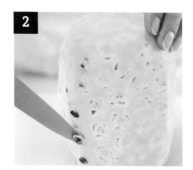

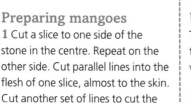

Preparing mangoes

1 Cut a slice to one side of the stone in the centre. Repeat on the other side. Cut parallel lines into the flesh of one slice, almost to the skin. Cut another set of lines to cut the flesh into squares.

2 Press on the skin side to turn the fruit inside out, so that the flesh is thrust outwards. Cut off the chunks close to the skin. Repeat with the other half.

Using passion fruit

The seeds are edible but if you want the fruit for a purée or sauce, you will need to sieve them.

1 Halve the fruit and scoop the seeds and pulp into a food processor or blender. Whiz for 30 seconds, until the mixture looks soupy. Alternatively, just scoop the seeds and pulp into a sieve, as step 2.

2 Pour into a sieve over a bowl and press the pulp hard with the back of a spoon to release the juice.

Using fruit

Most fruit tastes marvellous raw, although a few always need to be cooked. Nearly all fruits make superb desserts when they are baked, poached or stewed, and many are equally good made into smoothies.

Making smoothies and purées

Fruit, either cooked or raw, can be transformed into a smooth sauce by puréeing. Fruit also makes a healthy breakfast or snack that is bursting with flavour when used in a smoothie.

Puréeing in a blender

Some fruit can be puréed raw, while others are better cooked. Leave cooked fruit to cool before puréeing.

1 Put a large spoonful of fruit in the jug and blend until smooth, then add another spoonful and blend again. Add rest of fruit in batches.

2 For a very smooth purée, pass the fruit through a fine sieve.

Puréeing using a mouli

The fine plate of a mouli-légumes does a good job of puréeing, although it is slightly more laborious than a blender.

1 Set the mouli over a bowl and, working in batches, ladle in the fruit.

2 Turn the handle until the fruit has gone through, then repeat until all the fruit has been puréed.

Basic smoothie

To serve four, you will need:
4 passion fruit, 150g (5oz) low-fat yogurt, 4 bananas, 225g (8oz) grapes.
1 Halve the passion fruit and scoop the pulp into a blender. Add the remaining ingredients. Crush 8 ice cubes and add to the blender.

2 Process until smooth and pour into glasses. Serve immediately.

GOOD FRUITS FOR BAKING

FRUIT	PREPARATION
Apples (dessert or cooking)	cored and halved or quartered
Apricots	whole or halved and stoned
Bananas	peeled and halved, or in their skins
Berries	whole
Nectarines and peaches	halved and stoned
Pears	cored and halved or quartered
Pineapple	cored and cut into large chunks
Plums	whole or halved and stoned

Baking

The key to success to baking fruit is in keeping the cooking time short, so that the delicate flesh of the fruit doesn't break down completely. Preheat the oven to 200°C (180°C fan oven) mark 6.

1 Prepare the fruit and put in a single layer in a greased baking dish or individual dishes. Put a splash of water in the bottom of the dish(es). (For extra flavour, you can use fruit juice or wine instead of water.) Sprinkle the tops with sugar (and other flavourings such as spices, citrus zest or vanilla, if you like). Dot with butter.

2 Bake the fruit until just tender when pierced with a knife or skewer; this should take 15–25 minutes depending on the fruit and the size of the pieces. Leave to rest for a few minutes before serving.

Poached fruit

To serve four, you will need:
300g (11oz) sugar, 450g (1lb) fruit (pears, plums, peaches, nectarines, apricots), juice of 1 lemon.

1 Put the sugar in a large measuring jug and fill with cold water to make 1 litre (1½ pints). Transfer to a pan and heat gently, stirring now and then, until the sugar has dissolved.

2 Peel and halve the fruit, core pears, remove the stones from stone fruit, and gently toss with lemon juice.

3 Bring the sugar syrup to a simmer in a wide-based pan. Put in the fruit, cut sides down. It should be completely covered with syrup; add a little more water if necessary.

4 Simmer very gently for 30–40 minutes until soft when pierced with a knife. Serve hot or cold.

Grilling

Cooking fruit under the grill is a quick and delicious method for fruit such as pineapple, peaches and figs.

1 Preheat the grill to high. Prepare the fruit and put in the grill pan (or a roasting tin) in a single layer. Sprinkle generously with sugar.

2 Set the grill pan under the grill about 10cm (4in) from the heat. Grill for 5–8 minutes until the top is lightly caramelised and the fruit has softened. Serve hot or warm.

Stewed fruit

To serve four, you will need:
450g (1lb) prepared fruit (chunks of apples and rhubarb, whole gooseberries, halved plums), 1 tbsp lemon juice, sugar to taste.

1 Put the fruit in a non-stick stainless steel pan with the lemon juice and sugar. Add 2 tbsp water. Bring to the boil over a medium heat, then reduce the heat and simmer gently, partly covered, until the fruit is soft, stirring often.

Preparing and using nuts

Nuts feature in many desserts and puddings. Some can be bought ready prepared, but here are various tips and techniques that may be helpful.

Blanching and skinning

After nuts have been shelled, they are still coated with a skin, which, although edible, tastes bitter. This is easier to remove if the nuts are blanched.

1 Put the shelled nuts into a bowl and cover with boiling water. Leave for 2 minutes, then drain.

2 Remove the skins by rubbing the nuts in a teatowel or by squeezing them between your thumb and index finger.

Chopping

Only chop about 75g (3oz) of nuts at a time. Unless you want very large pieces, the easiest way to chop nuts is in the food processor. Store chopped nuts in an airtight container for up to two weeks. **Note:** Leave nuts to cool completely after skinning and before chopping.

1 Put the nuts into a food processor and pulse at 10-second intervals. Chop to the size of coarse breadcrumbs.

2 Alternatively, place a chopping board on a folded teatowel on the worksurface to give stability and use a cook's knife.

STORING NUTS

★ Because of their high fat content, nuts do not keep particularly well and turn rancid if kept for too long.
★ Always buy nuts from a shop with a high turnover of stock so you know they're likely to be fresh.
★ Store in an airtight container in a cool, dark place, or in the fridge, and use by the 'best before' date on the pack.

Nut Praline

Use crushed or ground to flavour ice creams and desserts.

To serve four, you will need:
250g (9oz) golden caster sugar,
175g (6oz) nuts.

1 Line a baking sheet with baking parchment and fill a bowl with very cold water. Put the sugar into a heavy-based pan over a low heat. Shake the pan gently to dissolve the sugar. When the sugar has turned a dark golden brown, pour in the nuts and stir once with a wooden spoon.

2 Dip the base of the pan into cold water to prevent the praline from burning, then quickly pour the praline on to the parchment and spread out. Cool for 20 minutes, then break into pieces with a rolling pin.

Slicing and slivering

Although you can buy sliced and slivered nuts, they're easy to make.

1 To slice, put the skinned nuts on a board. Using a cook's knife, slice the nuts as thinly as required.

2 To make slivers, carefully cut the slices to make narrow matchsticks.

Toasting

Toasting improves the flavour of many nuts; if you toast nuts in their skins, the skins will rub off easily after toasting.

1 Preheat the oven to 200°C (180°C fan oven) mark 6. Put the shelled nuts on a baking sheet in a single layer and bake for 8–15 minutes until the skins are lightly coloured.

2 Remove the skins by rubbing the nuts in a teatowel.

Index

CONVERSION TABLES

TEMPERATURE

°C	FAN OVEN	GAS MARK	°C	FAN OVEN	GAS MARK
110	90	¼	190	170	5
130	110	½	200	180	6
140	120	1	220	200	7
150	130	2	230	210	8
170	150	3	240	220	9
180	160	4			

LIQUIDS

METRIC	IMPERIAL	METRIC	IMPERIAL
5ml	1 tsp	200ml	7fl oz
15ml	1 tbsp	250ml	9fl oz
25ml	1fl oz	300ml	½ pint
50ml	2fl oz	500ml	18fl oz
100ml	3½ fl oz	600ml	1 pint
125ml	4fl oz	900ml	1½ pints
150ml	5fl oz / ¼ pint	1 litre	1¾ pints
175ml	6fl oz		

MEASURES

Metric	Imperial	Metric	Imperial
5mm	¼ in	10cm	4in
1cm	½ in	15cm	6in
2cm	¾ in	18cm	7in
2.5cm	1in	20.5cm	8in
3cm	1¼ in	23cm	9in
4cm	1½ in	25.5cm	10in
5cm	2in	28cm	11in
7.5cm	3in	30.5cm	12in